D0563976

Into the Blue

Susan Edsall

Into the Blue

*A Father's Flight
and a Daughter's Return*

St. Martin's Press
New York

www.stmartins.com

Design by Kathryn Parise

Photographs courtesy of the author

LIBRARY OF CONGRESS CATALOGING-IN-PUBLICATION DATA

Edsall, Susan.
   Into the blue : a father's flight and a daughter's return / Susan Edsall.
    p cm.
   ISBN 0-312-32141-4
   EAN 978-0312-32141-3
   1. Edsall, Wayne—Health. 2. Cerebrovascular disease—Patients—United States—Montana—Biography. I. Title.
   RC388.5.E324 2004
   362.196'81'0092—dc22

                               2003026483

10 9 8 7 6 5 4 3 2

For my dazzling family,
for Bud, who might as well be (family, that is),
and for Betsy, from the bottom of my grateful heart

Note to the Reader

This is a true story, and names of family members and close friends are unchanged. However, the names and identities of other individuals mentioned in the book have been changed.

Contents

Acknowledgments

I have always wanted to write. The trouble was—and this was big—I had nothing to say. Not that this prevented me from engaging in spirited dinner conversation, but for some reason it got in the way of me writing. For this we should all be grateful.

But when I finally thought I *did* have something to say, I then discovered that *wanting* to write and actually writing were not the same thing. I got kind, stern, unyielding help from Tim Brookes, author, essayist, and professor at the University of Vermont, who took me on as an adult student and, with humor and clarity, repeatedly pointed out to me my bad writing habits. (I have finally forgiven him for putting undue stress in my life by asking for a writing sample before he agreed to be my coach. What was he thinking? It took me nearly a week to work up the nerve.) I simply would not have been able to get started—or to finish—without his unflagging guidance. Amazingly, I think he managed his unenviable tutoring task without once pointing to a chapter I wrote and saying, "This totally sucks."

He introduced me to Betsy Rapoport, freelance editor supreme, who took on my manuscript as if it were her own. She not only shaped the book, meticulously editing it at least four times, but fed me in her astounding kitchen, housed me, encouraged me, made me howl with laughter, baked me birthday flan, bought me presents, introduced me to some new, very bad habits, and became one of my dearest friends. I have never met anyone as intrepid in rooting for the underdog (that would be me) and being stopped by nothing. This book would not have made it to press without her. It is sheer beginner's luck that I made it this far in my life without her, or without her husband, Ken, who kept me laughing (and still does), and her children, Sam and Katie, who kept me entertained and amazed (and still do).

She introduced me to Jim Levine, my sensational agent, who champions me and the book, churns out ideas like he's a manufacturing plant, and promptly returns my e-mails. I feel lucky as a novice writer to have such a savvy, experienced, happy agent.

Many friends provided support along the way. Phyllis Theroux provided needed encouragement at her writer's retreat in Italy. Joanne Warner let me write in her Italian villa and brought me biscotti and vin santo every afternoon. Sarah Stewart Taylor walked me through the publishing and publicity process from a writer's perspective and kept me from falling into every single muddy ditch along the way. Kim Meredith kept my house clean—no small feat in either effort or importance. Who can craft a sentence when the dishes in the sink plead without pause to be washed?

Barbara Wagner, Carol Evans, Phoebe Toland, Jane Breyer, Holly Barry, Anna Benassi, Sue Jamback, Beth Lee, Cary Joseph, Lisa Marella, and Joanie Herwig each read the manuscript in its early stages and gave very helpful feedback.

I couldn't have told this story without Bud. His memory of events, his turn of phrase, and his hilarious e-mails gave me the fodder I needed to get the story down.

Thanks to Gene Graf and Steve Kleimer, who spent an October afternoon with Dad and me snapping photos in the air and on the ground to get the jacket shot for the book. Thanks beyond measure to the entire flying community in Montana, who supported my father and our family in countless ways. I can't imagine any other group of people who could care more, cheer more enthusiastically, or hold their breath as long. I fell headlong in love with them all.

There isn't enough thanks in the world for my family—my parents, my sister, and my brother—who let the story be told, chaff and grain together. We did not sprint across the finish line with grace and an admirable shimmer of sweat on our brow. We yanked, shoved, and hauled ourselves across it, gasping and heaving, and this is the story they let me tell without any spit shine. Special thanks to my sister, Sharon, whom I fell in love with all over again in the recovery process with Dad and in the writing of this book.

Diane Higgins, my attentive and unharried editor, cared about the book way past the editing process. Nichole Argyres, the associate editor, made everything seem effortless, although I know that on her end it certainly couldn't have been. Brenda Woodward meticulously copyedited the manuscript with an attention to detail that was nothing short of a marvel to me. I believe she might actually be an angel or in some way supernatural.

Abundant thanks to Avery Roberts, my awesome flight instructor and friend, who taught me how to fly, a dream that was awakened when I began writing this book. I have never had so much fun in my life. Thankfully I have not had to buy him a beer for every bad landing.

Finally, deepest, fondest thanks to my husband, Rick, who stood willingly in every breach, and there were many. After reading this book you might correctly surmise that I am not exactly a peach. He believed in my father, he believed in me, he believed in my book. All of this meant the world to me and made so much of what happened possible. I am profoundly grateful to him for his companionship. I would not have wanted to do any of this alone.

Into the Blue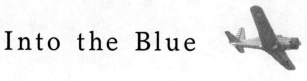

Dad flying the BT-13 over the Rocky Mountains

1

Prologue

In March of 2000, spring arrived early in Montana. Melting snow and clear skies were the only signals pilots of small planes needed to know winter was sufficiently over. They were like crocuses in that way—wired to head for the sky at the tiniest indication of spring.

I was in Bozeman to visit my parents. As always, Dad and I planned to go flying, this time in his BT-13, a huge silver plane shaped like a bullet, built in 1942, and used to train pilots in World War II. Dad in front; I in back. This plane was magnificent—imposing and muscular. It had a 450-horsepower engine, which meant it could deliver the same oomph as a team of horses hitched up two-by-two and stretching on for half a mile. It was twenty-nine feet from its round engine to its rudder and had a wingspan of forty-two feet—bigger than a three-car garage. Made of sheets of aluminum riveted together along every edge, it blazed like a metal sun at high noon. You could fly with the cockpit open or pull a Plexiglas canopy from back to front to close yourself off from the wind, but never from the view.

The BT was one of two antique airplanes Dad owned. He'd been collecting and rebuilding them for nearly twenty years. He and his best friend, Bud Hall, had rebuilt nine together and were in the middle of rebuilding another.

Collecting antique airplanes differs from collecting stamps or Hummels or spoons. This hobby hurtles past fascination and curiosity, creating enough passion to make hardened men swoon. It also takes up more space and is riskier by a Montana mile. Stamp collectors or retirees breeding African violets rarely concern themselves with hangar space—or crashing.

Dad kept his prized planes in three hangars—one at the house and two at the airport. The hangar at the house had been taken over by his current project, rebuilding an old 1941 Airmaster. The BT and his beloved Fleet Series 9—the only one left in the whole world still flying—were parked at one airport hangar. Another held his Cessna 185, what we called his "regular plane" because, in our minds, it was ordinary—only one set of wings, engine properly stored inside the fuselage, closed cockpit, full instrument panel—practically a station wagon.

Dad was crazy about his BT, which he'd bought and rebuilt in 1993. It was the same plane he'd flown on the Freedom Flight in 1995—a cross-country trip he and two hundred other pilots of antique airplanes took from Los Angeles to Washington, D.C., to commemorate the fiftieth anniversary of the end of World War II. My brother, Steve, flew on the first leg from Los Angeles into Kansas City. My sister, Sharon, flew the second leg from Kansas City to the Wright-Patterson Air Force Base in Dayton, Ohio, where I joined up with them.

In Dayton, Sharon and I met dozens of World War II veterans, some of them so gnarled they could barely stand. The vets, former pilots, asked Dad if they could sit in his BT. We braced them with our shoulders, hoisting them into a plane that, as young men, they had flown expertly to prepare themselves to fly over German territory. They sank into the tiny cockpit, the feel as familiar as an old coat, faces lit up with memories going back more than fifty years as distinct as this moment. "I flew this plane," they each would say, some of them tearfully, pulling the knobs, touching the indicators. "I flew this plane years ago," they told us.

I flew the final leg into Andrews Air Force Base in Washington, D.C. We swung past the Twin Towers in New York City, then everyone dropped long-stemmed red roses into the harbor as we circled the Statue of Liberty. I remember the wind blowing the skin on my arms into little accordion folds.

The morning after my midnight arrival in Bozeman, Dad and I headed for the airport. As always, his hangar was spit-shined and organized. Photographs, posters, old airplane parts, and memorabilia from air shows hung on the walls. A sizable American flag hung from the rafters. Four canvas deck chairs sat on a den-sized square of Berber carpet near the front, and provisions were stocked in the back. A microwave oven, shouldering a glut of ready-to-pop popcorn, perched next to a white refrigerator with the model name Coolerator sweeping in metal cursive across the door, a bumper sticker reading Semper Fi its only other adornment.

To move the Fleet or the Cessna out of the hangar, we'd each get behind a wing, put one hand on the wing and one on the strut, lean in, and shove. The plane rolled out of the hangar easily once we got it moving. Not so the BT. It was too huge. For it, Dad hooked a tow bar to his pickup and used it like a tugboat.

When the BT rolled from the windowless hangar out into the watery light of spring, it blazed, sunlight skittering off every surface, putting the devil to shame. Climbing in, I read again the words Dad had painted on the fuselage, written by poet and pilot Gill Robb Wilson, an inscription so apt that everyone in the family had it memorized: ". . . and of the living, none, not one, who truly loves the sky, would trade a hundred earth-bound hours for one that he could fly."

He meant it.

Dad had wanted to fly since he was six years old and he and his older brother, Everett, had snuck down to the fairgrounds outside of town where The Barnstormers had set up shop for the weekend. The Barnstormers were pilots who patched together a living by giving people joyrides in World War I airplanes at two bits a pop, a lot of money in 1935. A full day's wages for some. Somehow, without a whiff of his plans reaching their parents, Everett had scraped together enough money for one ride—for himself—leaving Dad on the ground looking up, outranked and wishing. From that moment on, he wanted more than anything to fly.

When he was a kid living in Missoula, Montana, Dad would often ride his bike to the airport after school and stand in the weeds outside the barbed wire fence to watch the planes land. Granddad, recognizing Dad's love of flying, gave Dad a ride in an airplane as a birthday gift when he was eleven years old. It was an open cockpit plane, and in March it was biting cold once they got in the air. The airplane, covered in a tight-weave linen, was a working plane—hauling cargo to various outposts in Montana—and the cloth cover had suffered. Dad looked down between his feet through a hole in the floor the size of a candy bar and saw the ground whiz past him thousands of feet below. Scary stuff. Thrilling. Flying got into his bones. It never left.

As soon as Dad towed the BT out of the hangar, I climbed onto the wing and swung my legs over the side onto the yellow leather seat directly behind the pilot's seat. I slid down, threaded the seat belt through the loops on the shoulder straps, and secured the buckle. Then I grabbed the shoulder straps and pulled them down hard, pushing myself firmly against the back of my seat. I stretched my legs way out in front of me, keeping my feet clear of the pedals. The joystick, used to maneuver the plane, stuck straight up out of the floor between my legs. Dad handed back the avocado-green headsets and I plugged them in. We would use these to talk to each other.

We taxied out to the airstrip, the nose of the plane so long that Dad had to make S-turns to see the runway in front of him. Dad lifted his finger in a wave to the other pilots getting ready to fly. As always, I felt lucky to be the kid in the back. What did other kids do on

Saturdays? Dad checked all his instruments, ran the rpm's up on his engine to make sure the magentos were working, then he cycled the propeller, set the flaps for takeoff, and set the elevator trim to remove the back pressure on the joystick during the climb out. He called the tower to tell them he was ready to go, rolled out onto the runway, positioned the BT smack on the center line, and hit the throttle lever. As the speed picked up, he maneuvered the rudder with his feet to keep the plane straight. When he reached flying speed, about 70 miles per hour, he cranked a handle on his left, lifting the flaps to eliminate drag, changed the propeller from takeoff position to flying position, and we were in the air.

We lifted, lifted up over the farmers' fields, the malls, the football stadium, the grid of city streets, climbing past the clutches of gravity and obligation. The broad valley quickly changed from fields of alfalfa and wheat and barley into a patchwork quilt of green and beige and black. We left it all behind. All the worry and confinement and chatter couldn't keep up with us as we climbed into the sky. Below, everything looked like a tiny toy train set. Nothing to bother about.

I shouted and thrust my fists into the air and laughed, like I always did. I couldn't help it. The thrill of flying made it burst out of me.

"Where to?" Dad asked.

"Show me around!" I answered. I never cared where we went, as long as we flew.

So Dad took me over to Harrison Lake, where we camped as kids, past the headwaters of the Missouri to spot bald eagles nesting and coyotes on the prowl. We buzzed fellow pilot Jim Green's house on the way back, diving toward his barn and pulling up into a steep bank and climb. It took my breath away. I had learned to counter my instincts and lean into the turn for the best view and the biggest thrill. With only a smear of sheet metal between me and the sky, I felt like a bird.

"Let's find a place for you to live!" Dad said. He took every opportunity to get me to move back west. "Three Forks," he said. "That's the place to buy."

We flew over Three Forks and buzzed a farmhouse. "That's a nice place," Dad said.

"Is it for sale?"

"Everything's for sale."

We took off across the valley and over to Bridger Bowl, the ski area outside of town. Grazing the ridge of the Bridgers, the plane jumped and lifted with the air currents. I shrieked and laughed just like I'd done as a kid, gripping the edge of the seat as if it would make a difference.

We stayed in the air nearly an hour. As always, on our way back to the airport Dad headed for home, dropping out of the sky to buzz the house low and fast on the west side, then pulling up and away, leaving that distinct thumpety-growl of an antique engine in his wake, a signal to Mom that we'd be home soon.

Over the years, Dad and a loose gaggle of pilots have developed a Sunday ritual of flying to remote places for breakfast. Of course it's not about breakfast—it's about flying. Three of them will head over to Lewistown, a forty-minute flight. Or fifteen will fly the two hours to a grass airstrip in Sydney, where local pilots stand ready with plywood tables, metal folding chairs, and big griddles to cook up sausages and piles of pancakes. Sometimes Dad will call up my brother, who lives near Sun Valley, and suggest breakfast or lunch. "It's only a ninety-minute flight. We'll just fly over," he'll say as casually as I might suggest meeting for coffee at the café downtown.

As much as he enjoys flying with me, I know Dad has his greatest fun when he's flying with his fellow pilots. Up in the air these guys play for hours. They tune their headsets into radio frequency 122.75, the "bullshit frequency," and they're in a world of their own making.

On one typical Saturday, Dad and Bud were out flying their planes, tuned into the bullshit frequency to see who else was out there. They could pick up Steve Kleimer, but just barely, so Kleimer tried climbing to see if he could establish better reception.

"Where you guys at?" Kleimer crackled over the radio.

"Right there by the red barn next to the railroad track where the road turns left to go to Smitty's," Dad said. Dad had been flying for over fifty years, and for him these landmarks were as precise as a global positioning system.

"Where the hell is that?" Kleimer shot back, laughing. In his early fifties, Kleimer was still young. He'd only been flying for twelve years. He flew a Cessna 180 and was in the middle of rebuilding a 1940 Stearman.

"We're coming up on Madlow," Bud offered. He was nearly sixty-five and pussyfooting around retirement like it was a rattlesnake. He had a mat of gray curly hair that stuck so resolutely to his scalp it looked sculpted there. His tanned skin draped like melted caramel into soft pouches under his eyes and around his cheeks. He could fit his entire wardrobe into the glove compartment of his Jeep. Jeans and a T-shirt, white socks and tennis shoes, a baseball cap, and plenty of gum. Bud always, always chewed gum—it was the only exercise he got.

Although he'd been flying for over thirty years, Bud navigated strictly by towns and major highways, a source of ceaseless ribbing. The trouble was, even when he navigated with his road atlas he got lost, a word he refused to use, preferring instead "getting temporarily misplaced in foreign airspace."

Now they were looking for Kleimer, and Bud was mostly tagging along, glad to have someone else doing the looking while he concentrated on keeping track of Dad's plane.

Dad banked his plane steeply and craned his neck toward the windshield, scanning the skies for Kleimer's plane. "Where you at?" If Kleimer couldn't find them, maybe Dad could find Kleimer.

"I'm just coming over the Bunkhouse Bar," Kleimer ribbed Dad. How many Bunkhouse Bars were there in Montana? Hundreds?

That's it! Dad knew exactly which Bunkhouse Bar and he headed his plane in that direction. Bud followed, incredulous.

"What's your altitude?" Dad asked.

"Six thousand five hundred, coming south," Kleimer responded.

"We'll stay at six thousand, going north." Dad was zeroing in.

"Okay, we gotcha, you're at ten o'clock," Dad said, then added, "There's bald eagles below at about five o'clock. You see 'em?"

"Hell, no, I don't see 'em, Edsall. I'm having a hard enough time finding you!"

"Hey, boys!" Widebody broke in. He'd picked them up on the bullshit frequency and caught up with them. "Looks like Jack Frost visited the river last night. I'm going down to take a look." Widebody was young too, wild and good-natured, nicknamed for his squatty build. Bud often described him as "all ass and no body." He was the butt of merciless wisecracks about his hangar. Though Widebody was an avid beer drinker, there wasn't a garbage can in sight there. He just threw the cans on the floor and they were now ankle deep. Pilots always called his hangar the one with the aluminum floor. He had two antiques—a 1947 Culver and the plane he was flying now, a 1947 Vagabond painted bright yellow.

"Okay, I'll stay at ten o'clock," Kleimer answered Dad.

"What a great deal when Wilbur and Orville got together and shit-canned the bicycle shop, eh boys?" Bud summed up their collective happiness.

"What do you think about heading over toward Helena for a bowl of soup?" Guido piped in. Helena was only about a thirty-minute flight, and they were regulars at a good café. Guido was a lithe Italian who was a pilot for Delta Airlines. In addition to his "regular plane," a Piper Super Cruiser, he owned two antiques—a 1943 AT6, very similar to Dad's BT-13, and the one he was flying now, a 1944 Howard, which Dad and Bud had rebuilt for him several years ago. He was coming up on sixty-five years old, mandatory retirement age for Delta pilots, and it gnawed at him. All he'd ever done was fly.

"I'm hungry enough," Dad responded. "Let's go do her!"

"Let's go by Townsend first and take a look at Mike's new hangar." Mike had just retired from the Montana Aeronautics Division. He'd set a world distance record flying nonstop from Hawaii to Oshkosh years back. He was a member of the unofficial "Crash Club"—having had an engine failure in his Bonanza airplane over Utah. He and his girlfriend, also a pilot, set it up in a slight nose-down glide. It was snowing hard. They never saw the ground until they hit it. It destroyed the plane, but they walked away without a scratch. Bud calls them "shithouse lucky."

The five planes took the twenty-minute detour to Townsend, buzzed Mike, then swung over to Helena and had "a bowl of soup," which usually meant a burger and fries, gave the waitress hell, she gave them hell back, then they did the whole thing again only in reverse.

A typical Saturday.

I knew how these guys spent their time. I even knew some of the banter. But I had only the faintest inkling of what it felt like to be a pilot. Dad had the power to go anywhere he pleased, alone. He flew through canyons at 140 miles per hour, tipping the plane up on its edge to crank through a tight turn. He flew over places no one had ever been before, tracking herds of elk in the hundreds, grizzly bears and their cubs, bald eagles nesting, red-furred baby buffalo in the spring. He was a masterful pilot and chock-full of joy when he flew. He was free.

When we landed at the airport and taxied back to the hangar, Dad repeated what he said after every flight. "Got her down one more time!" as if it was a miracle. He logged his flight in his worn leather log book, stashed the headphones, and clicked all the switches off. I climbed out and stretched my arms high over my head, swinging my body left to right to get out all the kinks. We hitched the BT to the tow bar and moved it into the hangar, wedging it in next to the Fleet, closed the big hangar door, and headed home for lunch, like we always did. Like I assumed we always would.

Dad copiloting a B-17, 1997

2

SNAFU

I figure when the phone rings in the middle of the night, it probably means something bad. When it rings in the middle of the day, it probably doesn't. So when the phone rang at noon on Saturday, March 25, 2000, I ignored it. I couldn't think of anyone I wanted to talk to. I let the machine pick it up.

"Hi honey. It's Mom." Mother paused, but not long enough for the machine to cut her off. "Honey, are you there?"

I reached for the phone. "Hi, Mom!"

"Oh! Hi, honey!" She sounded momentarily disoriented. "Did I catch you at a bad time? Are you in the middle of lunch?"

"I'm all yours, Mom," I said, pinning the phone against my ear with my shoulder while I continued perusing the headlines of the *New York Times*. "I'm just reading the paper. What's up? How's Dad?" My father had undergone bypass surgery four days ago and was doing well. He was scheduled to go home on Monday. I hadn't flown out to Montana for the surgery, since my brother and sister were there. My husband had had open heart surgery to replace his aorta and valve five years ago. Mom had had bypass surgery four years ago. Open heart surgery had become something of a family thing, and I'd stopped wringing my hands about it.

"Well, we've had a little setback, honey. I don't think it's anything to worry about, but we'll be at the hospital a little longer than we thought."

"What do you mean, Mom? What does 'little setback' mean?"

"Well, he's just had a small stroke, honey."

"What do you mean 'small,' Mother? How is it possible for a stroke to be small?" I closed the newspaper and tore a page off the pad that hung from the fridge. I pictured Dad paralyzed, mute, and wearing Depends. I could hear the sounds of other people talking in the background, and I figured Mother was at a pay phone in a public hallway in the hospital. I was probably the last person she called because she knew I would have endless questions she wouldn't have the answers to. It would leave her feeling inadequate, wondering if it wasn't all her fault.

"It will be fine, honey," Mom said firmly. "We're looking on the bright side. It's just going to take a little time, that's all."

"That's all?" I shot back. "*All?* You telling me that Dad has just had 'a little setback, a little stroke' is not all, Mother."

"It will be fine, honey." Mom had memorized this line decades ago. All things being fine meant order, and Mother loved order. She considered fighting clutter a noble cause; tidiness was her Holy Grail. Her pantry had about six cans of food in it, arranged alphabetically. She had salmon steaks cut and wrapped in individual portions in the freezer. Her Tupperware nested in uniform stacks and there wasn't a single missing or melted lid. All her clothes were hung up, her socks came out of the dryer in pairs, and she never misplaced her shoes.

Dad's stroke was an assault on Mom's hard-won law-and-order sensibility, and she was relying on an old standby—thinking positive—to keep from running aground.

"Okay, Mom. I'm sure it will be fine. But what happened?" I knew that in no time flat everyone would find out that it was not going to be fine.

"Well, your sister walked into your father's hospital room this morning and—"

"When this morning, Mom? What time? Be specific," I snapped.

"Well, I don't know, honey. The morning's been such a blur. About seven-thirty, I guess. I don't know. It was before breakfast. Sometime before breakfast, I guess."

"Okay. So sometime before breakfast Sharon walked into his hospital room. Then what happened? What happened next?" I wrote, "breakfast—Sharon walks into room."

"Well, he was sitting on the edge of the bed pouring water into the phone and—"

"Pouring water into the phone?" I squeaked, the pitch of my voice raised so high it sounded like a child's. A small stream of clear snot ran out my nose and onto my upper lip.

"Well, honey, he had his water pitcher and he was just pouring it into the receiver. I don't know what else to tell you. That's all there is, really. What else do you want to know?"

"Is he paralyzed? Can he talk?"

"No. He can't talk. That's another thing. Not really. The nurse asked him what kind of toast he wanted, white or wheat, and he said, 'Wood.' So he can talk, but he doesn't make any sense. I don't know what they call that—it sounds like aphrodisiac, but I know that's not it. A medical word. Anyway, it means he can't talk. And he seems to have, what did they call it? Something. They called it something. Anyway, he has trouble with his right side. Neglect. That's it. He has neglect on his right side. But we don't really know much yet, honey. It's the weekend, you know. It's hard to get any help on the weekend. We're just waiting until Monday, and then Dr. Lilly will be back."

I used a tone of voice reserved for occasions when I was enraged. It had the exterior veneer of reason and calm but was overlaid with a fearsome sarcasm that made me appear unhinged, dangerous. "I see.

Dad can't talk, and you're waiting for the doctor to mosey on in Monday? I guess we wouldn't want to disturb him on his beeper, for Christ's sake, him being a doctor and all."

Mother hated it when I swore. "I'm sure he has a beeper, honey, but this all takes time."

"Dad has had a stroke, Mom, not a little acne flare-up."

"It's just a matter of time," she said. "Dr. Wynload said—"

"Who the hell is Dr. Wynload? I thought you said there was no doctor until Monday!" I barked.

"Well, there's a doctor." Mom didn't want to thrash through this thicket of detail. "But Dr. Wynload is the surgeon, honey, he's not the actual doctor. I mean, he's a doctor, but he's not the doctor that deals with the stroke. Anyway, Dr. Wynload *the surgeon* said the whole stroke might reverse itself within twenty-four hours." Mother was grasping mightily at this thin straw. "He'll be fine, honey. Really, it could be a lot worse."

It could not be a lot worse. I knew what stroke meant. I had seen it. Stroke meant wheelchair, drooling, hands flapping in frustration, being fed, being strapped in, being treated like a pet. "Gorked out" is what we called it. Stroke meant it would have been better just to die.

"I'm coming home," I told Mom.

"Oh, honey, it's not necessary, really. We'll manage. Sharon's here." I couldn't tell if that was a family inventory or a warning. Mom could probably handle Dad having a stroke. What she couldn't handle was having both daughters home at once.

"How's she doing?"

"Well, better than she was. When Dr. Wynload told her your dad had a stroke, she went out into the hallway and sat down on the floor and bawled. I mean bellowed. Loud. It's all you could hear. She was out of control. Bless her heart. I thought I was going to have to turn her over my knee."

"Mother!" I said in mock horror. She laughed, but I imagined that she longed for the days when that was all it took to keep us managed.

It is well known in our family that Sharon can't squelch her impulse to cry. She cries all the time. On the phone. In person. During the news. While driving. Anytime, anywhere. She can't help it. She bawls like an Olympian—loud and long, head thrown back, mouth open, sound wrenching up from her gut in rhythmic waves.

I was certain she was doing that now. What I wasn't certain about was whether it meant anything. Did Sharon know how desperate the situation was? Or was she simply crying like she always cried? That level of hairsplitting made no difference to Mother—she just wanted a lid on it. "The doctor went over to her and told her to get her act together," Mom continued. "He told her that how she reacted was how your father would react. That seemed to straighten her up."

I could see Mom trying to present a Sunday best family to the hospital staff. Polite and deferential. A family the staff would want to be nice to. A family they would have reason to help. A family they would not deliberately kill. To accomplish that, Mom had to keep me in Vermont. She knew me as my father's daughter, which meant there would be too little regard for decorum. I would botch her game plan.

It's not that Mother didn't want me there. I had a strong back and a good mind and she could use the help. But I had no grace. With Dad out of the picture, at least for the short term, she knew I would easily slip in to take his place—charging in, banging and clattering, swiftly summing up what was wrong and why. Mother would find it not only disruptive but a shameful reflection on her, on her motherhood.

"Just stay put, honey. I'll let you know if you need to be here. I will. Really." Mom was practically pleading. I imagined her fingering the mustard seed encased in a plastic cross that hung from a gold chain around her neck. It reminded her that faith this small could move mountains. She'd banked her faith for decades, piling up good deeds like green stamps. She went to church, tithed, was thankful, read good books, did not swear, and sent packages of medical supplies to the missionaries. She was prepared to cash it all in now. God she could count on. I was a much dicier prospect. "There's nothing you can do, honey. I mean it."

I ignored Mother's pleadings. Of course she needed me, she just couldn't admit it. "I need to be there, Mom. I know there's nothing I can do," I said, writing "To Do" on the sheet of paper in front of me.

After we hung up, I walked out on the porch to find my husband, Rick, a big bear of a man with a wiry bush of bristles for beard and mustache. He'd given up the daily ritual of shaving almost twenty-five years ago, so neither one of us knew what his face really looked like. Disdaining "salons," he presented me with a professional set of electric clippers, grousing that if anyone was going to fuss over his hair and blow in his ear, it was going to be his wife, on the porch, in good weather or bad. He's had some rough approximation of an army haircut ever since. He looked more like a lumberjack than the medical librarian he was. Nevertheless, he was a master at research and knew the ins and outs of all kinds of medical conditions. I knew his reaction would tell me plenty. He was walking up from the yard.

"Dad's had a stroke," I blurted.

He stopped for just a moment, his eyes widening as he sucked in air, like he'd gotten hit in the stomach and was trying to hide that it hurt.

I knew then that our lives would change.

"Help me," I said as he wrapped his arms around me. But I had no time for comfort. I squirmed out of his hold, frantic. "I need to know what to ask, what to know."

We sat at the kitchen table, where only hours earlier we'd feasted greedily on a Yankee breakfast of warmed-up apple pie with a slice of cheese, a weekend indulgence, talking over the plans for the garden, deciding which plants to start from seed in the basement and which to buy at the local farm stand. Although we had a comfortable dining room open to the kitchen, we rarely ate there. Not even when we had company. We liked the small table in the kitchen surrounded by the windows, the light, and the view of the gardens, the apple trees, and the meadow where a mowed path snaked down to the woods and pond.

It was at this table that we planned vacations, made decisions about our mutual funds, futzed with our list of the movies we wanted to rent. When I made breakfast, Rick would read the weird or quirky from the paper. When he cooked dinner, I would do the same. It was at this table that I would ask the etymology of almost any word and Rick would know it. It was here that I learned from Rick that the word *snafu* was really an acronym from World War II meaning "situation normal: all fucked up," an apt word for the moment, I thought. I never believed Rick actually knew this stuff—and could remember it. I was always newly astonished, pointing a disbelieving finger at him and laughing, "You're so smart! How do you know this stuff?" He always replied, "Finest schools."

Rick had three standard answers and one backup: "Finest schools," for why he had the answers to particularly goofy questions; "Cab driver, Pittsburgh," for why he could find his way anywhere under any conditions; and "My soul speaks," for when I was winning an argument and he needed a way out. His backup was "Where I come from, girls don't do that sort of thing," shortened to "Where I come from. . . ." He rarely dusted that one off because it had long ceased to get a rise out of me.

We'd never sat at this table to solve a problem of this sort before, but it was where our family life occurred and it was where we huddled now.

Within fifteen minutes we'd generated a page and a half of questions and tasks for me once I got to Montana: who to see, what to ask, how to proceed. Rick had made a list of questions he would research on the Web and another set of questions he would ask his medical colleagues at work.

There was no doubt in either of our minds that going to Montana was the right thing to do. But Rick's knowledge of stroke and recovery heightened his awareness of the urgency. He knew I needed to get there immediately and press for action. "It's important your dad get started in rehab as soon as possible," Rick emphasized. "That needs to be your top priority. Get him into rehab. There's no time to lose. The sooner his brain starts learning a new way to operate, the better off he'll be." Rick was walking a fine line between urging me to do what he knew was important and jacking up my anxiety level so high I would throw up from the vertigo.

"You're exactly what your dad needs right now," Rick said, knowing my dog-with-a-bone tendencies. "I'll get your suitcase. You get reservations."

Rick brought my suitcase up from the basement while I opened my appointment book, called the voice mail of my clients to cancel the next ten days of work, and booked the first flight out.

Dad with his Piper Clipper in Alaska, 1953

3

This Is Not My Father

The next day, Sunday, a cab dropped me off at the emergency room entrance to the hospital, a sprawling complex of buildings joined by skywalks and underground tunnels. I asked the emergency room clerk seated behind a pinkish counter how to find room 232, Edwards Annex. "Head down this hall, second left, through the double doors, up the stairs, your first right after the coffee shop, take the elevator to the second floor, and follow the signs. Can't miss it." He went back to his manila folder where he continued counting something.

I didn't move. "I'm sorry. But I am really bad at directions, could you—"

"Here." He snapped a six-page booklet titled "Campus Map" from a stand on the counter and pushed it across at me. He yanked the cap off a yellow highlighter and put an aggressive **X** on one spot on the map. "You are here." Then he mashed the blunt tip of the marker onto the page and dragged it across the map, going left, right, and up little stair icons, leaving a shimmering trail for me to follow. "It's not that hard. Really."

When I found Edwards Annex I stopped short of the nurses' station. I couldn't make myself go to my father's room.

I went to the women's bathroom instead and stood in front of the mirror. I looked like an unmade bed. The bags under my eyes looked like udders, my clothes were wrinkled, my short blond hair stuck to my skull like it was painted on. I had that rural pallor from having spent too many days in bad weather. I blamed it on the fluorescent lights and fluffed my fingers through my hair, trying without success to give it a little lift. I could see now that my decision, since turning forty, to dress for comfort and not style had serious drawbacks. My stretchy black pants—finishing short of the goal, a few inches above my ankles—bagged at the knees. My clever tactic of wearing black socks and black shoes to cover for their length—or lack of it—fooled no one. The bright pink fleece top, clownishly out of sync with the gloomy surroundings, made me look like a mascot for the children's ward.

If I thought I looked bad now, it was nothing compared to how I'd look next to my sister, Sharon. She had perpetual style—black jeans crisply ironed, starched white shirts, a big black leather belt, and black ankle-high boots, her black hair cut to three-eighths of an inch, with a little feathering down over her forehead. Tiring of this look, she had recently dyed it red. When she called to tell me about it, she fell down the stairs during the conversation because she had the phone in one hand and was admiring herself in a handheld mirror in the other.

Sharon's only makeup was deep red lipstick, applied in layers starting with a pencil and finishing off with high gloss. Maybe that's the trick, I thought, digging around in my backpack to find my lipstick. Lipstick was, in my mind, a wonder cosmetic. Hopeful for something of a miracle cure, I rolled it up from the tube. Matte grayish-mauve. Surely I hadn't bought this color. I turned over the tube to look at the name—Double Truffle. This was not my lipstick. This was Mother's lipstick. How had it gotten in my backpack? I dug around for something else. Another tube. Double Truffle. Marveling at the depth and breadth of my fashion mistakes, I smeared on Double Truffle and smoothed it around. As everyone had been telling me for years, I looked exactly like my mother.

I wiped the water from around the basin. "You're stalling," I scolded my reflection.

I walked reluctantly back to Dad's doorway and peered in. My father sat on the edge of the bed, his head slumped forward, a lock of greasy graying hair hanging down into his eyes. He wore blue cotton hospital pants and a hospital pajama top that was tied at the back of his neck but otherwise hung open. His pale belly hung over the waistband of his pajamas. The flesh of his upper arms hung down in swaying, wrinkled folds. He needed a shave.

This was not my father. My father had flown me in his plane three weeks ago. This man was whipped and soul-sick and hoary with age.

My father wasn't old. He had turned seventy-one just four days ago. He was over six feet tall, a big guy—beefy but not fat. He was strong, energetic, always engaged in a project—messing with the sprinklers, mowing the lawn in the summer or snowblowing the driveway in winter, spreading grass seed on the airstrip, working on his airplanes. He whistled all the time—strange songs. Sometimes in the middle of spring he would whistle a Christmas jingle—the song those irritating little chipmunks would sing around the holidays. In desperation we'd turn on the radio to try to bump him musically into a current season or at least a more recent decade.

When I looked at this gray, limp man slumped on the side of the bed I felt unholy undiluted terror, as if my tether to the earth had been severed and I were floating helplessly away from everything I had ever known to be true. Grotesque worries crossed my mind. What if I have to kill him, I thought, put a pillow over his face or something worse? He would want it done, and no one else would do it.

The room smelled sodden and sour, like something had leaked into a hard-to-reach place. Sweat and pee and stale breath. The overhead lights were on even though it was midday. Heavy plastic curtains, patterned with swirls of maroon and pink the color of internal organs, obscured most of the natural light.

Mother sat reading a paperback book, trapped in a high-backed green plastic chair large enough to hold a person three times her size. I'd never seen her look so small.

Sharon sat next to him, rubbing his back, smiling and nodding as my father struggled to speak. She frequently interjected an eager "uh-huh . . . uh-huh" as if she understood what he was saying.

"I"—he shook his head hard and rough—"The tire. No." He shook his head again, angry. He couldn't get things straight. "The clerk?" He looked at Sharon, pleading, his eyes fierce beams broadcasting alarm. He gestured impatiently toward a low counter covered with plants in baskets, fading bouquets of flowers, plastic jugs, toiletries, folded clothes, wadded-up Kleenex, and various stacks of papers and mail.

Nobody had the remotest idea what he wanted.

I eased into the room.

"Oh! Look who's here! It's Susan!" Sharon greeted me as if I had risen from the dead. "Hey, Dad, Susan's here! He's doing great, aren't you, Dad? He's had his lunch and we're sitting here talking, aren't we, Dad?" Sharon leaned over to him and kissed his cheek, leaving a proprietary red smudge. She turned back to me and smiled, lips slightly parted, eyebrows raised in an optimistic arch.

"Hi, everyone. Hi, Mom," I said flatly.

"Hi, honey," she peeped. We were here. Practically the whole family.

I never grew accustomed to how perfectly groomed Mom and Sharon always were—even under grueling circumstances. In the few minutes it had taken me to get to Dad's room, my lipstick had already migrated off my lips and onto my front teeth, as Sharon had quickly alerted me by baring her teeth and whisking her index finger across them instructionally.

But here was Mom, several days into a devastating blow, and she looked, as always, picture-perfect. Her ginger hair was cut, permed, combed, and in place. She never left the house without holding up a handheld mirror to her bathroom mirror so she could see the back. She was looking for "holes in her head"—places where her hair didn't curl in just the right way. Mother had been the smallest baby ever born in the Butte, Montana, hospital in 1929. She only weighed four pounds at birth, and by the time she was a year old she weighed only twelve. Now she was still small—five feet two inches tall—and unlike many women her age, whose considerable spread reflected their accommodation to the easy world of the elastic waistband, Mother was abstemious and thin. Sharon and I both towered above her, eclipsing her by eight inches and a good twenty-five pounds apiece.

While I had one purse—a small black leather bag I could shove into my backpack—Mother had multiple purses that matched her outfits. Her shoes matched her clothes, which matched her purse. Looking "presentable" ranked high in her world, and she always looked presentable, even now.

"The wanna!" Dad tried again, this time gesturing emphatically toward the crowded counter and shaking his head.

"You betcha!" Sharon chirped. "We'll take care of that for you right away, won't we!" Her too-big, too-red smile looked garish against the dull pink decor of the room. The starched whiteness of her pima cotton shirt made the sheets look like shabby, shameful underwear.

I looked at my father. He didn't even glance my way, but persisted in trying to get someone to understand what he wanted.

"Get the clert." His face looked momentarily hopeful, thinking he had finally gotten the word out, then his head dropped. "No," he said, clenching his fists, his shoulders drooping. He was giving up.

I thought he might cry. I had only seen him cry twice in my life—once when I married the wrong man and the second time when my sister did. It was from him that I had learned not to cry. I took it as a point of pride that I had not cried in nine years. The crying jag then came as a result of a severely dislocated shoulder. Anyone would have cried. Even a guy would have cried, though I doubt that Dad would have.

Sharon popped off the bed to give me some room, patting the

space next to Dad, all gung ho. "I'll get these pillows fluffed up!" she announced. "They're a little flat, don't you think? Huh? Yeah, they sure are! No wonder you have a crick in your neck!" Then she turned to Mom. "Mom, tell them we need fresh pillowcases," she ordered. "Dad can't sleep on these. They smell and they're sweaty." She turned back to my father, regaining the lilt in her voice. "Aren't they, Dad? Good thing you have me around or you'd be sleeping on dirty sheets!" She kissed Dad again and squeezed his hand, smiling, giddy as a goose.

I sank onto the plastic-covered mattress, filled with horror. My mother and sister stared back at me. It was my turn.

"You're in a real shit hole of a mess, aren't you, Dad?"

He clutched my hand and shook his head from side to side. "Outta luck," he declared, clear as the crack of a rifle on a cold day, then looked me in the eyes. By force of will I did not cry.

"Fuck," he said. I had never in my life heard him say that word.

Mother closed her eyes momentarily, putting her finger in her book so as not to lose her place. She could feel the whole situation coming unhinged and starting to tilt and reel. "Please don't swear, honey."

"Who are you talking to, Mom? Me or Dad?"

The whole family at the cabin, Hyalite Canyon, Montana

4

Size Matters

Later that afternoon, my spiral notebook in hand, I flew into action. How bad was Dad's stroke? Was this a subjective judgment or a classification that was the result of a test? What were the prospects for recovery? How long would it take?

What the hell had happened here?

I started with the nurses and got vague answers that made me both more furious and more insistent. "It's too early to tell," smiled Martha, the head nurse, putting her hand on my shoulder in an attempt to comfort me. I'm sure she thought I would nod, acknowledge the mystery of it all, and shamble back to Dad's room.

"Well, okay," I said, "how soon before it's not too early anymore, and what will you know then, and what will that tell us?"

Martha nodded. I simplified. "Is Dad's stroke, say, large, medium, or small?"

"Perhaps you should talk to Dr. Lilly. He'll be able to answer your questions."

The next day was Monday and the doctors were back. Sharon had taken on the role of keeping Dad occupied—taking him on wobbly walks down the hall, fetching bowls of soft-serve ice cream, ordering his meals, holding his hand. I was the self-appointed gatherer of information, and I was beginning to feel more like a gleaner than a researcher. So when Dr. Lilly came in to check on Dad, I followed him out into the hall. "I need some information about Dad's stroke. I'm trying to understand what happened—biologically. You know, what the damage was in the brain, where it was, and how that might impact his recovery."

Dr. Lilly looked at his watch. "I'll tell you what I know, but please understand, I'm not the neurologist. My specialty is rehabilitation. You'll want to talk with Dr. Moore for more specific answers to your questions." It was inconceivable to me that someone who specialized in rehabilitation from brain injury wouldn't have more to say about stroke, but I didn't argue the point.

He popped his pen in his pocket and shot out his answers. "Your father's stroke was embolic rather than thrombotic. The bad news is that with embolic strokes it is possible another stroke might follow. We are watching closely for that."

"Another stroke?"

"What you need to know is that when a stroke is thrombotic, it's basically a closing off of the artery wall. An embolic stroke is a result of debris traveling into the brain, and it is possible for more debris to be on its way, so to speak."

"Debris?"

"Clot. From what I can tell from the symptoms, your father has had an ischemic attack to Broca's area of the brain. . . ."

I was writing furiously.

"The lack of blood supply to the brain was of sufficient duration to cause an infarct—"

"I don't know 'infarct.'"

"*Infarct* is simply the tissue that dies from lack of oxygen. This lesion in your father's brain . . ."

I did not ask what a lesion was, but I wrote it down to ask someone else.

"... is, as I said, in Broca's area."

"I'm not sure where that is." I dearly hoped he didn't think I was prolonging this screed as a dumb blonde's high-minded attempt at flirting.

"Broca's area is the location of many of the language centers of the brain, which is why your father is aphasic as well as suffering from agraphia, alexia, mild apraxia, and some paraphasic speech. At least that's what I've observed. The therapists have noted to me that he has a tendency to perseverate. He also has some ataxia on his right side, although I see signs of improvement there."

"You know," I said, trying to sound as stupid as he clearly thought I was, "I don't have a clue what you're talking about. In fact, the only words you say that I understand are 'and,' 'the,' and 'suffering.' Can you say that same speech without all the flimflam?" I looked at him wide-eyed and blond.

"Haven't they given you the pamphlet on aphasia?" He rummaged around in the brochure rack and came up dry. "Ask Martha to give you that pamphlet for family members. The blue one."

"I'll do that. But I'm not asking general questions here. I'm trying to find out specifically about my dad."

"I can't tell you that. You'll need to ask Dr. Moore." Dr. Lilly strode purposefully down the hall, probably wishing for the return of strictly enforced visitors' hours.

I hate being treated like a speck. I felt keen fury—fury way past emotion and on toward strategy. Dr. Lilly didn't know that he hadn't succeeded in shoving me back to my rightful spot as a whimpering, compliant family member. He had merely steeled my resolve. I would raise hell and put a brick under it if I had to.

The next day when Martha came in I decided to sheathe my claws until I could find a doctor. I relied heavily on my background in improvisational theater. For nearly an entire morning I holstered my fury and acted like a nice person—like Mother, in fact. I put on my dress-up clothes and pleaded. What were Dad's prospects? Surely they could generalize in some way. Why couldn't they give me a ballpark prognosis? What was this indirection all about? Why was everyone avoiding the topic?

"I know you're anxious." Martha purred, as if there were a thunderstorm and I was a trembling pup, quaint in my simple fear and needing comfort. I worried that she might forget herself and pet me. "Your father does have deficits and he always will. But all strokes are different. It's really too hard to say."

"Okay, so if every stroke is different, why is everybody here getting treated the same way?" I wasn't being snotty, I was stating what seemed to me an observable fact.

"Would you like me to set up an appointment for you with Dr. James? She's our neuropsychologist. She might be able to give you some coping mechanisms."

I wasn't looking for coping mechanisms. I was looking for information. I tracked down Dr. Moore and got a smallish little speech on general stroke, but nothing specific to Dad and nothing about the rehab process (he was, after all, the *neurologist,* not the rehab specialist). I went to the hospital library, where the librarian was very helpful, but there wasn't any useful information there beyond the blue aphasia pamphlet for families. By this time, Jeff, my sister's husband, had arrived from North Carolina. He found me in the library and bounded to the computers, logging onto the Internet. A physician's assistant in cardiovascular surgery, he would surely dig up something fabulous that would help Dad. I was so relieved I shuddered with goosebumps.

"Look at this! De-luxe!" he said, bouncing in his chair and pointing at the screen, transfixed. I pulled up a chair, my pen poised over my notebook to write down everything. Jeff clicked a button on the screen and I watched as the Seattle King Dome imploded and fell to the ground, as if in slow motion. They were making room to build another stadium.

"I don't care about this, Jeff."

"How can you not care?" he said, his Long Island accent even more pronounced now that he was in the west. "This is fantastic! It's the King Dome! This is a once-in-a-lifetime experience! You gotta care!" he implored, as if the problem was that I didn't understand. "Wanna see it again?" he turned his attention back to the screen and replayed the action.

I knew Jeff well enough to know that as soon as this little diversion had passed I would have his full attention, so I ignored him.

I spent my morning and the first part of the afternoon trying to get information that was more helpful than Stroke 101. I failed. The less willing the hospital staff were to budge with the goods, the more I wanted it and the more I assumed the worst. Did they know something dreadful that they just didn't have the nerve to disclose? But mostly I was frantic about the passing of time. I knew we needed to get Dad into rehab *now*. Rick had been urgently clear: the brain needed to work to rewire itself right away or it might be too late. I could picture Dad's brain solidifying into a nonfunctioning lump, as useless as the clay ashtrays I had sculpted for my nonsmoking parents as a child. Rick's parting instructions to me pursued me like a hag: *This needs to be your top priority. Get your dad into rehab as soon as possible.*

We made an appointment with Dr. James for that afternoon—me, my sister, and my mom. I'm sure it was odious to Mom. Sharon and I had routinely sought the help of shrinks to get us through our divorces and various other life hurdles. Mother, however, had never in her life set foot in the office of a psychiatrist. Mom and Dad's dinner club, called The Over the Hill Gang, met once a month for a potluck dinner, and Bob and Gloria Smith were part of the regular crew. Bob was a psychiatrist, and Mom probably thought that was risk enough. Who knew what kind of silent psychoanalysis he was doing during the dinner conversation and how the various interactions of the evening got parsed as he and his wife sat up in bed at night? But this was the real thing. There was no getting out of it. A stranger was about to ask her personal questions in front of her daughters.

Dr. James arranged four chairs in a little circle in her cramped office. "So!" She smiled tranquilly, her voice as soothing as white noise. This must seem like factory work to her, I thought. "How are you feeling?" Yes, factory work.

"I feel fine," Mother answered, truthfully. "I think Wayne is progressing well and I have a feeling that everything will work out." She clasped her hands in her lap, like she was in school.

"That's bullshit, Mother. Complete bullshit," I blurted. "You know what, Mom? You're in denial. You think that if you say everything's fine often enough it will be true! It's ridiculous!"

"Honey," Mom said, part warning, part rebuke.

"Really, Mom. I cannot figure how you can say that. You know the problem?" I turned my accusing eye to Dr. James. "Nobody around here will tell us anything. Believe it or not, I'd be perfectly happy for everything to be just fine. Really! I'm not a negative person! The problem is that we have no information. None! Zero! Zilch! Zip! Big goose egg!" I hit the last half-dozen words hard.

"Now, honey, that's not true. They're telling us as much as they know. These things take time."

"You know what I think? If they're telling us as much as they know, they shouldn't be in this business. They should know more. I would simply like a teensy weensy bit of information. A morsel." I mashed my thumb and index finger together to indicate how much. "Evidently that is just too much to ask for around here."

"Sounds like you feel upset," warbled Dr. James.

"Funny thing," I sang back. If she got paid by the blinding insight, she'd be homeless, I thought.

"Now let's hear from Sharon!" she directed, all aflutter about full participation.

Better get your raincoat, I thought, and I hope to God nothing in here is prone to rust. Before I could even look sympathetically at Sharon, she had burst into howling wet sobs.

"All I care about is Dad!" she bawled. "Isn't that what this is about?" Her face was screwing up into a splotchy little clod, her lips swollen and purplish. "I just don't understand why it's so hard to get

Dad into Sunnyside for rehab. That's what he needs." She squeaked out what she had to say, her voice needle sharp and thin, drawing out the last word into three whining syllables.

Mother was fine. I was furious. Sharon was crying. Had there been any waffling on the issue before, we were removing all doubt now: we were not the Waltons.

"So!" I piped up, feeling a tiny bit of responsibility for getting things back on track. "We're looking for coping mechanisms!"

Dr. James stopped holding her pen like it was a weapon and relaxed back into her chair. "Yes. Well," she hummed. "There are a variety of ways families approach the loss of capability in their loved one." She had shipped out, full sail, into the billowy pastel cloud of her mind.

By the time we used up our hour, Dr. James had delivered neither information nor coping mechanisms.

And now Mom was mad. She waited until we were out of the shrink's office to say so.

"Susan." I knew that one-word sentence. "We need to talk." I was in trouble and I didn't care. We marched to the hospital cafeteria, ordered coffee, and faced off at a table. A meeting of medical staff occupied the opposite corner.

Mom started in, battling through my frequent blasting interruptions of "That's bullshit!" and "That's the biggest bunch of bullshit I have ever heard in my whole life!" She was furious and embarrassed. In her view my ire not only had left hard feelings in my wake but in the end hadn't helped Dad. She delivered an ultimatum: I needed to behave myself. "You are an angry young woman," she concluded.

A fine point was put on Mother's conclusion when a tall, wiry man in a white coat with a stethoscope swinging authoritatively from around his neck strode up to our table. "Would you two women mind carrying on your argument in a less public place? We're trying to have a meeting."

"If you don't like it, maybe you should have your meeting in a less public place," I snapped back. Mother shot out of her seat and sprang for the door. I stayed in solitary protest and finished my coffee. I resisted the sensible urge to put my head down on the formica tabletop and bawl a rain barrel full. I didn't want to be acting like a pig, but how could I possibly behave better? I felt out of control in a situation that was out of control. Jeff joined me at my table in the cafeteria. Mother must have told him I was there.

Now that the King Dome was down, I would have to rely on him as my only remaining hope. Comprehensible and serene, he explained to me in plain language what had happened to Dad. Once he took out all the fancy words I understood it completely.

He told me that since Dad had heart disease, it meant he had clogged arteries. So what most likely happened was that a piece of fat that had built up in Dad's arteries broke off and wangled its way to his brain. It was also possible that the stroke could have been caused by a blood clot.

He explained that what makes a stroke big is simply how big the clot or piece of fat is. The bigger the blockage, the earlier in the brain it gets stuck. When it gets stuck early, more brain tissue gets cut off from oxygen and dies. The more of the brain that dies, the more problems the stroke survivor has because he loses whatever function that part of the brain was in charge of, from speech to swallowing to walking to writing to everything. That's what *embolic* and *infarct* and *lesion* and *ischemia* and *debris* and *deficits* were all about.

"Learn the words," Jeff advised. "It makes them nervous and they'll take you more seriously." He took my spiral notebook and wrote down the most important ones for me to know and use.

"Okay, I get the basic science, Jeff, now get to the bottom line," I pressed. "What can Dad do and what can't he do?"

As far as Jeff could tell, the major damage in Dad's brain had affected all aspects of his speech. Basically, his whole language system was blown. He couldn't talk. He could *think* the words, but his brain had lost the connection between the thought and the verbal expression of that thought, so his brain couldn't send signals to his mouth and tongue. The train tracks didn't meet. Sometimes he could pop out a word that was right, but more often he couldn't. Oddly, this only added to the frustration—if he could get it right once, you'd think he'd be able to get it right again. But "getting it right" was often random and unpredictable, providing hope when really it was just luck.

Dad also couldn't read. He'd lost his ability to recognize letters of the alphabet and words as anything that had meaning. He could see them as lines and shapes, but he couldn't see *B* as a letter of the alphabet that had a specific sound, let alone recognize the combination of letters *ball* as signifying a toy that bounces.

Which meant Dad also couldn't write. He could think the words, but since he didn't know that *B* corresponded to the sound "buh," he had no ability to put anything down on paper.

His ability to write was further compromised by numbness on his right side. His left brain was affected, which meant his right side was affected. It looked to Jeff as if the physical effects on his right side were not nearly as severe as the language effects. Still, he couldn't coordinate his motion well enough to, for example, grip a pencil. That explained why he spilled his milk every time he tried to pour it from a carton into a glass, and couldn't spread jam on his toast. The damage to his left brain also affected his vision on his right side, so he'd run into things because he couldn't see them in his peripheral vision. Since his right side was also numb, he would walk the way people do when their foot has fallen asleep, which would affect his balance. He would probably fall over a lot, at least at first.

Dad could understand what was said to him. That was the good news. But it had to be one person at a time talking very slowly. More than one person talking and he wouldn't be able to track the conversation. It was as if the comprehension part of his brain went from a four-lane interstate to a country road.

Right now, the whole "system failure" in his brain had left Dad disoriented and confused. That's why he did things like pour water into the phone, which would be indescribably frustrating and terrifying to him.

"So, I take it Dad's stroke was big," I summarized.

"Big enough."

Oddly, even though the news on Dad wasn't good, I felt relieved just to know.

Jeff, on the other hand, looked uncharacteristically worried. He was generally so slaphappy that I often thought being married to him would be like being married to a six-month-old golden Lab. He confided that his biggest concern wasn't what caused the stroke, or even what deficits Dad had, but how long before Dad got started on rehab. Although the dead brain tissue couldn't be brought back to life, other parts of the brain could be retrained to take up reading, writing, and speaking. Jeff was anxious because the retraining needed to start immediately. If the brain got used to being broken, it would be harder to retrain.

He didn't know why things were stalled in a neutral gear and was determined to find out.

"My father had a stroke," Jeff said, thinking back. "He never really recovered. But I think he could have. If things had been done right." He looked up at me, challenging me. "You ready for this?"

"Yes," I responded, not knowing what it meant to be ready.

He slapped the table and popped up out of his seat. "Let's go raise a little hell."

Me, four years old, Easter morning

5

Give Me a Year

I don't know what Jeff's idea of raising hell was, but for the next three days the whole family did nothing but wait.

We asked about when Dad would begin rehab and they said they were working on a schedule. We asked about the schedule and they said they were waiting for a room in the Sunnyside rehab unit. We asked about a time frame and they said "shortly." I asked what "shortly" meant. They said "soon." I asked if they could be more precise. They couldn't.

Rick's pressing counsel, *There's no time to lose*, was a curse that kept time with my pulse, measuring out the wasted minutes beat by beat.

Dr. Lilly, the rehab specialist, came around once a day, held up a pen, and asked Dad what it was. Dad squeezed his eyes shut, tightened his jaw, and forced out "a . . . p-p-p-ehh-n." When the doctor left, Dad looked at us and rolled his eyes as if to say "What does he think I am, dumb?"

Other than that daily distraction, there appeared to be no plan. We tried to fill the time.

"How about some ice cream, Dad?" I said this at about two o'clock every afternoon.

"Crit. C-c-crittle. 'Kay," he'd respond, heaving his legs off the side of the bed and pulling his sweatshirt down over his stomach, taking in a deep, sighing breath. I'd hold on to him and we'd walk down to the cafeteria.

I described to him the weather, easing him over to a window so he could see for himself. I told him about Rick's latest furniture project and thrust photos into his hands so he could see for himself. He understood, but he could offer nothing back. Except mumbo jumbo.

Several times a day Sharon suggested to Dad that they take a walk. She held on to a belt tied around his waist to steady him if he started to fall. Desperate to communicate what he wanted, he used his finger to write on his hand, then he looked at Sharon and gibberish came out of his mouth. She held his hand and looked at him and said, "Dad, I don't understand you right now." It only made my father's sense of frantic terror grow.

By Friday we'd been sitting there for six days. All of us. The days eking themselves out one reluctant second after the next.

At last the transfer process ground around to us, and by the end of the sixth morning after his stroke, Dad was moved from the medical ward to Sunnyside Rehabilitation Center. What a relief to see Dad's name go up on the white board! His name on the left and names and times of his various therapy sessions in columns to the right. Speech, Recreational, Occupational, Physical. Finally, finally, it felt like things were starting to move. We walked with him to the first session—Orientation to Recreational Therapy.

Dad was surprisingly steady on his feet. He concentrated fiercely on putting one foot ahead of the other, trying not to betray to anyone that he had been physically compromised. We rode the elevator to the basement and walked down a long cinderblock corridor dimly lit with flickering fluorescent lights. Our conversation petered out as we began to hear it echoing back to us off the walls and ceiling. The smell of the place brought back dreadful distant memories of Bible school in the church basement.

We turned left into the Recreational Therapy room. The "recreations" were organized into stations so patients could move from one activity to another. I spotted the shop station first. Its central feature was its surreal neatness. Two clear plastic bins held screws and matching bolts. A screwdriver, wrench, and several strips of wood with matching holes in them completed the set. A third bin contained nails and roosted alongside a hammer and several two-by-fours, each about eight inches long and pocked with dents from numerous missed opportunities. A longer two-by-four spanned two risers, firmly secured, with a small practice saw at the ready underneath. There was not a mote of sawdust. I was accustomed to Dad's busy, messy, real workshop, and the preternatural Playskool tidiness of the ersatz station made it look menacing. I felt suddenly superstitious, seized with the fear that this station was a reverse Rosetta Stone. If Dad touched it, it would make him supremely stupid forever.

Beyond that was the home ec station, which showcased an apartment-sized electric stove, a tiny hip-high refrigerator, a few open cupboards holding several plates, cups, and glasses, a small metal sink, a wooden cutting board in the shape of a pig with a small dull knife on top, and a plastic ring below the sink that held a red-checked dish towel. Another open cupboard held a jar of peanut butter, a plastic bag of white bread, and a colander of oranges alongside four or five plastic storage containers of various sizes. I surmised that the several drawers contained an unmatched array of silverware and probably plastic wrap and foil. A green formica table with ribbed metal edging nestled between two brown metal folding chairs. I guess Dad would learn to make lunch here. And eat it, too. And clean up after himself. I contained my enthusiasm.

Neighboring home ec was the games station. A game of checkers, the red and black disks set up for immediate play, rested on a round formica table along with two decks of cards. A bookcase, listing against the wall, was crammed with other games—Chinese Checkers, Scrabble, Yahtzee—all in frayed cardboard boxes held closed by big red rubber bands. Sand-filled egg timers, score pads, and dice, all loose from their moorings, were crammed in another plastic bin.

Behind that sat the computer station with an ancient beige PC. A genuine typewriter—a blue IBM Selectric, the exact model I'd used to type term papers in high school twenty-five years ago—sat beside the computer, as if competing for suitors. I had a hunch there hadn't been any for a long, long time.

The final station was a sitting area dominated by a brown plaid couch, a coffee table of the style that Sharon and I dubbed Trailer Court Chic, and a television set teetering heavily on a metal kitchen cart. An old man, white bristles sprouting all over his face like rime frost, sat slumped on the couch, pitched to one side. His red scaly legs, so swollen that his skin pulled tight against his ropy purple veins, poked out like brittle tree branches from beneath his bathrobe. His hands, fingers twisted at odd angles from arthritis, flopped and jumped aimlessly in his lap while he talked sluggish, uninspired gibberish to someone who wasn't there.

I took all this in with one sweep of my eyes and a big inhale of church basement air. Spontaneously, my teeth began chattering as if I had a fever. This whole place was making me truly, physically sick.

Paul, an ardent and cheerful recreational therapist, greeted us. He was probably a recent college graduate, but from my distant vantage point of forty-four years, he looked about twelve. He had short blond hair, gently spiked so it looked perpetually wet, an earring in one ear, and a muddy green tattoo circling his wrist—a snake eating its tail from what I could make out. His muscled forearms and mild strut seemed like advance press for nicely rippling pecs hidden beneath his cotton shirt. I supposed that it was an important job qualification to be strong. I knew it was a job qualification to be enthusiastic, which he was, categorically.

"Well, Mr. Edsall!" beamed Paul. "Do you like cards? Have you ever played solitaire? How would you like to learn to play solitaire? Would you like that?"

"No, Dad would not like that," I said, with sinister calm. "He plays cribbage and he wins."

"Well! We'll get you back to using a computer! You can write letters to your friends!" It was irrelevant to him that Dad had never used a computer in his life—or a typewriter. Nor had he ever written a letter to his friends. He flew to small towns in Montana on Sundays for breakfast with his friends.

I was so brokenhearted that all I wanted to do was haul off and smack that guy. I needed someone to blame for how desperate I felt and how desperate I knew Dad felt. We had been fighting for nearly a week to get Dad into rehab. Now that we were finally here, it seemed like the centerpiece of their plan was to wheedle Dad into lowering his standards, prepare him for a more sedentary life, teach him to settle for making peanut butter and jelly sandwiches and not falling down in the shower. It seemed to me that this therapeutic setup was the beginning of trying to fob off on Dad the notion of pleasant puttering as a lifestyle. I could barely take it in.

I looked at Dad. I could tell that he wanted to sock someone too. His back was rigid, his jaw was held in close to his neck, his lips had shriveled into a thin gray line. He frowned. This was worse than the day he had to walk me down the church aisle and give me away to a man neither one of us loved. At least in marriage there was a way out.

Paul put his arm behind my mother's back and directed her to the card table, patting its wood-grain formica surface. Dad followed. But he wouldn't sit until Paul nearly shoved him into the metal chair, misunderstanding Dad's slowness, which was not because he didn't understand but because he did. Dad understood exactly.

Dad eyeballed the home ec station. A morbidly cheerful therapist in a brightly colored smock was trying to coax food into the mouth of a woman who was strapped into a wheelchair.

"Goddamn shit hell son of a bitch fuck assholes assholes goddamn son of a bitching assholes assholes assholes goddamn sheeee-it shit shit shit shit!" someone was shouting in the hall. I sidled toward the door. A man, probably in his mid-sixties and another stroke victim, was strapped into a chair. He'd lost all power of speech except for swearing. The nurse was trying to quiet him, which only propelled his frustration, and in consequence his swearing, into high gear. This could be my father, I thought. I was certain that Dad was thinking the same thing.

I looked for clues to what Dad was feeling. His eyebrows seemed to have slipped down the edges of his face to frame flat black pebbles for eyes that kept darting over to me, to Sharon, to Mom as if he were sending an SOS in Morse code. His shoulders disappeared into his body, leaving a gentle unbroken line from his neck to his elbow. He looked like something held together in a sack, drained of all shape. A husk.

A vague feeling of foreboding clung to me. We were up against a medical monolith, a rehab machine whose crowning purpose seemed to be to strip us of all expectation as quickly as possible and then set about helping us be at peace with the hopeless situation. Watching my accomplished, virile father fight against the fear of being buried alive loosed in me a force I had never known before. I could tell Sharon was feeling it too. In that moment we became the Furies, those mythical winged women who punish crimes against their kin by hounding their victims until they die in madness.

Frank, another recreational therapist, made the first mistake early the next day.

Dad was slumped in a pink plastic chair with thin metal arms outside the speech therapist's office waiting for his thirty-minute session. Sharon and I stood next to him—not because we wanted to stand but because there was only one chair. Frank, a good six feet tall, dressed in boot-cut Levis, a tooled leather belt, and a denim shirt, moseyed on up to Dad, put his hand out, and bellowed as if calling cattle, "Hello, Mr. Edsall! Say! Who've you got here with you?" Dad looked at us. His eyebrows drew together in concentration and worry. He looked down at his hands, his fingers rubbing the pads of his thumbs as if to conjure thoughts, words, names.

"Sh-sh-ar-ron," he posed, feebly. Then he looked at me. Blank. Rubbing his thumbs smooth. He squeezed his eyes shut to focus his thoughts, and shook his head. He let out a long stream of exhausted breath and slumped even further down.

"Susan," I offered, reaching for one of Dad's hands to stop the rubbing. Frank plowed on.

"I heard you used to be a pilot! Well, you'll never be able to do that again. But we'll find something else for you to do."

Sharon moved so quickly I was surprised I didn't hear a sonic boom. She grabbed Frank by the elbow, her long red fingernails sinking into his biceps, wheeled him around on the heel of his cowboy boot, and yanked him down the hall. Had she been taller, she would have grabbed him by the ear or the hair.

"Dad *is* a pilot, Frank. He didn't *used to be* a pilot." She jabbed at his face, her polished fingernail like a red-hot stiletto. "Got that? He *is* a pilot." She let that sink in. "If you tell him that he'll never fly again you might as well cut his throat," she snarled.

She stormed back, ablaze with righteousness.

"Nailed that puppy," she reported to me and Dad.

But Dad hadn't even noticed Sharon's departure or indignant return. He was probably still trying to absorb the ferocious fact that he used to be a pilot.

We never saw Frank again. But it hardly mattered. Each therapist pounded out the same monotonous drumbeat. Dad would not recover much. He would learn to find happiness in the subtler things in life like playing checkers and making meals without using the stove.

They gave him a set of cards that said, "Please be patient. I have had a stroke and have trouble speaking," trying to persuade Dad to gambol around the therapy room role-playing how he would use these in public situations so he wouldn't be mistaken for a degenerate. "You wouldn't want people to think you were on drugs or an alcoholic, would you?" the therapist asked Dad.

The next day in Sunnyside we met Ann, an occupational therapist. She sprang into the room as if propelled by a slingshot. She was tall and athletic, wearing red sport pants with a white racing stripe down the side, white tennies with soles that wedged out at the bottom for a good solid grip, and a T-shirt tucked into her elastic waistband. A thick elastic band held her long dark hair in a high ponytail that bounced and swung when she walked. Her cheeks were naturally rosy, her lips soft. I could just tell she ate a big bowl of cereal for breakfast, plunging her oversized spoon into it with gusto and slurping. I imagined there would be lots of jobs she'd be perfect for—doggie day care, summer camp for overweight children, handing out food samples at Costco.

"Hel-lo, Mr. Edsall!" she yelped. "How are we doing today, huh? Okey-dokey! We'll work on balance today, okay? Balance? O-kay?"

"Can I talk to you for a minute?" It was my turn. Ann followed me out of the room. I turned to face her. "Dad's not retarded and he's not deaf. You're talking to him like he's both and it's not helping."

"Patients like us to be peppy and encouraging!" Ann chirped. "It gives them a shot in the arm!" She bounced up and down on her toes, grinning.

When they weren't engaging Dad in activities he found irrelevant, like building birdhouses out of tongue depressors, they scheduled him in group activities that simply gave him the creeps. Dad would roll his eyes before going into a session or give a rip-roaring Bronx cheer after a session to let us know what he thought. We got the message. Amy, a recreational therapist with a big red dog, wanted Dad to sit in a circle and try to talk with other stroke patients about how they were feeling. In an admirable effort of orchestrated mismanagement we ensured that Dad missed every one of those sessions. We didn't even tell him about them.

My growing fear was that Dad was beginning to believe in his own disability. The humdrum expectations of the medical professionals, people we'd counted on to be the experts, were debilitating. I continued to press for answers. How long do people improve before they level off? Does recovery progress through predictable stages? What's the best we can hope for? All I got was a contemptibly fainthearted vagueness.

We soon came to realize that, as a family, we had to be our own lodestar. We had to set our compass on one destination: Dad would fly again. On this we chose to agree.

We didn't talk as a family about whether Dad would fly again. Ever. To do so would have been a bald act of betrayal. Dad flew. That's how we understood who we were as a family and who Dad was as a man. It wasn't something you questioned, it was just a fact. Like agreeing on gravity. Sharon had already staked her claim that Dad would fly again in her shoot-out with Frank, coming at it full throttle and straight from the heart. Mom was reliably in the camp of thinking positive, so she didn't have to struggle to believe with all her unwavering might that Dad would fly.

That left me. And Dad.

I tried to imagine what life would be like for him—and us—if he didn't return to piloting. There was nothing—*nothing*—to imagine. I needed some time to think—alone—and found the hospital's family lounge. It was mercifully empty, and I slouched onto the beige plastic couch. A wiggly brown water stain on the ceiling framed my view.

It's at times like these that many people want to pray. Right then I was among them. I wanted to be in a soothing, roomy chapel, able just to pray and feel awash in grace and composure and certainty. But I couldn't believe in some well-intentioned Somebody who didn't have enough power to keep things afloat in the first place but would pitch in now that we were drowning. While I couldn't bring myself to pray, I was willing to say out loud what I wanted, and if God wanted to eavesdrop, there wasn't anything I could do about it anyway.

I stared at the water stain and said out loud, "Dad will fly again." I had planned for that to be my little ritual, my mark of commitment, the declaration I would utter and then hustle back to Dad's room to resume my duties. But it didn't go like I thought it would. Quite unexpectedly, my heart started to race and great waves of feeling made me shudder and shake. "Dad will fly again," I forced out again, repeating this over and over until I was overtaken by racking sobs that left me with the hiccups.

In the strangest way, I felt that only in this very moment had I truly chosen to be in this thing—that I was no longer snatched away from my real life to fight a reluctant battle but choosing to take this trip, wherever it might lead. I had no idea how we would ever get Dad to fly again. I just knew we had to figure out how to make it happen.

Then I grabbed the Kleenex and blew my nose. Now we just needed Dad. He needed to choose to be in this thing too.

The next day, yet another occupational therapist bounded toward where Dad and I waited in the hallway, Dad in the single pink plastic chair, me on the floor beside him. Mike looked like he belonged on a box of Cheerios. His blond hair was cropped close to his ears, his striped cotton shirt tucked neatly into pressed khaki pants. His polished brown loafers made the slightest squeak when he walked. His face was soft and pink, and he smelled pleasantly of soap and mouthwash and deodorant.

He held out his hand to Dad in greeting. "Hello, Mr. Edsall! I'm Mike! Gosh! I hear you're a pilot! That's a heck of a talent, isn't it?" Dad leaned forward, his elbows resting on his thighs, his hands clasped between his knees. He was dog-tired. He gripped his hands together, the muscles in his face tightened, and his head dropped. His eyes squeezed shut in the by now familiar effort just to talk. "That's h-h-h-is-tory." Then he exhaled, the thought completed, his face as lonesome as a burned-down barn.

"Well, I'll see you at three o'clock! Just wanted to stop by and say hi!" Mike slapped Dad on the knee and hurried down the hall to another appointment.

I crawled over to Dad. I knelt in front of him and grabbed both his hands in mine.

"Look at me, Dad. Look at me." I waited. He stared at the floor. I couldn't control the trembling of my elbows and knees. Never before had I been so intimate with my father. Ours was a sort of man-to-man relationship. I was much more likely to sock him in the arm to show my affection than give him a long warm hug. He returned the affection by routinely poking his stubby finger in my ear and making an irritating swishing sound whenever I was engrossed in a book. I had never grabbed both his hands and looked him square in the eyes, except maybe when I was four and I stood on his feet, holding tight so we could dance together.

"Look at me," I pleaded, clutching his hands. I waited, the silence piling up by the pound, pressuring me to abandon the promise I was about to make. "Please Dad," I whispered, willing myself not to cry.

Slowly, Dad moved his head up so his eyes met mine. Was he afraid of me? Of what I might say? "It's *not* history, Dad, and you have to stop saying that. You *will* fly again. I know that. I promise. You are a pilot and you will fly."

"I'm outta luck, h-h-h-oney. Bet-ter get u-u-used t-t-to . . . it."

"No, Dad, you are *not* out of luck. I *know* you will fly. You have to believe that too, do you hear me? You have to believe that you will fly. Do you understand me?"

I was on my knees. I didn't know if I was begging or praying or raving. Maybe they're all the same thing. But I wouldn't let go of my father's hands. My pink fingers, the nails ragged from years of nervous chewing, enveloped by his big calloused hands, couldn't have looked that much different than when I was a child. "You will fly again, Dad. In one year. You will fly. You will fly me for my birthday. We will do this together. Okay? I promise."

Silence. Dad stared down at the floor.

I leaned forward. I would not let go. "Okay, Dad?"

Dreadful, lengthy silence spooled out before me.

"Please, Dad. One year."

I could feel his warm hands tighten around my own. He squeezed them hard, decisively, and then looked up.

"O-k-k-k-ay. Wuh—wuh—one year." He was spent.

Dad with a Piper Pacer, Alaska, 1954

6

Uncharted Territory

That night I walked the mile back to my hotel room in the numbing rain and in the dark, my mittenless hands stuffed into my coat pockets, my shoulders hunched ineffectually against the drizzle. I felt forlorn, consumed by our formidable task.

The day's events played through my mind like a CNN Special Report, complete with urgent, pounding commentary and incendiary video clips.

After Dad and I made our pact, we'd gone to see Cheri, the speech therapist. I trusted Cheri because she looked sensible. She wore khaki pants, brown loafers, a sage green crewneck sweater, and a small bobble on a simple gold chain. Her earrings were restrained little gold dots peeking out discreetly from blond hair cut short to frame her sweet, scrubbed face. Her serviceable fingernails were trimmed short—neither chewed nor fashionable. She could use them to pick up dimes or paper clips off the desk, but she couldn't injure you with them. I liked her.

Dad worked next to her at the table. I watched from a chair by the wall, writing down every single thing she did, every single thing she said. I needed to learn what to do, what not to do, what to say, and how to say it. If Dad was going to fly in one year, I needed to learn everything.

Cheri pointed out a word—*cat*—and Dad worked at pronouncing it, unsuccessfully. Then she'd put a picture of a cat next to it. Dad continued to struggle.

"Look at me," Cheri said, tapping her finger against her mouth. "Cat," she said, slowly and distinctly. "Cat," she repeated while Dad stared at her.

"Cat," Dad mimicked.

"Good! Very good!" Cheri pointed back at the word. "Do you understand what it means?"

Dad shook his head no.

I couldn't get this scene out of my mind. Dad didn't know what *cat* meant. How could he ever learn to fly again? I fought back the worry that we were in the Bermuda Triangle, that my-dad-the-pilot had been lost without a trace.

Where had Dad's fearlessness begun? Where were the headwaters of his passion to fly?

Dad had taken to flying as if he were a direct descendant of the Wright brothers, starting lessons soon after he and Mom arrived in Anchorage, Alaska. They went there six months after they were married so Dad could work on building the Air Force hospital. It was a romantic and adventurous beginning—Mom riding off into the wilderness with her man.

The first time Mother ever noticed Dad was the spring of 1945, her sophomore year in high school, when he and Granddad stopped by the dairy farm where Mom lived. Dad's family had just moved back to Bozeman from Missoula and they needed a milk cow, so they bought Lavancha, an endearing cow with only one stubby horn. Mom, hovering around the edges of the barn, spied Dad, noticed his chipped front tooth, and thought he was cute.

Six weeks later was the Spinster Spree, the one time each year when girls would ask guys to a dance. Mother hung with a group of ten popular girls who got together every other weekend for slumber parties, where they would listen to records, sing songs, and everyone but Mom would smoke until the air turned blue. All they talked about the weekend before the Spinster Spree was who would ask whom. Mother was scared witless. She'd never asked a boy to anything! But the bevy of girls had settled it—Mother would ask Wayne Edsall.

But how? She felt like she was on the third floor of a house on fire. She couldn't call him on the phone—they were on a party line with nine other families. She'd have the entire farm community listening in, each click registering another lifted receiver, stifled giggles and laughter sure to unnerve her past repair. With only three days left until the dance, her clutch of friends threatened reckless action—they would do the asking for her. Fear propelled her. Passing Wayne in the hall between classes, her books hugged to her chest to stay the idiotic tremble of her hands, Mom popped the question.

They did more than dance. They went steady off and on until graduation—breaking up whenever Mom looked sideways at another guy. Or he at another girl. Standard high school dating misery.

After high school, Dad enlisted for two years in the Navy and served a third year in Guam during the Korean War. In May of 1952, he came home for a two-week leave, bringing with him a diamond ring. This time there was no off-and-on. Wayne and Marcia got engaged. They married in late December and combined their honeymoon with a drive to San Diego where Dad finished the six months remaining in his tour of duty. They returned to Bozeman in June to buy a brand-new 1952 International pickup, and within a week they were waving good-bye from the back window of the truck.

Mom admits to having one crying spell as they drove out of Bozeman. She was determined not to squall in front of her mother, so she acted eager for her new adventure when saying good-bye to her folks. But the minute they crossed the town line, she put her head in her hands and bawled. She cried for a solid fifteen minutes and then it was over with. She was on her way to Alaska.

It took them four full days to drive the AlCan Highway—twenty-five hundred miles of dirt road that connected Montana through Alberta and the Yukon Territory to Alaska. All they expected to need for the trip—including gasoline, food, water, and sleeping bags—plus all they expected to need to make a home in Alaska was wedged into the truck bed and covered with a tarp. Since there were no motels, at night they pulled out their sleeping bags and slept under bridges.

When they got to Anchorage, they moved into the basement apartment of the house where Dad's parents lived—Granddad was the construction superintendent of the Air Force hospital. It had a living room with chrome furniture, two padded folding chairs, and a wingback chair in desperate need of reupholstering. They bought a small television set, which had programming for one hour each day. The kitchen had metal cupboards, a small sink and stove, and exactly eight inches of counter space between the stove and the fridge. They wedged a washer and dryer into the hallway and that was it. Mom learned to adjust to the cramped apartment. Accommodating Grandma took more seasoning.

Grandma had exacting standards. I fantasize that she had "Idle hands are the Devil's workshop" tattooed on her inner thigh, where she could see it every morning. She embroidered a set of seven dish towels that summed up her view of things: Monday, Laundry; Tuesday, Ironing; Wednesday, Cleaning; Thursday, Marketing; Friday, Baking; Saturday, Mending; Sunday, Worship.

Even someone as fastidious as Mom didn't adhere strictly enough to the antiseptic standards that Grandma set. It irked Grandma, for instance, that Mom didn't clean the rubber treads on the stairs every day. Mom was pregnant with Steve and would have harked up her lunch at every step if she'd bent down with a wet sponge, the smell of rubber shooting up her nostrils like a stream of acid. This excuse didn't wash with Grandma. For one thing, she didn't believe in morning sickness, which meant she didn't believe in naps either—

two things Mother engaged in on a daily basis. Not that Grandma actually said anything. She just made it known. Lots of conversations with Grandma took place that way—in full and articulate silence.

Mom didn't think of it as a rugged beginning. Being poor was old hat to her, and Anchorage had more going on than the dairy farm she'd left. But managing the winter took some ingenuity. The sun didn't come up before ten and didn't stay up much past midafternoon—that she could handle. But construction on the hospital shut down until it was warm enough and light enough to work outdoors, which meant that Dad was home. All day. Every day. That's what needed to be managed.

They did their best. Mom reupholstered the wingback chair, teaching herself from a do-it-yourself book. Dad bought a large paint-by-numbers kit of a deer in the woods. He worked on that at night, but it wasn't doing the trick during the day. He got the itch to learn to fly.

There was probably no rougher country to learn in for lots of reasons. The weather was unpredictable and changed quickly, the cloud ceiling often dropped below one hundred feet, the mountains and glaciers were precipitous, and much of the country was uncharted, one big expanse of yellow on the maps.

It was February when Dad signed up for flying lessons. His flying instructor was Roy Lindsay, a slender, laconic man from South Dakota known for letting his students get into trouble and then get themselves out of it. Roy didn't waste any time getting Dad in the air. On his second lesson Dad was in the pilot's seat of a Piper J3, a small two-seater on skis with the pilot in the front and the rider in the back. Several minutes into this student flight, the crankshaft broke, which meant the engine quit, which meant Dad was in trouble.

"You'll just have to handle it," Roy shouted from the backseat.

Without an engine, Dad had to look for the best place to land. Gradually losing altitude, he circled back to find a road that had recently been snowplowed to use as his landing strip.

"It was no big deal," Dad said. "In that part of the country, airplanes landed on the road all the time. There weren't that many cars.

Not really. You just had to keep your head plugged in, that was all."
"Keep your head plugged in" was a constant refrain at home, advice
applied to everything from ice skating to dating boys.

For Dad, being in the air was as comfortable as being on the
ground. He got a bead on that road-turned-airstrip as easily as if he'd
been operating a backhoe. He landed the airplane, pushed it off to
one side, and he and Roy dismantled it.

"We had it on a trailer and back at the airport in under two
hours," Dad bragged, as if the speed of dispatching the crippled
plane was the impressive part of the story.

By the end of his fourth lesson he soloed. He had his operator's
license within three months. The following summer his dad bought
him his first plane—a Piper Clipper with floats and skis. It cost two
thousand five hundred dollars, almost four months' salary. Dad was
twenty-three years old, and he's never been without a plane since.

Lots of the guys Dad knew had planes, and they often took off to
go fishing for the day or hunting for the weekend. His first winter
there, they built themselves a ten- by twelve-foot ice fishing cabin on
Red Shirt Lake and went out once a week during the winter. They
took off and landed on the ice, guided by the makeshift runway
lights they strung out onto the lake and powered with a battery.

The day after Christmas in 1953, Dad, Bob, Kip, and Jack decided to go fishing for the day. Daylight only lasted from about ten in
the morning until three in the afternoon if they stretched it, so they
had to get off as soon as they could after the sun rose. Mom was nine
months pregnant by then, due any day. Dad promised to be back by
nightfall. Kip and Jack left first in Kip's plane. Dad and Bob followed.

Dad and Bob stopped at Nancy Lake to pick up bait. When they
landed, Dad discovered the snow was so sticky he couldn't get
enough speed to take off with the weight of two men in the plane.
Dad pitched out all the emergency gear that he routinely carried in
his plane—a tent, sleeping bag, stove, and packets of dried food—
and told Bob that someone would be by to get him. Maybe today.
Maybe tomorrow. Not to worry. Dad took off to fly to Red Shirt
Lake, about a twenty-minute trip.

By that time the weather was starting to deteriorate quickly. Clouds were coming in, visibility was a good ten feet, and it was starting to snow. Dad landed at Red Shirt Lake and dispatched Kip with the more powerful plane to pick up Bob. The weather was so lousy that Kip and Bob had to "grid it" to stay oriented at Red Shirt Lake. That meant Kip had to make his way up the lake by flying the width of the lake, making a ninety-degree turn to the right, making another ninety-degree turn to the right, flying the width of the lake again, and so on, using up precious fuel, until he could see the runway lights. He landed and they secured both planes, a miserable wind gaining force. They pulled Dad's plane up against the fishing cabin and connected the stovepipe from the oil stove to the plane engine to keep it warm.

The next day, December 27, the weather was too bad to fly. The day after that, December 28, my parents' second wedding anniversary, was more of the same. The cloud ceiling was at four hundred feet. They decided that Kip and Dad would try to make the one-hour flight to Anchorage in Kip's plane, leaving Bob and Jack behind. Kip and Dad would be back to pick them up, packing extra plane fuel, when the weather cleared in the next few days.

On the flight back to Anchorage the cloud ceilings continued to fall, an impenetrable thick dough pushing the plane to lower and lower altitudes. But at this point Dad and Kip were committed. They only had enough fuel to make it to Anchorage, and they were running out of daylight—they couldn't turn back. When they flew into Anchorage, about one-thirty that afternoon, as dusk was starting to fall, the cloud ceiling was so low that they flew past the fourth floor of the McKinley apartment building. If they'd had the presence of mind to stare they could probably have seen someone in the shower.

Dad walked into their basement apartment about three o'clock that afternoon to find Mom in labor. He bundled her up, took her to the hospital, and my brother, Steve, was born that night. Two days later the weather finally cleared, and Dad and Kip flew back to Red Shirt Lake to pick up their buddies and their gear.

We loved it when Dad would tell these stories. Sometimes Dad would launch in on a story and Mom would abruptly get up from the couch. "I can't stand this one," she'd announce, leaving the room hurriedly. "I almost lost you!" Nearly fifty years after the event, she still couldn't stomach the close calls.

Mom must be wondering if this might be the time we really do lose Dad, I thought, as I walked the remaining soggy blocks to my hotel room.

It was these stories that reminded me of who my father was. I would lash myself to these memories of his beginnings in Alaska. They would be my ballast.

Uncharted territory.

You'll just have to handle it.

Keep your head plugged in, that's all.

7

*Bud "lands" his Tiger Moth
on the interstate, 1987.*

Bud

"Where's Bud?" I asked Mother the following morning. "Why hasn't he been over? Has anyone called him?"

Sharon had called Bud the day of Dad's stroke, more than a week ago. She got as far as "Bud, this is Sharon" before she'd dissolved into a puddle of tears.

"Oh, shit," Bud said. He finished the conversation while Sharon cried, telling her to keep him posted as she knew more, that he would wait in Bozeman until she called and let him know when to come over, finishing with, "Hang in there, kid."

Bud and Dad were best friends, although I was sure they'd never actually said so. They worked every evening in the hangar out behind the house rebuilding their current project, the Airmaster. This model had been built in 1941 as a high-wing, four-seater charter plane, trumpeted at the time as the most efficient plane in the air. With only a 165-horsepower engine, it could fly at 155 miles per hour. There were only forty of them flying now, and Dad wanted his to be one of them.

This was the tenth antique airplane Dad and Bud had set out to rebuild and fly and the most confounding. The airplane was still strewn in little piles all over the shop, defying assembly. Dad had bought the Airmaster only three months earlier from a junk dealer in Colorado. With winter closing in, Dad was getting desperate to find a project. The junk dealer had been storing the wrecked plane for eighteen years. The funny thing about the Airmaster was that Dad and my brother, Steve, had seen this very plane sold eighteen years ago at an auction in Idaho. Dad wasn't looking for a project then, but he admired the plane. The pilot who bought it intended to fly it to his home in Seattle, but as he was preparing to take off, he'd taxied it into another plane and totaled it. The plane hadn't been in the air since.

Dad borrowed a trailer from Arlin, a pilot friend, and drove down to Colorado to buy the plane and haul home the fuselage and the "tailfeathers." Then he and Bud drove back down the following weekend to bring home the single wing, which was seven feet wide and thirty-four feet long.

Bud and Dad had been working on the wing right before Dad had his stroke. Every other plane they'd rebuilt had wings that were in two sections that they would bolt to the body of the airplane. Two wings are much easier to rebuild and reassemble than one large wing—they're just less unwieldy. This awkwardness of the Airmaster's large cantilevered wing made working on it miserable in every regard, from rebuilding it, to recovering it, and especially to mounting it on the fuselage.

Worse yet, unlike previous planes they had built, the nosepieces on the wing were tapered in such a way that each one had a slightly different angle. Every single nosepiece had to be custom measured and cut and then assembled so that the wing angled correctly while the leading edge "ran true." Dad and Bud had disassembled the wing and were cutting individual nosepieces to replace the damaged ones, but they had no patterns to work from. It was a tedious mathematical problem.

Rebuilding these antiques was the grown-up version of what Dad had done as a child. When he was in grade school he would order model airplanes to assemble. A tube of one-sixteenth-inch balsawood strips would arrive in the mail along with a blueprint. Dad would pull the blueprint out of the tube and unroll it like it was a secret code. He would tack the blueprint to a piece of plywood laid out on a table and cover it with waxed paper so he could see through it but not get glue all over it. Using the blueprint as his guide, he would cut and assemble the ribs, the struts, the fuselage, and the body of the plane, creating a frame. Then he would cover the frame with tissue paper, carefully cutting the paper to fit around curves and joints. "I never could get them to fly," he would tell us, still mystified by why. But it didn't daunt him. He kept ordering model planes, assembling them, and trying to get them in the air.

He never had trouble getting his real projects to fly. But he and Bud were having a devil of a time getting the Airmaster rebuilt. It wasn't as easy as a set of mail-order plans shimmering under a protective sheet of waxed paper. They consulted old pictures, old descriptions, and took careful notes as they disassembled the plane, but they had no blueprints. It was slow work. They tackled it every night in the hangar, which Dad called "the sandbox."

That's where Bud and Dad had spent nearly every evening for the past twenty years. Now more than ever Dad needed to see Bud. And Bud, I could only imagine, needed just as much to see Dad.

Mom looked weary as I pestered her about it. "Honey, we don't need Bud. We've got plenty to keep track of around here."

I disagreed.

"He works, Susan. He's on the road. We'll call him when Dad gets better and things settle down a little."

"That's bad, Mom. Bud needs to be here. It's weird that he's not."

"What would he do, honey? It's a long drive. What could he do over here, really? We already have too many cooks in the kitchen."

Mom was afraid that if Bud showed up it would seem to Dad as if the vultures were gathering. She was thinking he would be thinking that we were thinking he was about to die but we weren't saying anything because we didn't want him to think that's what we were thinking. Sometimes that was the convoluted way we reasoned and communicated, so she wasn't entirely off.

Maybe Mom wanted to protect Dad. Maybe she was afraid of rumors whispered about Dad around town. *Did you hear? Wayne Edsall can't talk. When he walks they have to hold on to a strap tied around his waist in case he falls. Isn't it sad? Poor Marcia.* I don't know, maybe she was hoping he'd snap out of it and nobody would have to know anything. I have no idea what she was thinking. She wouldn't say. Or couldn't. Or maybe she did say and I couldn't hear. In any case, I found a phone booth.

"Bud, this is Susan. I'm calling from the hospital. I'm wondering if you would come over and see Dad."

"I've been waiting for your mom to call. I didn't know if it was okay for me to come. I've kept the guys at the airport apprised of what I know, but I've been pretty general." Bud always spoke like he was just about to fall asleep—slow and calm, with plenty of space between sentences. Unlike me, nothing worked him up into a higher gear, let alone a frenzy. "How is he?" Bud asked, without inflection, like he was wincing in advance of getting hit. He didn't want to know the answer.

"He's bad, Bud. He's real bad." My throat closed up and I could only speak with a squeak. "He needs you to come over. He needs to see you."

Bud was silent. "You know, your dad and I, we've talked over a lot of things." He paused again. "He always told me if he ever got Alzheimer's he wanted me to lead him into the pond. I never thought I'd have to, that it would come to this." He was silent again, then let out a big anguished sigh. "I don't know if I can do this."

"You're his best friend, Bud."

"I am?"

"Of course you are, you dope."

"I guess I am. Yeah, he's my best friend, too."

Dad and Bud met over thirty years ago. They were competitors. Dad was running his own construction company and Bud was an estimator at Haggerty-Messmer Construction. Although Bud had wanted to learn to fly his whole life, it wasn't until he was thirty-three years old that he bought a plane and took lessons—in that order. Dad invited Bud to land at his grass airstrip out behind the house. So Bud did. Then Dad invited Bud to keep his plane in the empty hangar Dad had out there. So Bud did. In the winter Bud put skis on the plane and invited Dad to fly it anytime he wanted to. So Dad did. Flying a plane with skis brought back all Dad's memories of Alaska, and Bud and Dad fell into trading stories about the construction industry, about flying, about Dad's service in the Korean war and Bud's service as a Marine. A friendship developed.

They had gobs of fun out there in the hangar. One winter they were rebuilding the Waco, a World War II ambulance plane built in 1936. It was in bad shape. They had to rebuild the left wing entirely from scratch. While doing research on who had owned the plane previously, Dad discovered that the Waco he had just purchased was the exact plane he had flown when he was up in Alaska forty years earlier. Up there he flew it with skis.

Occasionally Bud would bring Tyler, his school-age grandson, along with him to the hangar. Tyler was devoted to Bud, loved airplanes, and was real pals with Dad, whom he called "Edsall." When he was in the hangar, Tyler acted like another one of the guys. One evening all three of them were in there and Tyler plunked himself down in the pilot's seat at the controls of the Waco. He strapped on goggles and a headset, and although his feet didn't reach the floor, he was punching buttons and pulling levers and flying that airplane, complete with his own supply of engine sounds. Dad caught Bud's attention. While Tyler was absorbed in his role as pilot, Dad lifted up the tail of the plane and shook it, turning it in the hangar. Tyler exploded out of that seat, clambered down over the edge of the open cockpit, scaled the body, slid onto the wing and down onto the hangar floor. When his feet hit solid ground he spun around and hit Dad with a raven's glare. "Edsall!" he barked, gathering his wits and discovering that he had not, after all, taken off. "I didn't like that!" He switched from pilot to mechanic for the rest of the evening.

I never spent much time in the sandbox with Bud and Dad, except as an invited guest. I'm sure lots of time passed without a word being spoken, big band music playing on the radio and Dad whistling along with it, Bud bouncing around like a fart in a mitten, keeping busy.

Dad wins most of the arguments, but Bud's wins become prized—their scarcity increasing their value. Years ago they were rebuilding one of their first antiques. The rudder was crushed up like a ball of tinfoil, and fixing it had them buffaloed. Luck showed up in Harold Hamm, another pilot from Helena. He offered to take it to his shop, straighten it up, and recover it. When Harold brought it back, Dad tried to fit it onto the plane, but there was so much paint and unidentifiable glop in the holes that he couldn't set the pins. Over Bud's objections, he applied the Wayne Edsall method and clobbered it. He would bully it into position. Bud watched as the rudder collapsed under the drubbing.

Dad slid a sidelong look at Bud.

"You are a dumb shit," Bud said.

They argue about how to approach covering a wing, how to attach a wing to a fuselage, where to take an engine to get it reconditioned. Usually Dad has an idea about how to approach the job. Bud thinks it won't work. Dad can't explain exactly why he thinks it will work, he just knows it will. Bud says bullshit. Dad waits a day or two, then does it his own way. Sometimes it works, sometimes it doesn't. That's the way it goes.

They do more than spar in those evenings and weekends together, though. They talk about all kinds of things that are personal and important to them—how to help a pilot with cancer, worries about friends who've fallen off the wagon, fear of getting

Alzheimer's, plans for going on the air search for a missing plane in the Bitterroots.

Somehow Sharon and I developed a snarky relationship with Bud that we carried on in the realm usually reserved for junior high boys with an underdeveloped sense of humor. Bud calls us "the Blister Sisters." We've hurled a bucket of cold water over the shower stall while he was cleaning up, snuck into his room and short-sheeted his bed, made him a sandwich and slipped a piece of brown paper in between the slices of meat. Truly shopworn teenage antics. Bud complains, but he couldn't imagine a happy life without us.

Occasionally Bud provokes us beyond camp pranks into the category of loud public embarrassment. One afternoon Bud spotted Sharon and Mom getting into their car in a grocery store parking lot. Bud hollered at the top of his lungs, "Get the hell out of that car or I'll call the cops!"

Mother, mortified, checked to make sure she was in the right car, but Sharon's instincts kicked in and she let loose. "You keep your flapping jaw shut, you fat ugly toad. Don't even come near me because I have an order from the judge, you pervert."

Shoppers had stopped barreling to their cars with their grocery carts. With no alternative, and certain to lose if he pressed further, Bud walked back to his Jeep and muttered to the parking lot at large, "She's out on work release from a mental hospital, folks. I'm sure they'll pick her up shortly. Move along. Move along."

Bud could never quite anticipate which corner we might fly out of, so he always got caught flat-footed and he always lost. But intrepid and overconfident, he kept on trying. It was the most reliable way he had of letting us know he loved us.

One of the things we most enjoyed ribbing him about was his deathly fear of water. Bud was so afraid of water that he wouldn't fly over lakes. He often said that he wore three life jackets in the shower. How on earth had he ever become a Marine? Why had he *wanted* to become a Marine? Why would they have wanted him? It was bewildering.

He told us that in basic training, he hated Fridays the most. That was the day everyone had to walk off the end of the diving board with all their gear on. Bud couldn't swim. He couldn't even dog-paddle. But he could hold his breath. So he'd sink to the bottom of the pool, and eventually somebody would stick a pole in for him to grab and they would drag him to the side.

Bud would tell this story as if he were a perfectly reasonable person caught weekly in a ridiculous but unavoidable situation from which he had found a clever way out every time. He was proud of it. Darned proud. We tipped over from laughing. Finally, Sharon would wipe her eyes and conclude, "We knew you were stupid, but we didn't think you were *that* stupid." Then she would pause for dramatic effect and add, "Huh. I guess you are."

When we would go up to the cabin for a weekend, Bud would fly over Sunday mornings and chuck the paper out of the plane, trying his best to hit the porch. He came close sometimes. One Easter weekend he put in some colored hard-boiled eggs along with the Sunday News.

At some point early on, Dad and Bud developed a habit that persists to this day—they talk to each other on the phone every night: to puzzle through the plans for their current project, rehash a controversy on the airport board, growl about some throttlebottom at city hall, or dole out tasks for the Belgrade Air Show, a huge annual event that they sink themselves into.

The Belgrade Air Show is electrifying. Old-timer pilots can see in one weekend how far we've come in aviation. They have vintage airplanes from World War II right next to jet fighters used on aircraft carriers today. Pilots that look young enough to be delivering your morning paper strap themselves into jets and take off from the runway going straight up in the air at nearly ninety degrees. They bring in the Blue Angels, eight Navy jet pilots who perform spectacular and minutely timed maneuvers in the sky. Another bunch of planes simulates a battle from the Korean War between Russian Mig fighters and

American F86s. The crowd, numbering more than thirty thousand over two days, comes from all over the state for the excitement.

Bud, Dad, and Steve Kleimer coordinate getting in the antique planes. Dad and Kleimer arrange for the local pilots, and Bud makes the calls to pilots with antique planes in distant states. They give people rides and do demonstrations for the crowd.

Every night they talk about this and just about any other thing—even when one of them is out of town. The phone always rings.

So it made me smile when Bud suddenly noticed that, after twenty years of spending practically every waking evening together, they had become best friends. Bud was quick to answer my request. "I'll be over tomorrow. Is tomorrow soon enough? I'll leave right after lunch. If I leave Bozeman at noon I'll be at the hospital by two-thirty." Just as I was hanging up he blurted out, "You know, don'tcha. Your dad's always been my John Wayne."

I guess I did know that. There were certainly plenty of John Wayne moments in the friendship between these two. In 1982 Bud bought a wrecked 1943 Tiger Moth biplane, which was a World War II Royal Air Force trainer. They spent two years and four months rebuilding it from top to bottom. It was July 1985. Sunday was to be its maiden voyage. They often took maiden voyages on Sunday mornings, and Mom never, ever stayed to watch. She would happily tag along in the passenger seat of his rock-solid Cessna, but she wanted nothing to do with test-flying antiques. For her part, she always hotfooted it to church to pray.

So on that Sunday morning, while Mom was off begging the Lord to spare her husband an early death, Bud was supposed to be flying the Tiger Moth. Only he clutched. When the time came, he was too scared to fly it. He had never flown a biplane before, and it was giving him the heebie-jeebies. So he invited Jack out, an old pilot in town who had flown lots of old planes.

They wheeled the plane out of the hangar. Dad was there with his video camera, providing a running commentary of the date, the time, the weather, the airplane's specs. The plane was catiwampus to the runway, but that didn't matter since Dad and Bud naturally expected Jack to take a few slow preliminary runs up and down to get his bearings. But he didn't. Instead, he hit the gas and the plane roared full bore down the runway. Dad bellowed, "Jack? Jack?" and then smack. The plane veered into the wheat field on the right side of the strip and crashed, flipping completely upside down, wheels straight up in the air, fuselage crumpled, wings bent and broken, and gas and oil pouring out onto the plane. By that point Dad had dropped the camera.

What we see next on the videotape is Bud draining a beer, clearly not his first of the afternoon.

"Bad day," he announced. Then he put his hands out to his sides like an airplane and reenacted what had happened several times.

The tape cut to Dad and Bud up at our cabin on Hyalite Lake. Bud is standing in the kitchen with a beer in his hand, slurring, "Yes. We're up here getting an attitude adjustment." Then he let out a long, ghastly belch and continued, "Yes, folks. Debriefing. Trying to feel good."

They spent the next eight months fixing the Tiger Moth—reconstructing what was broken and recovering what was torn—until it was ready to fly again.

It was April 1986. This time Warren, a friend of Bud and Dad's, was rolling the tape. Bud was dressed in his leather flight jacket, leather helmet, and goggles, his white silk scarf tied rakishly around his neck. This time it was his plane to crash. He taxied up and down the runway countless times, getting a feel for things. The trouble with the Tiger Moth was its brakes. Dad said the Tiger Moth was the second dumbest plane he'd ever flown—it was so hard to steer, you had to sort of slide it through the air using the rudder to do half the steering. Those old airplanes look disconcertingly like wild turkeys trying to fly, flopping and wobbling and lurching as if they'd rather do anything than travel by air.

Finally Bud lifted off. "He's in the air! Beautiful! Isn't that beautiful!" Dad shouted, watching his friend lift off into the Montana sky. "Whadaya think of that! I knew he could do it!"

After flying all over the valley, Bud came in for a bumpy landing. Dad walked up to the cockpit, they consulted together, and then Bud took off again. He needed to try for a better landing. The second time around was perfect. Bud taxied up to the hangar and hopped out of the plane. He bounded up to Dad and put his hand out to shake it, blurting out, "I'm so happy! Thanks, Edsall, you big bastard. I love ya, goddamn it." Then he couldn't help himself. He gave Dad a big hug. Thrilled, he spun around and pumped his arm up and down in jubilant victory. "That's great!" he shouted. Then Dad and Bud went right back to business. They walked over to the airplane, analyzing the rudder and the brakes and how it banked and how it flew and what it was like to land. They went up to the cabin that night, too. They called those trips to the cabin "getting in their cups." I'm quite sure that means they drank too much.

The next summer they decided to fly to Yakima, Washington, for the air show. Bud flew the Tiger Moth and Dad flew the Fleet Series 9, an open cockpit biplane built for pure sport in 1932.

Only eleven Fleet Series 9 planes were ever built, and as far as Dad knew, his was the only one left flying. Of all the planes Dad bought and rebuilt, this was his prize. He says he can sell the planes he buys and rebuilds because he doesn't fall in love with them. But the Fleet was the one plane that captured his heart. So much so that whenever the temperature got about sixty degrees he called it Fleet weather, and when he flew he called it "Fleeting," which he did whenever the weather allowed.

Because the Fleet was a bigger and more powerful plane than the Tiger Moth, Bud flew a straight line to Yakima and Dad flew in big circles around him to stay with him all the way there. On the return trip, Dad came back around from one of his big circles and couldn't find Bud anywhere.

They were headed east, planning to land in Missoula to get gas. They were down in a river canyon, mountains banding them on both sides. Then all of a sudden gray glop was flying out of Bud's engine and he had no power. The first thing he decided was that however he landed that damn plane, he wouldn't hurt anybody. He tried to glide back to a hay field, but he was losing altitude too fast. He looked down at the interstate, which was bumper-to-bumper traffic. Then he spotted a gap between two cars and he counted on that gap staying there. He skated down.

When he was about to put it down, he went right over the top of a camper and then he saw a VW Beetle straight ahead of him. All he could think was "Lady, please don't look in your rearview mirror." He put the plane down and thought, "Son of a bitch, I'm going to live."

Then those squirrelly brakes on the Tiger Moth finally did him in. As he tried to brake, the right wing tipped and dragged on the guardrail, and then it was all over. The plane tipped up and landed on its nose, straight up in the air, once again gas and oil pouring out all over the plane.

Bud was standing on the interstate with his leather helmet and goggles still on, his white silk pilot's scarf tied around his neck, when a woman hurried up and asked, "Was the pilot killed?"

Bud looked at her, his flight goggles perched on his forehead, and said, "I'm not sure, but I don't think so. Not yet, anyway. Would you mind putting out that cigarette?"

Dad found out what happened when he landed in Missoula. He got a ride out to the crash site, looked at the plane, and heard Bud tell about it.

"You did a good job, Hall," Dad said.

They took the next year rebuilding the Tiger Moth. For the third time.

Mother tried to be supportive in all this, but it was like watching boys play with fire. Her anxiety was not entirely unjustified. In 1987 three news reporters were out at our house videotaping a special on the Belgrade Air Show. Al Newby was flying his 1932 Great Lakes Trainer, doing loops and rolls for the television promotion. Al was known in the region as the Grandfather of Flying. Seventy-two years old, he had been flying his whole life. He was doing one last roll past the cameras when something went terribly wrong. He was flying too slow. He knew he was in trouble and got the plane upright, but not before he hit a guy wire and the roof of Dad's office on the way down, shearing off a wing. The plane's engine slowed to a thumpety-thumpety-thumpety as he tried to bring it down safely. When it crashed in the yard—not twenty feet from the porch—it sounded eerily soft, like the sound of a soda can crumpling under someone's shoe. Then there was a slide, almost a squeak, across the wet grass before a long hiss faded to silence.

With all that airplane fuel there was a real chance of fire. Anyone smoking immediately put out their cigarettes and rushed for the plane. Bud got there first and tried to get Al out. But Al had a good luck ritual that was thwarting their efforts. Before his stunt flights he always tied a leather thong from his belt to his harness. Bud couldn't get the knot untied. The force of the crash had only pulled the knots tighter and they held fast. Finally Bud pulled out his pocket knife and cut through the leather. They laid Al out on the grass, probably every rib in his chest broken. I watched as Bud pushed down on his chest to give him CPR. Others had fetched every fire extinguisher in the house and shop and stood ready, riveted to and sickened by the scene. I had called 911 and the ambulance sirens were howling in the distance. Even in the sunlight I could see their flashing lights two miles up our dirt road, a cloud of dust marking their progress.

Al was dead when he got to the hospital.

That, probably more than anything, soured Mom on old planes. Pilots of antique planes crash-landed on the highway, "dead sticking" their planes into farmer's fields or any flat place they could spot from the air. They regaled each other with the tales at airport potlucks while eating at makeshift tables made of plywood balanced on saw-horses. But their joking didn't sweeten the stories for Mother. Flying was risky business. Flying old planes was riskier. People died. She didn't want to hear us rattle off statistics about how much safer it was to fly than to walk. She had a lot more faith in solid ground than in insubstantial air, and she wanted her whole family on solid ground. Still, even after Al's death, Mom could never ask Dad to give it up. It was too much a part of who he was. She learned to live with the worry.

Bud, more than anyone, understood what flying meant to Dad. Now finally, after a week of waiting, Bud was on his way.

Sharon and I were in the hall when Bud stepped off the elevator. "Well, if it isn't the Blister Sisters!" he taunted.

"It's about time you showed up, Harold," Sharon hurled back. Bud hates being called Harold. We were trying to be our same old bantering selves, dishing out grief to each other and yucking it up, but it was falling flat. "He's in room one ninety-two, Bud. He's waiting for you," Sharon said. Bud went in by himself.

Dad looked at him, unable to utter a single word of sense.

"Hey, Edsall," he croaked out. "How ya doin'?" Then he covered his eyes with his hands and cried. Dad hung his head and cried too.

Bud stayed with Dad a couple of hours that day at the hospital, and I met him when he walked out of the room. He looked edgy, smacking his tongue against his dry mouth, sucking in big gulps of air, his eyes darting from me back to Dad's room. He was bled of all humor. "Goddamn," he said, stuffing his hands in his pockets to still them. "That's my buddy. The terror. Goddamn."

"He'll fly his plane again, Bud. We promised him."

"I know it." His voice was low and clipped and he wouldn't look me in the eye. "If anybody can do it, he can. Goddamn."

But I knew Bud. I knew he was holing up in his mute heart something so unthinkable he couldn't bring himself to say it out loud: Dad would never pilot a plane again. Neither of their lives would ever be the same.

He confirmed my fears. As he turned to go, he finally looked at me, his lip quivering. "Goddamn," he repeated. "We had a good thing going and it's over. Goddamn."

8

I finally found Sharon the most perfect gift ever—Bitch brand detergent, Christmas 2002.

Square One

It had been eight days since Dad's stroke. I was scheduled to leave in two days. Dad was scheduled to leave in five days. He was in a panic. So was I.

He was better off physically. Although he still didn't have much feeling in his right leg, the exercises had made him steadier on his feet. He could dress himself and could eat without spilling much. He still couldn't talk, however. Intense speech therapy had moved him along, but at a leaden pace.

Tackling his speech was the obvious and overriding priority for all of us. But Dad was the most impatient of all. He made it clear that he would tolerate no breathing room, no time to settle in back home, no dillydallying. He wanted to start cracking with his first speech therapy session no less than fifteen minutes after we pulled into the driveway.

I had no idea what home therapy looked like. What would the speech therapist do? What was our role? Betty, the social worker in charge, had gathered Mom, Sharon, and me in Dad's room for the handoff from hospital to home. She presented me with a single sheet of hospital letterhead on which she had handwritten the names of three therapists.

"That's it?" I asked, stupefied. They were sending us home with a 230-pound man who couldn't stand up in the shower or say "See Jane run," and this little sheet of paper with the names of three strangers on it was supposed to do the trick? It would be like Dad giving me the keys to the plane and suggesting, heck, why didn't I just give it a whirl. I turned the paper over to see if the real goods were on the other side—blank. "This is the plan?" I asked.

"I'm not familiar with the therapists in your community so I can't recommend one, but really, I'm sure any of these will be fine. Wayne is doing so well." Betty rubbed his shoulder and gave him two pats on the back. She put a check mark in a little square on the form adorning her clipboard and then sent a final sweeping gaze around the room, smiling confidently.

"Good luck!" she cheered. Her job was finished.

"Maybe Dad could stay here a little bit longer so he can continue with intensive speech therapy," I urged, grasping for mercy or kindness, thinking, too late, that had I been a less annoying family member they might extend our stay. "He seems to be making good progress."

"That won't be possible," Betty responded. "We need his bed for other patients who are in more serious condition than your father is in." It sounded to me like she had memorized this line. "Our job is to make sure your father is safe and then to discharge him."

I wanted to scream that my father wasn't safe. He wasn't safe from depression or fear or a dramatically altered life. He wasn't safe from never flying again. And what about me? I wasn't safe either. I wasn't safe from shouldering on my own bare back a responsibility that this entire hospital could hardly accomplish competently. We didn't have workbooks and exercise equipment and game boards and *staff*. We didn't have a white board on which to parse out little thirty-minute therapy assignments to fresh-faced college graduates. We didn't have a soft-serve ice cream machine. We didn't have a plan.

Articulate, searing anger streamed out of me like expensive whiskey with a lethal edge. "Oh, I get it. As long as you can document that he's unlikely to fall down over an open flame, your job is done, is that it? Any little quality-of-life issues Dad might face are a challenge to our own ingenuity." Betty blinked and said nothing. Mother squirmed.

"Well!" Sharon said, a little too loudly. "I guess it's up to us! C'mon, Susan, let's go. We've gotten all the help here that we're likely to get." She flounced out of the room with dramatic purpose. Black jeans, black boots, erect posture, a long stride, perfect hair. I scampered behind her, mostly to maintain the effect, not because I had any idea where we were going. Mother must have been relieved to see us leave so she could set her shoulder to the wheel of doing the cleanup work—apologizing for her daughters and thanking Betty for all her help.

Sharon and I reconvened in the hospital cafeteria, huddled over steaming Styrofoam cups of coffee. Sharon arched an eyebrow and leaned in, her elbows on the table. "So, how did you decide to get home—on a commercial flight, or were you planning to fly your broom?"

"I thought I'd leave the broom for you," I shot back. "It goes so well with your outfit."

We both went silent, brooding over what on earth we were going to do. I sank into my muddy thoughts and brewed there until something hatched.

"Tell me your schedule," I said to Sharon, an idea forming on the far edge of my mind.

"I don't have a schedule," Sharon answered. "Except my pedicure every other Thursday—and every morning I go to the bakery for coffee."

I retrieved my datebook from my backpack and flipped to April. "Here's what I can do," I said, madly drawing slashes through free dates and circling meetings that I had confidence I could cancel, then flipping over to May and doing the same thing. "Can you be in Bozeman these dates?" I asked, turning my calendar so we could both see it and running my finger across two solid weeks.

"Yeah, I can. I'll do anything, but what do you have in mind?"

I explained that we would do Dad's therapy ourselves. We'd seen Cheri work with Dad. There was no reason we couldn't work with him the same way. Cheri would provide us with workbooks and materials. We would do a two-weeks-on, two-weeks-off rotation for three months, then reassess. We would have "school" for Dad every morning from eight o'clock until noon. The speech therapist in Bozeman would augment what Cheri gave us and take the lead in moving Dad forward, but we would work intensively with Dad between therapy sessions. Sharon would commute from North Carolina and I from Vermont. We would meet at the airport parking lot in Bozeman to exchange notes and plans. I was breathless from the spill of ideas and from talking myself into their worthiness even as I was making it all up on the spot.

Sharon thought I'd lost my mind. Neither of us had any medical background. She hated school. She was lucky she even graduated. Just the word *school* made her queasy. She had always screwed up school, and I'd just handed her a golden opportunity to do it again, only this time with sky-high stakes and no bailout allowed. I waited, knowing that this plan shoved Sharon into bitter territory. Finally, she just stared straight at me, disclosing not a flicker of her churning doubt, and said flat out, "I can do this."

I thought I'd lost my mind, too. I had no idea if Sharon could do it—or if I could, for that matter. I knew this would be rough on our marriages. I knew there had to be a better way. I just didn't know what it was.

What I didn't know then was that there was an outpatient intensive therapy program right next to the hospital that Dad could have participated in. I didn't know enough to ask, and nobody on staff said a word. I don't think they deliberately bamboozled us. I suppose it's possible they didn't want our family within one hundred miles of the place, but I think it's more likely that they forgot. Or didn't even know.

So we had the travel plan mapped out, but not a single inkling about what school would look like. Dad couldn't read, write, speak, add, subtract, reason, or even reliably remember our names. He was frozen in savage terror, with part of his brain damaged or missing. Were we crazy to expect recovery? Was keeping him safe all we could reasonably hope for?

I went to see Cheri, the speech therapist. I was certain she would give me the resources we needed. Her office was lined on three sides with bookcases crammed with workbooks, files, and videocassettes, her desk heaped with three-ring binders bulging with worksheets aimed at teaching people how to talk. I had come to the right place.

I enthusiastically outlined our plan to her. Two weeks in rotation. School for Dad every morning from eight o'clock until noon. Field trips in the afternoon to get him out in the community. Word games in the evening. We had already purchased the game Taboo, a synonym game that seemed fun. Three months of intense work, modeled on the work Cheri had been doing with Dad. I was resolute and optimistic. She would see us as a model family.

"Is there a program or curriculum we can purchase? Do you have suggestions for materials?" I expected Cheri to whip piles of possibilities off those chockablock shelves and bury me with a wealth of options.

Cheri looked blank. Silence filled the room thickly. Perhaps I hadn't explained it very well.

"You know, workbooks. Or worksheets. Like what you've been using with Dad. Like the workbooks you copied these from." I pulled out some worksheets she had given us to jog her memory. I nodded eagerly in her direction to nudge her along.

She pushed together the papers that were scattered about on her desk. "I'll see if I can come up with anything. I'll let you know."

She followed me out of her office. I hoofed it to the cafeteria for a strategy session with my sister. Cheri, I found out later, made a beeline for my mother.

"Mrs. Edsall," she'd said sternly, putting her foot down, "it is very important for you to know that your daughters cannot be your husband's speech therapists. It simply won't work. You all need to resume your roles as wife and daughters and leave the work of speech therapy to professionals."

Mother was too confused and scared to argue. She had trusted professionals all her life. She had learned to live with the experts' advice—what she owed in taxes, how much medicine to take, when to fertilize, how long to bake the brownies. She'd always complied. But now she faced the horror of caring for a seriously disabled man exactly twice her size, a man she loved and had always depended on. Now he would be utterly dependent on her. What did it mean to be a wife in those circumstances? Or a daughter? What was there left to resume? Every single thing had changed.

Mother held this professional advice as an awful secret for three months, a hex she carried as carefully as a live grenade. But I imagine she looked at Cheri expressionless, another splinter of worry lodging firmly in her heart.

Sharon and I, in the meantime, went on a tear—making lists, calling therapists from pay phones in the hospital, buying blank index cards, using our ramped-up organizational skills to make up for what we didn't know. I kept pestering Cheri for materials, leaving imploring messages on Post-It Notes stuck on her office door and on her voice mail. But I kept missing her.

I threw myself headlong into helping Dad. In the breaks between various therapy sessions in the rehab center we worked on our own in his hospital room. We sat together singing the alphabet song—"A B C D E F G . . ."—with all the lifts, lilts, pauses for deep breaths, and the rapid giggly descent into "LMNOP." Funny how that silly song seems to stay with you for life. But singing it with a seventy-one-year-old successful businessman whose advice you have routinely sought and followed was hideous. I had to work at sounding engaged, happy-go-lucky, normal. I began to appreciate the fine balance the therapists must continuously maintain between sounding encouraging and treating patients like bewildered and tantrum-prone toddlers on their first Monday of preschool.

Next, Dad perched on the edge of his brown plastic chair, the bed tray pulled across in front of him, we spread out the alphabet worksheets the therapists had provided. The letters were perfectly scribed with shaded guides to copy neatly, over and over again. He was willful and intent, his hair flopping over into his eyes like a schoolboy's. He gripped the pencil hard and tore through the paper as he laboriously copied the letters, the lopsided arcs of a *d* not quite meeting the crooked, zigzagging stem, which hurtled past its given stopping point. In the course of thirty minutes, the pencil lead broke five times.

Everyone starts out this way, I thought, don't they? I could teach him to read and write, couldn't I?

"*B*," I said, skipping *A* so I could have the advantage of a hard consonant sound. I pointed to the line with the *B* on it. "*B* is buh."

"Buh," Dad repeated. He looked lost. He was just repeating what I had said. It clearly had no meaning for him.

I was awash in fear. I pressed on, methodically.

"*B* is buh," I said again, as if he hadn't heard me the first time. Then I added hopefully, "As in *boy*."

"*Boy . . . boy!*" He nodded, catching on. "*B*. Buh. *Boy*." He repeated it three or four times to seal it in his memory. Then he moved with determination to *C*.

"*C* is kuh as in *cat*," I said, remembering all the references teachers used when teaching me to read as a child. But what about when *c* sometimes has the "s" sound, as in *city*? How would I explain that practically every letter has several sounds and sometimes no sound at all? How very complicated and arbitrary it all was.

"*C*. Kuh. *Cat*." Again Dad repeated it four or five times, storing it up, proud as a cardsharp methodically amassing all the poker chips on the table in front of himself.

We galloped through *dog, egg, farmer, girl,* and *hog*. Dad scraped out every letter with his soft lead pencil, leaving the newsprint in shreds. I recognized in him the familiar traits of impatience and immutable, infuriating stubbornness. They were traits we shared. As maddening as they had been to me as a child, they were now my talisman against despair.

When we got to *ice cream,* we decided a bowl of it would be a good idea—two flavors mixed together. Soft serve.

On my way to the cafeteria I sank into a telephone booth and called my friend Carol in New Hampshire. "I can't do this," I choked, then broke down into heaving sobs. "I can't do this. I don't know how to teach someone to read. What does *of* mean? You tell me!" I demanded of her. "Why do 'for sale' and 'on sale' mean two completely different things? What's the deal with *of* and *for* anyway?" I ranted on wildly while she listened. "Dad had to print the word *par* on his worksheet, which of course he did, and then he asked me what it meant. I couldn't tell him, Carol. All I could say was 'Well, it's like in golf. You know, par.' What an idiot I am! I can't do this. I. Cannot. Do. This." I pounded the glass doors of the phone booth with each word.

Carol clucked and purred in sympathy as I fell apart. Then she set me straight. "Don't be ridiculous, Susan. You don't have a choice. Since when is *can't* in your vocabulary anyway? You'll figure out how to do this. You have to."

I had to come to terms with the fact that whether I knew how to do this or not was absolutely irrelevant. I had to do it anyway. No muscled hero was busting down any doors to rescue my father—or me.

When I got back to Dad's room, I looked down at the worksheet he had completed that afternoon and noticed something I hadn't before—there was a pattern in what he did and didn't understand. The worksheet was designed with a single purpose: to get Dad to write three-letter words, practicing writing by copying. But the mind doesn't have a single purpose. The mind seeks meaning. Dad could copy all the words, but he only understood the meaning of concrete nouns—*van, boy, man, gum, wax.* Abstract words—like *try, out,* and *end*—befuddled him. He didn't know what they meant, and I couldn't explain, leaving us both frustrated and anxious. The next day

I made up my own worksheets with simple nouns that I could either point to or draw: *ball, dog, leg, mom, nut, pot.* This seemed to work, but how did I know? I felt on shaky ground and was desperate for guidance.

I kept hounding Cheri for help with materials but got no response. On the day I was to fly back to Vermont, I camped out in front of her office at 6:00 A.M. so I'd be sure to catch her when she came in. At 7:45 she tromped in juggling her canvas bag, a cup of coffee, and her keys. "Oh! Yes! I've been looking," she said soothingly, "but I really came up with nothing that can help the layperson. Everything I have is for trained professionals."

"But what about the workbooks? Those worksheets?" I sputtered, kicking myself for not simply stealing one or two of them off her desk when I had the chance.

"I'm sorry," she offered sweetly. "But good luck!"

Luck? I didn't feel like our family had been sailing along on a lucky streak. After her heartfelt well-wishing, Cheri disappeared behind her office door, closing it serenely in my face with a soft click. I stood there for a full minute, empty-handed.

The perfect hat for Dad

9

If You Can Read,
You Can Do Anything

When I got back to Vermont, Rick made dinner and we spent the evening at the kitchen table talking everything over. I knew Rick had been digging up information about stroke recovery and rehabilitation from his friends at the hospital, and I was ready for a slug of optimism.

"I talked to Charles," Rick reported. Charles was a renowned neurologist and personal friend of Rick's.

"Yeah?" I was waiting for the good part.

"He said speech therapy was useless."

"Yeah?"

"He said that either the brain would recover or it wouldn't. There was nothing therapy did but make the therapists feel like they were accomplishing something, which they weren't."

"Yeah?" I shoved my dinner plate to the side of the table, clearing a path in front of me. "What do you think?"

"I honestly don't know, honey. I don't know what to think."

I planted my forearms directly on the table and clasped my hands together so I wouldn't slam them through the windowpanes next to our kitchen table. I leaned in. "Well I'll tell you what I think," I spat out. "I think that's a crock of medical profession claptrap. I think you told me that starting Dad on rehab needed to be my top priority. That's what you said. I am sick of getting jerked around by everyone—everyone. I am sick to death of *everyone* giving me a shitload of we-give-up, he's-old-anyway-so-what-difference-does-it-make crap. That's what I think."

"I'm on your side, sweetheart," Rick said, meaning it.

Then I put my head down on the table and cried. "Then why do you have such stupid friends?" I beat my fists on the table. "It's so ridiculous to say that therapy won't help. It's ri-dic-u-lous!" Lately I had lost my edge when it came to squelching my impulse to cry. It seemed like I cried every day now, often more than once. I tried not to count.

He squatted down next to me, put his hand over my shoulder, and kissed me on the ear. "C'mon," he said, "let's work out a plan." Rick reminded me of my dad in so many ways. He was a big guy, broad-shouldered and tall. He liked building things. He had his own version of Dad's "sandbox," a workshop so big that people often mistook it for the house. I called it "the testosterone shop." He called it "the clubhouse" and nailed up a brass Laconia Rotary Club sign right next to the door just to be funny. He would have nailed up another sign that said No Girls Allowed but knew that if he did, when he needed my help moving plywood or shifting a palette of veneer, the sign would doom him to doing it on his own. I was a stickler when it came to these kinds of rules. Rick was a furniture maker in his spare time and was moving quickly toward quitting his job as a medical librarian to become a furniture maker full time, and I was cheering him on. He brought the same passion to his work that Dad brought to his. It was one of the things I cherished about him.

Wiping my nose and eyes on the sleeve of my sweatshirt, I fished my spiral notebook out of my backpack and we assigned duties. I would go to the bookstore tomorrow. He would look for specific teaching materials on the Web. We would rendezvous tomorrow night at the kitchen table to compare notes.

With a one-day plan in hand, I dropped into bed, exhausted.

The next day we set to work. I drove with purpose and urgency to the bookstore. The bookstore approach had always worked before, when I was learning to bake good cakes, organize my office, or put in a decent garden. Surely it would work for teaching a stroke survivor how to do—well, everything. My first stop was Borders, a thirty-mile drive south.

Nothing. There wasn't a single resource.

I went to Barnes and Noble, a ninety-mile drive north. Nothing. I approached the information desk. "I'm looking for a how-to book on recovering from a stroke."

Nothing.

"How about 'speech recovery'? Could you try that?"

Nothing.

"Aphasia? Try 'aphasia.' A-P-H-A-S-I-A. Aphasia. It means speech loss." It shouldn't be this hard, for crying out loud. How many people had strokes every year? Plenty. Enough that there should be books for them and their families.

Nothing. No resources. I left with a cookbook on low-fat meals.

Even the library didn't have one single book on aphasia, strokes, or speech recovery. I was furious in disbelief and roiling with worry. Then it suddenly hit me. The Dartmouth-Hitchcock Medical Center, the largest teaching hospital within one hundred miles of here, had a bookstore right at the hospital. Surely they would have something.

The next day I was at the door of the medical center bookstore fifteen minutes before they opened. Buoyed up by the prospects of the wealth lying within, I sipped my coffee and browsed the books on various diseases displayed in the window. This month's feature seemed to be female afflictions. Too bad Dad wasn't suffering from night sweats, hot flashes, or bone loss—we'd be sitting on an information gold mine. At the appointed minute I bounded through the door and asked to be directed to the section on stroke and speech recovery.

"We don't have a section on that per se," said the sales clerk, a bookish guy with ill-fitting glasses that he kept pressed to his face with an index finger, his brow furrowed.

He wandered around a few bookshelves, pulling out a book here and there and then shoving them back in. Each time I hurried to the rejected book to make sure nothing promising was passed over. *Spinal Cord Injury: Prospects in Research, Case Studies in Severe Brain Trauma, Neurological Indicators in Brain Surgery*. No treasures here.

After a few minutes of unsuccessful browsing, the clerk was ready to get on to other things. "No. I thought we had something, but we don't really deal with that here."

I boiled over. "What do you mean you don't deal with *that* here? Isn't this a teaching hospital? Of course you deal with *that* here!" I stared at him, expecting that my insistence would shame him into admitting they had a mother lode of stroke workbooks just around the corner. He was unmoved. He turned and walked to the checkout counter to sell a tin of mints to a college student.

I sailed out of the bookstore and plied my new habit of bursting into tears just outside the doors. Down the hall of the hospital, I noticed an office with pink curtains on the windows and a sign that read "Community Health Options," a program that apparently connected patients and their families to community resources. I veered in. "My father's had a stroke. He's not getting the help he needs and I have no idea what to do," I managed to squeak out.

Kim, the receptionist, looked me in the eye and said with unflinching confidence, "I will help you." I believed her, and felt so unexpectedly comforted—even loved, as if that's even possible by a stranger—that more tears splashed down my face and over my swelling lips. She promised to find me the right people to talk to. She took my e-mail address and phone number and said she'd be back in touch with me by that afternoon.

She was. A speech therapist called me the next day. Revitalized by this progress, I dove right in, filling her in on the details of Dad's story, emphasizing the lack of help we were getting. "We're losing time here!" I said. "I can't even imagine the consequences of these delays in Dad's therapy!"

"The first thing you need to do is calm down," she said quite firmly. She agreed to send me some information and suggested that I go to the "Games" section of a large bookstore and buy logic and word games, being careful to choose books that weren't too advanced. They needed to be games simple enough for him to solve, but complex enough to get his mind working.

"Mind games are like jumping-jacks or sit-ups only for the brain," she explained. "They might not seem *directly* related to what you are trying ultimately to accomplish—in your Dad's case, fluent speech—but they build the brain's capacity and strength so it has the right stuff to get the job done in the end. What you're trying to do is get the brain up and working, not unlike getting a person who has just had surgery up and walking as soon as possible. Logic and word games begin the long process of teaching the brain to use alternative pathways to accomplish speech, writing, and reasoning."

I relaxed, my voice sounding less like my hand was caught in a hay baler. "So this will help us rebuild the road?" I asked.

"Exactly."

The next afternoon I drove back to Borders. They had an entire section eight feet high and sixteen feet long devoted to games. Starting in the upper left-hand corner, I methodically looked at every single book in the section. I rejected those designed as little perk-me-ups for members of the Mensa Society. Given how much of Dad's speech abilities were knocked out of service, I was looking for something aimed at children from five to seven years old.

Going through those bookshelves was grueling work. I took a break every few hours for a cup of coffee. I called Rick to tell him about my progress. He had news to report too. He had found two Web sites—Wayne State University and the Visiting Nurses Association. They both had good materials.

I hung up and called both publishers and ordered every book they had on speech therapy.

Then I went back to my spot on the bookstore floor and continued my methodical sweep, moving from the games section to the section on teacher resources for reading, writing, and math for grades one and two. The whole process took me seven hours. I spent $387 and had pounds and pounds of material and easily an equal amount of hope.

As I browsed through these books I could begin to see how we could put a program together for Dad using these games and exercises as the building blocks. The books not only provided a comprehensive list of what people need to know—I had forgotten, for instance, that Dad would need to relearn how to tell time—they also provided a *format* for teaching him. I dreamed up thirty-minute segments centered around games and exercises designed to build specific skills step-by-step. I felt immense relief that I wouldn't have to make everything up.

The time was coming for my two-week tour of duty. Sharon and I had spoken every night for the past two weeks and she had given me the blow-by-blow. She had been following the lead of Sally, the speech therapist who met with Dad three times a week for an hour, dutifully going over the exercises she provided. Sharon wanted desperately to believe that Sally held the elixir for Dad, the magic program that would make him talk and read, but the hesitancy in her voice about how the therapy sessions were going made me wonder.

"What do you really think?" I asked. Sharon paused a moment too long.

"She's really nice."

"Is she any good?"

Sharon came clean. "I think she's in over her head."

There, she'd said it. Then she started to cry.

"But I don't know, Susan. What do I know? She has a heart of gold—she bounces in the door on time wearing sandals and little capri pants. She always has activities."

I could picture Sally, bubbling and jubilant.

"But nothing's adding up to a plan. Dad keeps asking for some kind of overall plan, and there doesn't seem to be one. When I ask Sally, it's like she doesn't understand the question. To tell you the truth, it's kind of like day camp around here—lots of activities."

Sally had Dad matching a picture of a phone with the word *phone* and was giving him a topic like "animals" and having him list as many animals as he could think of in one minute (he could list only one—dog). But she never explained to Sharon or Dad what these exercises were supposed to accomplish or what success looked like. What were we aiming for here?

"I don't ask any questions," Sharon said. "I feel like she has Dad's whole future in her hands, and I'm worried that if I piss her off she'll leave, and then what will we do?"

But we just weren't the sniveling type, and now was certainly not the time to give it a test run. "I found a lot of really good materials at the bookstore. I'll have a curriculum design by the time I get there," I promised. "So, is there anything I need to know that you haven't already told me?"

Her nightly stories had been so optimistic. Dad seemed to be making such good progress and the bond between Sharon and Dad seemed so positive that I worried I would fail, that Dad would face two weeks of treading water and wishing Sharon would come back.

"Well, Susan, it's pretty intense."

"Like what? What do you mean, 'intense'?" I clutched. I wanted this to be plain, straightforward, miserably hard physical labor, like plowing a field with a table fork. I was happy to sweat. I didn't need it to be inspiring. But I didn't think I could handle intense.

"Well, Dad and I went on a walk to the shop last night," she began, her voice dropping to a whisper. "Susan, he cried."

"Huh?" It was more a gulp than a question. So it wasn't just me who was crying. Dad was coming unglued too. I wondered if it was easier for him to let loose with Sharon because crying doesn't bother her. Maybe she connected better on matters of the heart. Maybe I had something to learn here, and in an uncharacteristic role reversal, she would be my teacher. I dodged that thought like I was swerving to miss a head-on crash.

"He said he had regrets," Sharon continued.

"He said 'regrets'? He could say the word *regrets*?" Two syllables! Progress! I decided to focus on what I knew more about—what was going on in Dad's brain, the concrete, if formidable, task of recovering his speech. Yes, I assured myself, this was the real work. Crying was not the real work. We needed to stay focused and not get mired in softhearted gobbledygook.

"Well, yeah, I sort of got it out of him. But Susan, he said he felt regrets that he hadn't spent more time with us as kids and that he got too involved in the business. He said he wished he hadn't put in such a big lawn—that it all didn't make any difference. And that he wished we had gone on more camping trips together."

"Why is he worried about the lawn?" Somehow I had to keep this focused on rational, pragmatic problems. Sharon was simply wandering off course here.

"I don't know, Susan. It's not about the lawn. It's that he's thinking about his life and his family. He just feels sad."

"What did you say?" I had never had a conversation like this with Dad. We talked about investment strategies and retirement portfolios.

"I told him I loved him. That I thought we had a great family and a great childhood. I told him that I loved our camping trips up to Sixteen Mile to go grouse hunting. I told him how I felt."

Of course she would know what she felt. I didn't have any idea what I felt. Except angry.

"What did he say?" I asked, my insecurity mushrooming.

"He said he loved me."

Oh, my God. I was panicking. I knew I would freeze up, skip right over the conversation and pretend I hadn't heard. It wasn't that I didn't want an intimate relationship with my father. It's what I had always wanted. But until now I could blame any deficiencies in that area on "Guyville"—what we jokingly referred to in my family as "Wayne's World."

I had learned at my father's knee how to buck up—and I had learned well. Bud once told me that I'd be Wayne Edsall Jr. if I'd had balls. I didn't say anything. I just grabbed my crotch and acted like I was shifting my gear around the way I'd seen guys do. He said, "You wish," and I said, "You're worried," and that was the end of it. But balls or no, I was Wayne Edsall Jr., and I had a big problem. My thick skin was proving unsuitable for what we were facing—arctic clothing in the tropics.

"Are you still there?" Sharon asked.

"Yeah. I'm here. I'm wondering if I can do this. I don't think I can do this, Shar."

"I didn't think I could either, honey. But you can. It's okay. It's good, really. It's intense."

If Dad cried while I was with him, I didn't know what I would do. My strategy would be to control the situation so that crying didn't occur. For starters, I wouldn't take Dad on walks to the shop. We'd keep the whole two weeks oriented toward the classroom. Structure was the answer. I crafted a beautiful daily schedule that accounted for every hour starting at 8:00 A.M. and ended right after *The O'Reilly Factor,* Dad's favorite television show, at 10:00 P.M. If I stayed true to the plan, we would make progress. And we most certainly wouldn't cry.

On the plane ride out, my two carry-on items were magazine cases packed with books. For every minute of the nine-hour flight I methodically assessed every page in every book for relevance to Dad's recovery. I put Post-It Notes on pages that would serve as worksheets and cross-referenced them to the lesson plans I'd made. I drew a grid with four columns titled "activity," "purpose," "examples," "outcome." I ensured that every skill we were trying to teach Dad was contained in this grid and that it detailed the exercises we would use and what goal we were trying to reach—110 words per minute while reading aloud, for example. Our teaching plan wouldn't be random or ad hoc. When Dad saw this he would feel confident.

By the time the plane landed, I had as much order extracted from those books and my head as was possible.

In the next two weeks I learned that order wasn't going to be enough to tackle this problem. I had to bring more to the process than that. Much more.

Not a worry in the world.
Me, Christmas 1962.

10

Running As
Fast As I Can

When I walked off the plane that night, Mom and Dad were waiting for me, even though I'd insisted that I could easily take a cab. I'd wanted to take a cab. Desperately. It would confine our meeting to the privacy of home. I was a wreck imagining the public display of my feelings.

I walked down the long windowed hall from the plane to the terminal. When I saw my parents behind the glass I burst into tears. I was astonished that I didn't feel sad. I felt grateful. I felt so grateful that I had a family and that everyone was alive. I was so grateful that I wasn't coming home to a funeral. I was so indescribably grateful that I would get to have some time with my father. In the midst of all this difficulty, the strangest feeling of all was feeling lucky.

I loaded my luggage into the trunk and Mom drove, swallowed up by the driver's seat of a car built for my father. She seemed to have shrunk five inches in the last month. On the drive home, Dad did all the talking, halting and lurching, but talking.

"You sound good, Dad. You're making progress."

"You trunk . . . no . . . trank? No. You spose so?"

"Yeah. I do. It's amazing. You weren't even talking two weeks ago."

"Work-ing so . . . hard."

It was after midnight when we got home and we were all shot. "See you in the morning," I said, kissing them both.

"Five. Six. Seven. No, eight o'clock," Dad announced, taking a running leap. He was relearning things the way he learned them in the first place. Starting at the beginning was the only way he could approach anything in a series—time, days of the week, months, the alphabet, numbers. How he learned initially was stored in his long-term memory, which was still intact. His short-term memory had taken the hit with the stroke. Once he had done all the heavy lifting of moving things from his long-term memory back into his short-term memory, he wouldn't need to rely so heavily on this strategy of starting at the beginning.

Mom and Dad went off to bed, and for a moment I stood in front of the eight-foot-long dining room table that had been converted into a classroom. Dad would sit on one side, I on the other. Sharon had left things well organized. Dad's completed worksheets were stacked neatly, all dated. Uncompleted worksheets waited in another stack. A sheet of paper with the alphabet written in block letters lay on the table facing Dad's chair. A canning jar bristled with sharpened pencils. Jelly beans overflowed a candy dish. I felt like I was at an altar.

I thumbed through the worksheets Dad had completed. He had drawn hard, crooked lines that lurched between a picture of a television in the left-hand column and the word *TV* in the right-hand column, between a picture of a collie and the word *dog*. On a second worksheet his job was to look at a picture of a cookie and circle the right answer: (a) you eat this, (b) you wash yourself with this, (c) you fix the car with this, (d) you read this. At least Dad got the answer right, but I wondered if it had been hard for him, if he had needed any hints. Knowing that Dad was a royal mess was one thing, but seeing it square-on—even after being gone only two weeks—packed a walloping punch. Julie Andrews mocked me from the choral archive in my brain, warbling, "Just start at the very beginning! A very good place to start!" the whole Trapp family joining in with leering, dressed-alike cheeriness.

Another worksheet was titled "Complete the Series with Items from the Same Category." He could only complete two before he ran out of steam. For the line beginning "plums, strawberries" he scrawled "banana" after repeated erasures. Sharon had written "banana" in the margin so he could copy it. After "kangaroo, zebra" he wrote "lion." His printing was rickety and uncertain, lacking elegance, like mine in kindergarten.

Kindergarten was the year I went on the first plane ride that I can remember. It was barely dawn when we left, Dad carrying me to the car bundled in a blanket against the skim of September frost, Mom talking quietly with Grandma, who was staying at the house with Sharon and Steve. Dad slid two suitcases into a little door in the plane that opened behind the seat. I wanted to go in there too. I liked hideaways. By the time we were buckled down and ready, the sun was blazing over the Bridgers, bleaching the black sky to a deep blue. We were flying to Spokane so I could get tested for allergies, four mornings of torment I didn't understand—a grid of needles poked into my back, a drop of poison in each to see if I would swell and itch, Mom trying to explain why it was important, while my lip quivered bravely. I would not cry.

On the flight over we hit rough air above the Bitterroot Mountains near Missoula. All I knew from my place in the backseat was that I felt sick. Mom was sympathetic, but there was nothing to be done. I got sick in cars, too—Dad would just pull over to the side of the road and I would puke in the weeds. In the plane there were other solutions. Mom unfolded a plastic-lined "sick sack" and I leaned my face over it, my quivering hands pressing it over my mouth, and closed my eyes until the deed was done.

Practically everything gets off to a rocky start, I thought, thumbing through more of Dad's work. Eventually I only got sick in cars—eagerly tagging along with Dad in his plane whenever I could, so small my head just barely rose above the passenger's window. Dad would look over at me and say, "Wanna play roller coaster?"

My eyes widened in answer. "Yeah!" I gripped the seat, clamped my teeth in a grimace, and squeezed my eyes shut to prepare.

Dad would push the control wheel forward to make the plane plunge in altitude, shouting "Wheeee!" and I would scream and giggle, pulling up as hard as I knew how on the sides of my seat to keep the plane in the air, thrill and fear turning my whole body into jelly. Then he would pull the control wheel back out again and we would climb just as quickly as we'd dropped. I could feel the air leave my lungs. All the wispy blond hairs on my arms stood straight up on end and the back of my neck bloomed with prickles. It was electrifying.

"Do it again, Dad!" I would beg, knowing he could never resist my sweet, eager face.

Sometimes he would bank the plane sharply, dipping perilously toward the ground, the world turning sideways in my vision. I leaned away this time, both hands grabbing the opposite side of my seat, just in case. "Helping me?" Dad would laugh and then surprise me by banking the other direction and I would press my hands on his legs to keep from pitching into the pilot's seat, turning to poke my nose up over the edge of my window. All I saw was blue sky. I could never figure how Dad kept everything straight—where up was and where down was.

Sometimes I would reach out and put my tiny hand on his brown and muscled arm, and when he leaned in to hear me over the sound of the plane I would shout, "Wanna do race car?"

"Sure!" he smiled, heading for a broad flat field that stretched on for miles. "Ready?"

I nodded, stuffing my hands under my seat belt and craning my head up to see out the front. Dad would dive toward the ground and skim the fields at 140 miles per hour while I squealed. "That's how fast they go at Indy!" he'd say, pulling up and away.

I was happy about everything then—about being with Dad, doing tricks that made my tummy tumble, and not wetting my pants. Which was real close to how I was feeling now. We didn't know back then how life would turn out—that nearly forty years later Dad would be less able to speak and write than I could in kindergarten.

We certainly never imagined this.

I saw that Sharon had graded each worksheet with A+! written at the top with multiple stars. It gave me the creeps that I would be required to confer the judgment of "Good Job!" on my father. How could Dad reasonably be expected to believe that given an entire blank page it was an A+! to come up with one fruit and one animal? He probably felt he deserved an F. He'd lost his speech, not his mind.

This whole school gig must be giving Sharon harrowing flashbacks. The poor kid had had piss-poor luck in school, getting teachers who looked down on her as the third sibling who simply wasn't up to snuff compared with her older brother and sister.

A playground rhyme from over thirty years ago singsonged through my head: "Old lady Sitch, fell in a ditch, found a penny and thought she was rich." Mrs. Sitch taught fifth-grade Language Arts and she was as mean as a wolverine. She was stout and pulled her aluminum-gray hair into a bun, tight as an onion, at the back of her head. Deep wrinkles in her face threaded down into the thin lines of her lips, creating canals into which her red lipstick seeped, making her mouth look as if it had been hit with a broken glass. She always wore a green wool dress with sleeves rolled to the elbows, a belt tied loosely where her waist would have been, and heavy black lace-up shoes with thick, stubby heels. Finding out whether you got Mrs. Sitch was the scariest thing every fifth-grader did on the first day of school. I squeaked by and got fat, bald, happy Mr. Elliot. Sharon was not so lucky.

In Sharon's fifth-grade year, Mrs. Sitch successfully wrung out any remaining enthusiasm Sharon had for reading, learning, or school. The end came on a Monday in early spring. Sharon had spent the weekend working on an advertising poster against smoking. She had cut out the Marlboro man from a *Time* magazine, sitting astride his horse and gazing off into the distance. Then she surrounded him with drawings of tombstones. Across the bottom she'd stenciled "Don't Let The Marlboro Man Take You!" the ominous warning positioned between two skulls and crossbones. She worked on it all weekend, getting up long before anyone else on Monday morning to admire her work, sitting on the couch, the poster propped on her knees. She was so proud of her effort that Mom drove her to school early that day, so she could show Mrs. Sitch her poster first thing. Mrs. Sitch, her reedy voice sharp as a lance, sneered, "You should have filled in the stencils, Sharon. For heaven's sake, it's common sense. You can't read the caption from the back of the room." She gave Sharon an F.

Small wonder that Sharon made up for it all now with her wild enthusiasm for Dad's work. Sharon was back in the classroom, only this time she was the teacher she never had, and heaven would come tumbling down before she would flunk anybody over anything. She was relentlessly encouraging and filled with can-do school spirit.

I flipped through more of the worksheets, adorned with Sharon's exclamation points, stars, and smiley faces, and came across eight stark pages of Dad's repeated, dogged attempts at his signature, the pencil pushed into the paper so hard it felt like Braille on the backside. More child's writing, labored and loopy. On the first page he spelled his name wrong seventeen times before hitting his stride. Sharon told me that at one point he called for Mother and asked her, as he wrote his name, if he had it right. He didn't recognize it. I flipped through page after page after page of his name. I counted the number of times he wrote "Wayne Edsall"—368.

My God. It was as if Dad were trying to establish that he existed, as if the stroke not only wiped out his capacity to speak, read, and write, but wiped out *him*. I couldn't begin to imagine what that must feel like. Dad had always been right about everything, even when he was dead wrong. Not even to be sure of his name must have been staggering.

We were all staggered, operating in arenas that years ago we had closed the door on—and rammed dresser drawers up against to make sure it stayed closed. Sharon was back in school, I was getting poached in an emotional cauldron, Dad was so visibly not in charge that he didn't even have a voice, let alone a vote, and Mom was shot out of a circus cannon into a world of chaos and bad grooming that was the equivalent of a reeking, leech-ridden swamp.

As if I were handling precious tablets, I punched holes in Dad's worksheets and slipped them into a three-ring binder in chronological order. Instinctively I thought that keeping track of his progress might be the only way to prove to him that he was making headway. Or to me. Besides, I wanted a record of what I believed was going to be the most important and meaningful work I had ever done in my life. That our family had ever done.

I laid out all my plans for the next day, the lessons in thirty-minute blocks. I made flash cards with the alphabet on them. I arranged my cache of books on the buffet table, which converted nicely into a makeshift library. I ate all the jelly beans, first sorting them into like-colored piles.

It was probably 3:00 A.M. before I finally went to bed. I was as ready as possible. I crawled under the freshly laundered sheets and cried myself to sleep—the only way I knew to express my dark ache for my father.

11

I always wanted to be a driver.

Reporting For Duty

It was April 21. On my first day on the job I was the first one up. I made a big pot of caffeinated coffee for me, and while I waited for it to brew I pulled every possible breakfast item out of the refrigerator and spread everything all over the counter—onions, peppers, mushrooms, smoked salmon, Egg Beaters, whole-grain bread, bananas, apples, pears, soy milk, and spray-on butter. I heated a pan on the stove and took out two cutting boards to chop vegetables and fruit. Dad needed sufficient protein to keep his brain working, and I was eager to supply it. Sharon had taken over the shopping duties and I had dictated my list to her, so all the necessary ingredients were on hand. Mom wasn't too wild about how that fouled up her kitchen and wasn't sure she bought the whole protein argument. A good solid bowl of oatmeal had always been sufficient in the past. But she didn't put up too much of a protest; out of spitting distance from medical personnel, Sharon and I were both on our best behavior.

I take that back. We weren't on our best behavior. We were polite. It's not good behavior to come into someone's house, completely mess it up three times a day, and do it every day for three months. If someone did that in my house—I don't care how much protein they put in the entrée—I would call the police. Especially if I cared as much about my kitchen as Mom did about hers.

Mom's house was never messed up. She made the bed every morning, the towels in the bathroom matched and were never damp, and every plant was alive. Her closets were so clean that if you were talking while you opened one up, you would hear an echo. Yet often when I called her on the phone I'd ask her what she was doing and she'd tell me she was cleaning the closets. I couldn't imagine which closets she was talking about—unless she had a secret stash of them squirreled away like other people hoarded Scotch.

She had a huge dieffenbachia they got when they were married. She had cut it back with a butcher knife countless times because it was getting "out of control," and every single time, to our amazement, it had sprung back to life, greener and sprightlier than before. It knew how to behave.

Not so the daughters. We took Mother's house by storm—locusts in midsummer.

Mom appeared in the kitchen just as I was beginning to make a pot of decaf in the smaller coffeemaker.

"Morning, Mom! Hey! You got a great new coffeemaker!"

"Sharon bought it when she was here. I guess I didn't have the right kind."

"Well, this is a nice one."

"I hope you found the right coffee. I bought the right kind of coffee for you. The one without any flavors. It's in the brown bag up there, not the red one, the one that your dad and I drink."

"I don't mind flavored coffee, Mom. You always mix that up. It's Sharon who doesn't drink flavored. I don't drink decaf. This is caffeinated, isn't it? By the way, what's with the Cling Wrap, Mom?"

"What's wrong with Cling Wrap?"

"Well, for one thing, it doesn't cling. Look!" I said, exaggerating my attempt to wrap the onion and throwing my hands in the air in disgust as the plastic wrap drifted off the onion and onto the floor. "It's worthless. Why do you buy this crap, Mom?" I shoved the roll back in the drawer.

"Well, it's always worked fine for me. It's a lot cheaper than Saran."

"What do you think, Mom, we're poor? I think you can afford Saran." I wrote "Saran" on the grocery list hanging from the fridge. "I'll buy some when I go to the store today. Give you a little upgrade. How about an omelet, Mom? Smoked salmon!"

"No, I'll make my own later."

"You don't need to make your own. I'll make one for you. I have everything out already."

"I'll make my own."

"Whatever you say!"

She'd obviously gotten up on the wrong side of the bed.

Dad and I started at eight on the dot. Dad didn't want any shilly-shallying at school. I put into practice all of what I'd learned so far. I'd read that when your mind is relaxed it has a better capacity to think, so when we went over the alphabet flash cards we moved to the comfortable chairs in the living room. I'd read that because of where language is located in your brain, you are more likely to stimulate the language center if you look to the right when you're searching for a word, especially if you squeeze something with your right hand. Since Dad looked out the window when he was searching for a word, I put the window to his right and got him a stress ball to squeeze. I didn't have a clue what I was doing. I would have sprinkled salt over my left shoulder or rubbed cooking grease on my knuckles and buried the rag if someone had told me they'd read somewhere that it worked.

We warmed up with a memory exercise. I would give him a category like "animals" or "sports" or "vegetables" or "things that are hot," and he would have to name as many items in that category as he could in one minute. This helped Dad put the random jumbles of words in his brain into distinct categories.

I gave him the category of "vegetables." In one minute he named beans, carrots, and peas.

"How many am I supposed to get?" Dad stammered, exhausted from the work of getting three.

"We're aiming for sixteen to twenty in one minute, Dad." I wanted to say "six."

"I didn't do very good, then, did I?"

"We're just beginning, Dad. You'll get better every day. You'll see." I hoped anyway. How did I know?

One thing Dad couldn't tolerate was being bullshitted. That was one area of his brain that was certainly left undamaged by the stroke. But the lure to do some version of "letting him win" was ever present. I needed strict rules to keep me honest. I set out three.

Rule 1: Don't lie. If Dad asked me how he was doing, I would tell him.

Rule 2: Design work to make sure he could be successful (this would help bring Rule 1 into play less often).

Rule 3: Constantly raise the bar; keep him challenged (this would bring Rule 1 into play more often).

Abiding by these three rules required astounding vigilance. Temptation was everywhere. At night, when Dad was tired, he would stumble and stutter more. "Why can't I get this?" he would growl, frustrated. "I had it this morning and now I can't remember a damn thing. Do you notice that I get worse at night?"

Oh, how I wanted to throw my arms around his neck and tell him how wonderful he was, how I had never seen anyone work so hard in all my life, how proud I was of him, and oh, by the way, no, I didn't think he was stumbling at all, I couldn't even tell he'd had a stroke. But he knew he was struggling. To deny it would render meaningless the times when I was able to say that he was doing well. "Yeah, Dad, you do seem to have more trouble when you're tired."

But that set up the next temptation—adding "But we all do. I have trouble when I'm tired, too." This was as bad as lying. For me to glibly join in the ranks of people suffering the effects of a stroke was getting admission without the price.

Worse, a me-too response basically shifted the focus from him to me. "Aw, Dad, no big deal! It happens to people all the time! Let me tell you about the time I left the phone in the refrigerator! Ha! Ha! Ha!" It was hard not to say "Yeah, me too" because I wanted so much for him to feel normal. But mostly it was a whole lot easier to shift the conversation to "no big deal" than to acknowledge what Dad was feeling and let that stand. My attempts to diminish the pain he was feeling were really aimed at making me feel better. My job was to listen without judgment. Which meant more than waiting until Dad finished his sentences.

At the time, I saw these as important rules for helping Dad recover from his stroke. It didn't occur to me until much later that they might be a better way to live in general.

Each morning we recorded how many in a given category he could name in one minute. The categories began with simple things like "animals," "vegetables," and "tools" and advanced to more difficult categories like "animals you hunt," "vegetables that are green," "tools you use to fix a car." By the end the categories were as silly as "things that you eat with a spoon," "things that are fuzzy," "things that make you mad," "things that bounce."

The next thirty minutes we practiced reading using the alphabet flash cards. He was getting good at *B* is buh, *C* is kuh, *D* is duh. But *W* was a problem. "Double you is duh." Well, I could see how he might think that—every other letter had the sound of the letter in its name. The more times we went over it, the more times he got it wrong and the more frustrated he got. I needed a new idea.

Each morning I got up at four forty-five and ran for an hour. It was cold, it was dark, and I was alone. I ran for an hour not because I was committed to the exercise but because it took me that long to get all the raging thoughts in my head to settle down into some kind of order. It usually took me a good three miles before my mind was able to wander freely and solve problems that had seemed intractable the day before.

How do I teach Dad that W is wuh? "Double-you-is-wuh, Dad, double-you-is-wuh." I kept repeating this to the rhythm of my run until it no longer made sense as words. Sometimes I would add a chorus of "wuh-wuh-wuh-wuh-wuh-wuh-wuh." Then it hit me. Wuh as in Wayne. How dumb could I be? W was the first letter in Dad's name. That was my ticket in. That morning when Dad got to W, he said again, "Double-you is duh" and I gave him a flash card with his name on it.

"What's that word?"

"It's my name."

"Say it."

"Wayne."

"What's it begin with?"

"W."

"Right. What's the sound of W?" I could hardly contain my excitement.

"Duh."

I did not have a plan B. My idea had seemed watertight. I decided to simply repeat myself. When in doubt, just do over again what didn't work the first time, kind of like summer school.

"How do you pronounce your name?"

"Wayne."

"Right. It begins with W. What is the first sound in your name?"

"Wuh."

"Right. So what is the sound of W?"

"Wuh."

"Right. Good."

Right on cue, the entire haloed and robed Mormon Tabernacle Choir emerged on a rising platform in my brain and launched into a surprisingly up-tempo rendition of the "Hallelujah Chorus" with such inspired gusto it was all I could do not to sing along.

Mother baked these kinds of cakes every year. (She also loved the idea of a Tony Permanent Wave.)

Dinner My Way

By the middle of the first week I knew that Mother's pantry needed considerable beefing up. When Dad was napping I scooted to town to get a few cooking staples. At the fish market I bought white miso, black bean paste, mirin, and toasted sesame oil. At the health food store I bought pumpkin seeds, big bunches of kale, four bulbs of fennel root, and arugula, endive, and frisee to add a little interest to the evening salad. At the deli I bought some good imported anchovies packed in salt and some decent balsamic vinegar.

Now I could get on with the business of cooking some good meals packed with protein and flavor. I was a food holy-roller, wild with intention.

For dinner I had decided to make sea bass braised with fennel bulbs and served with steamed kale and roasted vegetables on the side. I was just flying into action, singing "Go You Chicken Fat Go!" the song my fifth grade gym teacher made us sing while we were doing squat thrusts, when Bud sauntered into the house without knocking.

"Hey, Dweeb!" he chimed. "I saw a sign up the road advertising that you and your sister were for sale! I thought I'd come check it out."

"Don't bug me." I ignored him, pulling the bones out of the fish. "I'm busy."

"Down there at the Pay and Pack. Big sign. Said 'Ding Dongs, two for a dollar.' Thought it was pretty pricey for the two of you, but some sucker will probably come along. Hey, where's your dad?"

"He's in the living room. Just your speed to pick on somebody who can't talk back."

"I won't pick on him. I have a new Hillary joke to tell him. Somebody's gotta think about keeping up his sense of humor. Gotta make sure you don't squeeze right out what little he's got left in him. He didn't have much to begin with. You ever gonna let him come out and play?"

"Not with you."

Bud tracked all the mud he'd collected in the driveway into the living room. "Hey, Edsall!" He plopped down on the couch. "How ya doin'?"

I heard a big laugh from both of them, heralding the predictable success of his Hillary Clinton joke.

Bud came over nearly every evening, engaging Dad in a halting and exhausting conversation, giving him welcome interaction with someone other than family. The best thing about Bud was that he was so relaxed. He could sit for a solid three minutes while Dad worked to say what was on his mind and he wouldn't flinch once.

"You want to stay for dinner, Bud?" I called into the living room.

"You gonna be there?"

"You get three tries for the right answer."

"Nah. I think I'll pass."

"Good. We don't have enough food for a mouth as big as yours anyway."

I reached to turn on the oven. At my house, you turn on the oven by pushing a button that says BAKE and then turning a knob until the number on the oven indicator says the right temperature. Mother's oven was much more temperamental and I hated it. First you had to push UPPER OVEN or LOWER OVEN, then you had to push BAKE, then you had to push TEMP, then you had to enter the temperature, then you had to push TEMP again, then you had to push START. Clearly, this stove was designed by engineers who detested people who cooked.

"I hate this oven!" I yelled, stabbing every button I could see in front of me.

"It's not that hard, honey," Mom intervened, setting the oven up for me.

"Well, maybe it's obvious to you, but ovens can be made simpler than this. It's a stupid design. Did you know it was this stupid when you bought it?"

"There, the lower oven is ready. Let me first turn on the fan."

Mother hit a button and a metal wall emerged from the back of the countertop stove with a deafening whir.

"Do we really need the fan, Mom? The noise is so irritating."

"If we don't turn the fan on, this house will smell like fish for a week."

I knew the house wouldn't smell for a week. Lighting a candle and opening a few windows would do the trick within thirty minutes. Nevertheless, I acquiesced.

I resumed my whirlwind of activity. Determined to keep everything as organized as possible, I cooked and cleaned up all at the same time, despite Mother's protests.

"If you cook, I clean up!" Mother set out the rules cheerfully.

"Mom, I don't have anything else to do. There is nothing wrong with me rinsing out a few pans." I crammed the tops of the fennel root into the garbage disposal along with the stem ends of the kale. "Please don't nag me."

"I want to clean up. It gives me something to do." She plucked at my arm.

"Believe me, Mother, there will be plenty to do." I opened the dishwasher and put in several bowls I had used to prepare the vegetables. Then I swung open the cupboards and pulled out plates.

"Here! Let me do that! I'll set the table." Mother reached for the plates in my hands.

"I'm serving it at the stove, Mom. I need the plates here. Why don't you put the silverware on the table and get napkins." If she really needed something to do that bad, she could set the table.

The timer rang on the oven, indicating the vegetables were done. The fish was ready and the kale just needed a little toss with vinegar. I swung into action for the final assault. Remembering the produce greens in the garbage disposal, I jerked on the faucet, flipped the garbage disposal switch, and watched as the septic system backed up into the sink. The timer continued to ring because I didn't know which button to hit to turn it off. The filthy water level rose in the sink.

It was clear that dinner would be delayed.

"I think I plugged up the sink."

"We'll need a plumber for this," Mother diagnosed, peering into the sink, her nose wrinkled in reproof.

"We don't need a *plumber*, Mother. Just get me a plunger. I can fix this."

Mother handed me a plunger. I shoved and heaved and swore. The level of the stuff in the sink did not change.

"Okay, Mom," I said. "I think we need to call a plumber."

13   *Mom joins the Shower Cap Wars, Western Front.*

Gotcha

Every time Dad succeeded, I jacked things up a bit. I made flash cards with words that began with each letter of the alphabet.

Sometimes he recognized whole words—like Montana. Other words looked like a jumble of letters to him, and he would often stab at them frantically, like he was swatting mosquitoes in a swamp. The more he flailed, the more hopeless he felt.

"Cay-ble. Cayn-lon. Cayl-et. Cay—"

I would barge in. "What's the sound of the first letter?" He would cover up the word with his wide, fat thumb and unveil each letter one at a time. "Kuh-a-n-duh-l." He paused, frowning. "Huh," he said, bewildered. He tried again. "Kuh-a-n-duh-l." He shook his head from side to side as if he were trying to get better reception. "Oh! Candle! Candle. Kuh-a-n-duh-l. Candle! Yeah. Kuh-a-n-duh-l." The whole concept of sounding out was such a relief to him. He wouldn't have to memorize every word in the dictionary after all. He had the keys to the kingdom.

We could work through about fifteen words in thirty minutes. At which point Dad was exhausted and so was I.

"Time for a break!" Dad didn't want to break. He wanted us to keep working. He was stuck on the idea that by July 1—this was an arbitrary date he had fixed in his mind—he would have made all the progress he would ever be able to make. That at midnight on June 30 Sharon and I would pack up our books and leave, that his mind would have soaked up the last drop of learning possible, and that where he was at that moment was where he would be for the rest of his life.

I knew from my reading that Dad needed that break every half hour—if only for a few minutes. When he inevitably protested, I would take my time meandering to the bathroom or wandering into the kitchen to pour a glass of juice. By the time I got back to the table, his head was down on his worksheets and he was sound asleep. I would let him sleep for ten minutes before waking him up to start again.

Mom wanted us just to let the poor man sleep. She could see that he was tired and she thought we were driving him too hard. Of course he was tired—we were all tired. But for us—and especially for Dad—being tired was simply irrelevant. We had a job to do—tired or not tired. Part of the trouble was that even before the stroke Mom never thought anyone got enough sleep. When I would come home for a visit she protested against how much I packed into my schedule. "You need to *rest*," she would pine, as if she were trying to persuade me to please, please, please give up intravenous drug use. So I had learned to accept this as Mom's overlay—everyone needed more sleep no matter what.

I would sit across from Dad and look at him, his forehead cushioned by the back of his hands, and feel heartsick. My love for Dad was deep and thick and I felt so sad that he had been pushed back so, so far. His whole life he had found himself in one bind or another and he'd always found a way out. But he'd never been in a bind like this, where he had so little control. He'd always had options, even if they weren't ideal.

I remember flying with him in his Beechcraft Bonanza, a low-wing, four-seater airplane with retractable landing gear. It was a perfect summer day. Dad wanted to check on a job in Libby, in the northwest corner of the state way past Missoula, and asked me if I wanted to tag along. I loved these trips. Me and Dad, wearing hard hats, inspecting tile flooring, roof shingles, talking with the foreman about the schedule and whether things were on track. I stood right next to Dad like I was vice president of the company. We arrived at noon and ate with the workmen in a big trailer that was set up to serve lunch every day. A husky, hair-sprayed woman spread out a feast on a plywood table covered with oilcloth. "Now there's plenty more groceries where that came from if that ain't enough," she announced. "Eat up!"

Bologna sandwiches on white bread slathered with Miracle Whip were stacked like brickwork next to a big metal bowl of pork and beans fresh from the can. Sacks of barbecue-flavored potato chips gaped open within easy reach of any seat. Plastic trays of Oreo cookies weighted down each end of the table. We sat with the men and did what they did, peeling back the bread and sliding potato chips into the Miracle Whip, pouring plastic glasses full of Kool-Aid, and eating it all like it was a holiday.

On the way back, we flew the traplines, following a set course along rivers, lakes, and mountain ranges. Around dinnertime, we headed back to the airport. Dad pushed down the lever to lower the landing gear, waiting to hear the sound of them clicking in. Nothing happened. One hand on the control wheel, his eyes on the airspace in front of him, he pulled the lever up and pushed it down again, hard. Still nothing. I didn't know yet that something was wrong. He flew close to the tower, something I'd never seen him do before, and banked sharply, the bottom of the plane facing the flight controllers, like Dad was mooning them. They confirmed on the radio what he had feared: the landing gear wasn't down. He hit the lever hard. "Shit!" he barked. That's when I knew we were in trouble. Never before, when flying with Dad, had I heard him swear.

I looked out my window as far as I could see and scanned the fields for the best place to land belly-up. It needed to be as flat as possible with few buildings around. I personally wanted it to be soft, but I didn't think that was a big consideration—or even possible. I knew Dad would have me put my head between my knees, even though I wanted to watch the whole thing. I also knew we had plenty of gas, and Dad would try to solve the problem another way or scout good locations. I wondered if we would buzz Mom first or if we'd just go ahead and land. I imagined Dad would radio in where he was intending to put the plane down, in case they wanted someone there—like a fire truck or an ambulance. I wasn't scared out of my wits, as I probably should have been. It just seemed exciting, and anyhow, I knew Dad could do it.

We flew around for quite a while, Dad's attention fixed entirely on the plane—he couldn't be distracted trying to explain things to me and I knew this. I didn't ask a single question and I didn't bite my nails. In this situation I knew how to behave.

Then I heard a familiar grinding noise. Somehow Dad had gotten the landing gear to lower. We mooned the tower once more and they confirmed it: all set for landing.

"That could make you soil your shorts!" Dad grinned at me, dropping the plane out of the sky and onto the runway.

Dad's bread always landed butter side up, I thought as I watched him sleep. I just hoped his luck would hold now.

"Recess is over!" I would joke, rousing him from his nap. Then I would ask him to read headlines from the local newspaper. He could often get each word, but stringing them together in a smooth sentence that made sense took grinding effort. I bought *An Ornery Bunch*, a book of stories written by pioneers of the Old West, some tales as short as half a page—"The Misadventures of a Tenderfoot" or "Milking a Steer"—none longer than two pages, and each morning he would read one out loud. It often took forty-five minutes. He would write the time on each essay. Then I would copy the essay, date it, and put it in the three-ring binder.

Dad was anxious because he couldn't connect the exercises to real life; they didn't seem to add up to anything that would get him back up in his plane. The few thousand feet he wanted to be up in the sky must have seemed as far-flung as the Milky Way.

My morning run produced a list: Speaking, Reading, Writing, Listening, Thinking, Computing.

I taped the list to the table next to his workspace. Now, for every exercise Dad would tell me which of those areas he thought we were working on and how it related to his goal of flying.

I also drew a Continuum of Progress. On the left I wrote "Don't have a clue," progressing to "I can get it but it's a lot of work" to "I can get it but I still need help" to "I can get it most of the time" to "I feel pretty confident I have this." When we finished an exercise he would tell me where he thought he was on the continuum. He always ranked himself lower than I would have ranked him. He was his own vinegary taskmaster.

Reading was hard, but writing was even harder. Not only was it more difficult for Dad, it wasn't as immediately applicable. He didn't do a lot of writing in his life. We eased in with word games. I would ask, "Which item in this list doesn't belong?" Then I would list "shirt, pants, gloves, fork." He would say, "Fork," then I would ask him to write it. He struggled.

Or I would have him draw a word out of the pile of flash cards and write a phrase that contained the word. At first I asked him to write a sentence, but he couldn't do it—it wasn't just that he couldn't physically *write* the sentence, he couldn't even *think* of the sentence. His left brain, in charge of logical progression and sequencing, wasn't up to the task yet. I ratcheted the goal down to a phrase. It was hard for him.

He pulled the flash card *chair* from the deck. He wrote "chair." Underneath that he wrote "lawn chair." Below that he wrote "summer."

Next he drew the flash card *television*. He wrote, "I wach telephone." Whoops. He drew a hard, chiding line through that and tried again. Laboring over each letter, and after many erasures, he was able to write, "I watch television." A sentence. Progress.

Once he got good at this, I would have him draw two cards and write a sentence that had both words in it. He pulled *plumber* and *plunger*. We had been having trouble with the toilets constantly being plugged up and were developing various theories about how to avoid the problem. Mother's strategy was to fill a two-gallon bucket with water and hold it high over the toilet bowl, pouring the water in while it was flushing. Sharon's was to use public facilities as often as possible. Mine was to buy a really good plunger for every bathroom. Dad's was to go to Canada and buy toilets that did not conserve water and replace these low-flow contraptions that didn't work and never would. So when he pulled these two words, he had something to say. A sentence came easily. He wrote, "The problem with the toilet is that it's not big enough." Dad was proud. This was getting easier.

I looked at the flash cards and I looked at the sentence. "Well, that's pretty good, Dad, but you didn't use either word."

When he realized what he had done, we both laughed. As we got into a rhythm of work and saw that what we were doing was paying off, we laughed a lot. Often Dad was the one that was playing the jokes. One evening we were sitting around the table after dinner and I was bloviating about how mad it made me when people expected that Dad would be retarded or stupid or something. I was on quite a roll when I looked over at Dad. His eyes were rolled into the back of his head and his tongue was hanging out of his mouth. It stopped me cold.

"Gotcha!" Dad said, and we laughed like families do when the dog tries to lick peanut butter off the top of his mouth or the cat walks sideways when there's a sock on her tail.

But I would not be outdone. Fiercely competitive, it was my turn. The next day I was making vocabulary flash cards, with a word on one side and the word in a sentence on the other side. For our exercise, Dad would choose fifteen flash cards, read both sides, then write his own sentence using the word. "Vacation," he read from one side. "The family went to California on a vacation," I had written on the other. Then he would write, "I need a vacation." He went through about seven of these before getting to my surprise flash card. "Feminism," he said, sounding mildly stumped. No sentence of his own was forming in his head. He turned the card over and read, "Why would I ever have to know the word *feminism*?" He paused and then looked at me.

"Ain't that the truth," he declared and snapped the flash card down on the table.

"Gotcha!"

Easter Craft Night can be a dangerous thing.

14

Way Out Here

One morning I handed Dad a blank sheet of paper and a pencil. "Write a letter to Sharon," I instructed, making efficient, teacherly flourishes, busying myself with the setup. On the periphery of my vision I could see that he was looking at me with a puzzled, near-protesting expression. I knew as I was conjuring this exercise that he would put up a fuss, so I didn't even look at him. My eyes locked onto that blank sheet of paper with great, absorbed interest. I didn't know how this exercise applied to flying and I didn't want to be asked. I just knew that Dad had to learn to write.

Dad looked defeated, bullied even. I felt terribly sorry for him. I wanted to take it all back, to say I was just kidding. I didn't want to be mean. But I sat still with a confident and patient expression and hoped with all my heart that he would be able to do it and that my internal anxiety would not express itself in a rash.

"Hello to Share," he began. While he strained to think of something to say and then to write it, I sat at the table, still as the blue heron we watched every morning out by the landing strip. "The weather is nice today and it is going to be another nice day. Jeff is still gone. Sue is working hard on my voice. It takes a lot of work, but it is worth it." His writing slanted upward, the soft lead pencil smearing under the force of his hand. He wrote, erased, brushed eraser bits off the page, and began again. Beads of sweat rolled from his temples into his sideburns. "We will take mom to dinner for her birthday. A coupla of planes flew over. That was nice. Mom slept through church. We are all tired for today. Happy Easter—Dad."

Forty-five minutes.

I had never worked him this hard. But I wasn't finished. Had I not had a plan in advance, I never would have asked him to walk this extra mile with a stone in his shoe. I handed him an envelope and an index card with Sharon's address copied on it.

"You do it," he said, asserting his authoritarian privilege.

"No. You do it. It's your letter." Dad looked whipped. Maybe I was pushing him too hard. He wrote the address, laboring over each line. He handed the envelope back to me.

"What about the return address? Put your return address up there."

"Mom has a st-st-st-rap. No. A str-str-ipe. No. What is it?"

"You tell me. What is it? Describe it for me."

"You lick it."

"Yeah? What do you call a thing that you lick. Say it in a sentence." Dad could often get the word if he included it in a sentence.

"You lick a stamp," he forced out.

"Right. So Mom has a stamp with the address on it?"

"Yes."

"Well, we're learning to write here, so you should write the return address instead of using a stamp." I hated myself.

He did it, but he was so tired afterward that he lay down on the couch and slept until lunch. I went into my room, crawled under the covers with all my clothes on, and cried. I didn't want to be in charge. I wanted to go back to being the kid who everyone was glad had come home for a little visit. There was so much comfort in having Dad firmly in charge and Mom firmly backing him up. It was always that way in our family. We counted on it.

When Sharon and I were in high school, the hot new vandalism rage was to smash mailboxes with baseball bats in the middle of the night. The beauty of the prank was that it was primordially satisfying to bash in a mailbox. It felt powerful to inconvenience someone in that way, but the individual cost to the person who owned the mailbox wasn't high enough for them to pursue the crime with any vigor. So the guys who did it got away with it.

Until they happened upon my father.

It was about two in the morning. Mom and Dad's bedroom was in the basement near the front of the house, and Dad heard the mailbox being smashed. He flew out of bed, grabbed his jeans, and was hopping on one foot and then the other as he tried to put them on at the same time that he was running up the stairs and shouting at Mother, "Don't turn on the light! Don't turn on the light!"

By this time we were all up, groggy and rubbing our eyes and whining. We followed Mom up the stairs in time to see Dad smash into a wooden decorative ladder that held various plants on each step, the pots now broken on the floor, the potting soil sinking irretrievably into the shag carpeting. Dad was still hopping into his pants, having grabbed the keys to his truck and heading back down the stairs to the garage, still shouting, "Don't turn on the light! Don't turn on the light!" as if Mother was badgering him by chasing him down, her hand ominously on the switch.

Sasha, our West Highland terrier, always slept out in the back foyer, right where Dad was headed. Dad burst through the door and tripped over the dog, who went tumbling and yelping down the stairs with him as he headed for the truck.

We heard his truck door slam and saw him head out the driveway without his lights on. Then we all looked at each other and burst into laughter. Mother laughed so hard she collapsed on the couch, her head flung back, hooting. She dabbed at her eyes with her green jersey nightshirt. Sharon and I first laughed at Dad. Then we laughed at Mom laughing at Dad, and then, about twenty minutes later, when Dad drove in the driveway, this time with his lights on, we stopped laughing PDQ and agreed that we could not look at each other under threat of death.

Dad walked in and headed straight for the phone.

"Goddamn kids." He called the sheriff and reported the license plate number, type of vehicle, and number of kids in the car. I'm sure those kids never knew what hit them.

The next day the sheriff called and asked Dad what he wanted done with the kids. "What do I want done with them?" Dad snorted, astonished that there was any doubt. "Throw them in jail!"

I had grown up with Dad in charge, clarity about the rules, and knowing my place in the scheme of things. Now the whole kit and kaboodle was knocked out of whack. I had never pulled this much weight in my life. It wasn't so much that I was weary—although I was—but that I felt like so much was riding on me doing this right, and I was struggling to stay upright while my own ground was undergoing a tectonic shift.

I was coming to understand a very tiny fact: in the scheme of things, my job didn't matter. I don't mean in the scheme of the history of Western civilization. I mean in a very narrow scheme of things: my little life. If I no longer ran around the country in airplanes, staying in hotels and eating very small salads that cost nine dollars at expensive restaurants where the menu was often bigger than the table I was sitting at, nothing about the world would change very much except that I would have more time with my family. I could do good work within a two-hour drive of my KitchenAid mixer and my impact on the world would be about the same. That is, not very much. Once I got over the initial shock and disappointment, I felt liberated. I wasn't taking any more clients that required me to get on an airplane—I didn't care how exotic the place.

I had often been lured to take on work in distant cities by the promise that it would be so much fun to go to fill-in-the-blank location. There was so much to do! To see! What I ended up doing was working straight through from an early breakfast to long past dinner, and what I saw was the inside of hotel conference rooms. Home was where I belonged—whether that was Vermont or Montana. My family was not, I discovered with embarrassed astonishment, a silk flower arrangement that always looked fabulous and was so lifelike that you had to touch it to find out if it was real. My family was one of those old-timey plants that die without water, fertilizer, and sun. I would write NO in ink across whole days in my calendar. These days with my family I would not negotiate away.

Next, I was dropping the oppressive division of labor quotas in our fully actualized feminist household. I was coming out of the closet on the fact that I liked to shop for groceries, cut the vegetables, cook, and clean up. I liked it when Rick cleared the path to the car with a snowblower and hauled all our garbage to the dump and changed the oil in my car. I liked pink, too. The next time a friend from out of town came to visit and sneered, "I see you and Rick have divided your work strictly along gender lines," as if I were a half-evolved fish flopping around on the beach heaving and gasping while trying to get my lungs to kick in, I would sparkle, "Why, yes! We love it that way!" and offer to show them my collection of hand-embroidered aprons.

I knew more than ever that this was the most meaningful work of my life. What I didn't know was how the story would end. Huddled under the covers in my room, I cried with the burden and with the not knowing.

That evening we were in the living room after dinner doing synonym drills. Dad called them "sons-a-bitches" because he had a hard time saying "synonyms" but mostly because he really hated the exercises. They were a way for him to build his vocabulary so he could substitute a word when he got hung up. They were hard. This was like memorizing the dictionary. I would say a word like "quick," and he would have to say something like "fast" or "speedy" or "rapid." We would do ten at a time. Sometimes I asked him to give me two synonyms.

"Woman," I said, looking to him for a synonym.

"Tomatah," he responded, automatically.

I looked at him in feminist reproof, ready to demand a second try when we both burst into laughter.

When we were done, he was beat and he looked it. Clumps of hair stood like gray stucco peaks from the top of his head. The round collar of his T-shirt, rimmed gray from sweat, stretched and sagged from nervous plucking. A tenuous scaffolding of knee, elbow, palm, and chin were the only thing that kept him upright in his chair. One tiny bump of his wrist, one nudge to the base of his chair, would have sent him tumbling to the floor. He had the expended look of a rookie marathon runner who realizes too late that he should have stuck to a good brisk walk around the neighborhood.

When he got this tired, his speech slipped—he got hung up more often, he couldn't find good word substitutions, and he got frustrated and self-critical.

"I don't feel like I'm making any progress."

Although it didn't come naturally to me, I knew that it was at these times that it was my job to listen, no matter what. Even though listening is deceptively hard.

I was powerfully haunted by the fear that I might blurt out the cheerleading responses I had come to abhor from the speech therapists. I knew I shouldn't try to talk him out of it ("Oh! No! You're doing *great!*"), to persuade him to think differently ("You shouldn't think that, Dad"), to commiserate ("I know how you must feel. I felt that way when I was learning to play the piano"), or worst of all, to favorably compare his situation to others ("Think of all those people up in Sunnyside who didn't know shit from shinola. You're doing a lot better than them"). I knew I shouldn't discount anything he was feeling. My job was simply and solely to listen.

But I was seriously hampered by being tired most of the time myself, and because this need to listen was always sneaking up on me, I memorized a multipurpose line that bought me a little time while I got my act together. It was this line I used now.

"Really, Dad? What makes you say that?"

I waited through his lurching and halting speech while he took a good two minutes to explain. "I'm going over and over these flash cards and I keep making the same mistakes. Like *s* and *l*. I keep getting them wrong. I'm not making progress. It took me an hour to write that letter. It shouldn't take me so long."

"What's today, Dad?"

"Thursday, Friday, Saturday. No. Sunday. Sunday."

"Right. Sunday. Let me show you what you did last Sunday." I got the blue three-ring binder and opened up to the worksheet dated a week ago. It was the one with "banana" and "lion" on it. I laid the binder in his lap. "This is what you wrote a week ago." Then I handed him the copy I had made of the letter he mailed to Sharon. "This is what you wrote today. You tell me if you think you're making progress."

The binder rattled from the trembling of Dad's hands. Then he dropped it and put his face in his hands and sobbed.

I sank to my knees at his feet, feeling bewildered, guilty, and confused. "You've finally done it!" I roared at myself. "You pushed him right over the edge! You made your father cry!" I thought I might throw up from the horror of my own meanness.

Stiffly, I reached over to Dad and put my arms around his neck. I was bent over awkwardly, struggling to keep my balance, rigid with reluctance. Then I cried, too. "What's wrong, Dad? Do you feel like I'm not helping you enough? That you need someone who knows more about what they're doing?" I assumed Dad had concluded that he was making lousy progress and if he continued this whole school charade with his daughters as his teachers he would either end up retarded or psychologically damaged or both.

Dad grabbed me around the neck fiercely. He held on as if he were marooned in deep starless space and I were a steel cable, his only tether to earth. "I didn't realize how far back I really was, things could have been so bad. Was it only a week ago?"

"Yes, Dad. It's been only a week. You're making tremendous progress, Dad. You're going to be fine. Really, you are."

I picked up the binder and flipped through it to show him his progress. He wouldn't look at it. He just closed it and handed it back to me. "You keep that," he said, unable to take it in. Then he squeezed my hand hard and looked me in the eye. "You don't know what it's like way out here."

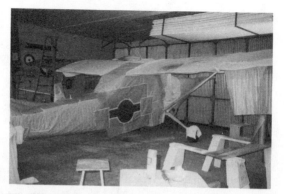

The Birddog in the hangar, ready to paint

15

Demons

The next morning Dad came dragging into the kitchen and something seemed to be wrong. He was late, for one thing, and Dad was never late. I had been standing there by the stove in my running shorts ready to pour the Egg Beaters into the pan for at least ten minutes when he finally showed.

"Hey Pop! How'd you sleep?"

"Okay, I guess," he said, rubbing his hands through his hair.

I laid out his breakfast on the place mat before him, along with a steaming cup of coffee. He hunched over his omelet, shoveling it in with the enthusiasm of Sisyphus. Big, dolorous sighs heaved out of him.

When breakfast was over, we waded into the day.

I thought we needed a little jollying up. "Name as many items as you can in one minute. The category is . . ." I raised my eyebrows, holding a note card out in front of me with a flourish to create suspense. I put on my Game Show Announcer voice, directing an invisible backup band. "Drumroll please! The category is! 'Things That Are Irritating!' Please be reminded that, as part of our strict contest rules, you cannot name your daughter because, as we all know, she is not an item!"

Dad reluctantly played along. "Don't quit your day job," he advised halfheartedly, stumbling headlong over every word. We both coughed out tepid laughs of mutual support.

"Things That Are Irritating," Dad repeated. "Things That Are Irritating." His attempt was lackluster. He only got ten in one minute, and we were aiming for nineteen.

The whole morning went that way. He did what I asked of him, but he had no heart for it. I worried that the prospect of spending every day like this for the next two months was too much for him to contemplate, to endure. I knew that the work of recovery was depleting. It was depleting me, and I wasn't the one recovering. It wasn't just that relearning everything was hard, though it was. It was that believing he could recover enough to get back to his old life was hard, believing that he would ever, ever fly again. None of us had been through anything this hard before.

Not that Dad had lived a charmed life. He'd toughened up young. Between the time he was in kindergarten and graduation from high school, his family had moved thirty-seven times. His dad, a construction superintendent, went where the work was—and so did his family. All Grandma ever took with her were her kids and her sewing machine. Dad joined the Navy when he was nineteen, went to Alaska when he was twenty-two, and went into business for himself when he was twenty-eight. He'd worked like a ditchdigger for everything he had, and very little of it came easily. He had the will of a bulldozer, and when his blade hit the ground, the best thing to do was get out of his way. He'd had plenty of hurdles as he built his business—labor strikes, lawsuits, bankrupt subcontractors—but if any of these were setbacks, he certainly didn't see them that way. They were just part of doing business, the heat in the kitchen. From watching Dad I learned that you kept putting one foot ahead of the other, that you just plain didn't take no for an answer, that you looked the devil square in the eye and spit. "Period," as Dad would say.

Except, maybe, for now. I knew Dad didn't want to take no for an answer, but I also knew that it must be killing him to muster, day after day after day, all that was needed to make even the most minuscule progress.

We worked until noon and then had lunch. We didn't do any errands that afternoon, but Dad did go on his daily walk down the airstrip.

I watched him out the picture windows of the living room. He was wearing the usual—his Edsall Construction Company baseball cap, his brown wool coat, and his jeans, baggy now that he was nearly twenty pounds thinner. Today his hands, curled into fists, were stuffed into his coat pockets, and he stared at the ground, leaning forward as if into the wind, although it was a balmy day. His shoulders lifted when he stopped to take in deep breaths, more sighs.

He always took his walk methodically, compensating for the weakness still dogging his right side, but today he seemed slower, sadder somehow.

He turned and plodded toward the hangar, stopping occasionally to look out at the Spanish Peaks—commanding purple ramparts of rock, snow-covered year round, that shot into the sky, as indomitable as the passage of time. When he got to the hangar, he riveted his eyes on the ground as if he could bore through the earth and get a clear shot to China. He hadn't been inside the hangar since his stroke. He wouldn't even look inside. He wouldn't lean his face up against the window, shielding his eyes from the sun with his cupped hands, to see the Airmaster in pieces, just as he had left it. He certainly wouldn't walk up the weedy, narrow path to the door, past the hand-lettered sign that read EDSALL INTERNATIONAL AIRPORT, ELEVATION 4,700 FEET, pull the key down from the top of the jamb, and go inside. The Airmaster was like a baby left on his porch. If he didn't open the door, he could pretend it wasn't there. If he did open the door, it forced on him all kinds of obligations.

The only person who could get Dad past that door was Bud. But Dad would have to be lured. He wouldn't be shock-shoved into the hangar. Bud would have to lean on Dad, bit by bit, working him up to it, getting Dad to think it was his idea. Bud was the only one with enough patience and stealth to take it slow and easy, circling and circling until they happened upon the hangar almost in passing. He'd have to use the same cowboy manner you'd need to catch a skittish calf outside the pen—chewing thoughtfully on the stem end of a weed, crouched down on your heels, crooning, "There now, that's it, nice and easy, babe, nice and easy," until the calf's snugly nose was nibbling the grain in your hand. Dad wasn't even close to being lulled. He was as wide-awake aware of the threat in the hangar as a calf is of the smoking-hot branding iron.

Dad trudged on past the hangar, down to the end of the strip, hefting one leaden foot past the other. His head dropped down to his chest as if pushed there and held immobile by some huge, hulking hand. I could practically see the cloud of doom circling him like carrion crows celebrating a sick lamb. I knew what he was thinking. He was wishing he had died. For him, dying was the only way out of this mess and it was an opportunity long past. There was little chance of him dying now, but every chance in the world that he would never fly at all, let alone in his beloved antique planes, and no chance in the world that he'd be able to tackle the Airmaster.

I had hoped that returning to the Airmaster would be the antidote to the slow-dripping poison seeping into his spirit. Now I could see that the Airmaster was ridiculing him, parading his loss by simply sitting there, unmoving, in the hangar, demanding to be rebuilt. She was too loud, too insistent, too there. He probably hated her.

When he turned, the hangar loomed like a dare, staring him down. Dad stared back, weak and aching. He was dueling with the devil, deciding whether to go on and how.

From a quarter-mile away, I was staring too. All I could see was Dad, standing stooped and stock-still at the end of the runway, his eyes fixed on the hangar, but I knew more than I saw.

I felt panicky, like I was hearing a hurried boatman shout "All Aboard!" for a little cruise down the River Styx, his hand pressed into the small of my back, nudging me, unwilling, into my seat right behind Dad. Then I crabbed at myself about exaggerating things to a fevered pitch. For crying out loud, this was just school, after all. This was just learning to talk and read and write, something everybody had to do at least once in their life. Dad just happened to have to do it twice, that's all. So what! This wasn't life and death.

I quizzed myself. What had I considered a setback in, say, the last two months? The list came easily, sliding out of my mind like a rotten banana from its skin. I'd been really ripped about a two-hour flight delay; stomped around for a few minutes when I forgot to videotape my favorite cooking show; felt inconvenienced when my housekeeper had to miss a week because her son was in some unmemorable sports tournament; huffed and puffed for a good ten miles when I found myself behind a snowplow on a road with no opportunity to pass. Then there was the really big stuff like the stock market decline and leaving my entire makeup bag in a hotel room and having a client comment that I "looked a little wan." The zenith of my humiliations, however, was returning to my hotel room after a full day of work and discovering pepper lodged in my front teeth. I wanted to die. Not to mention that, with all this traveling, it was very hard not to gain a pound or two.

It is not pretty to discover you are a trite little person living a very public trite little life.

I fixed my eyes on Dad. He stood there for a long time, wrestling with his thoughts. I knew he was asking himself what it would mean if he just gave up now. What it would mean if he failed. He knew who he was—a husband, a father, a friend, and a pilot. What he didn't know was who he might become. A burden? A bitter old man?

Dad lifted his eyes to take in the sweep of the Tobacco Root Mountain Range, pulled his collar up against the afternoon breeze, and put one foot ahead of the other to start his long walk home. I knew he'd made a decision. The bulldozer had lowered its blade to the ground. Wayne Edsall was going to look the devil in the eye and spit.

16

The Blister Sisters ready to take on the world, 1974

The Blister Sisters

My brother, Steve, has an equine veterinary practice in Bellevue, Idaho. I'd asked Dad to write a letter to Steve as well as the one to Sharon. Steve later told me that when he unfolded the white sheet of typing paper and saw the childish, faltering handwriting, the repeated erasures, the elementary school narrative, he was devastated. Rather than evidence of how far Dad had come, the letter was proof that Dad was worse than he thought, proof that Dad would never fly again. Faced with such bitter news, Steve retreated into silence. Finally, I called him.

"Did you get Dad's letter?"

"Yeah. I didn't realize he was so bad."

"What do you mean, so bad?"

"I just thought he was better than this, for some reason."

"Steve, two weeks ago Dad couldn't string three words together. Now he's writing letters. He's doing great. Why don't you come over? I think it would be good for you to see him."

"I wish I could, but I can't get away. Spring's my busiest time of year. I've got foals coming."

"Not even for a weekend?"

"No, I really can't." He took a deep sigh and came out with it. "I don't think I could handle it, Sue."

"You were there for his surgery, weren't you?"

"Yeah, but I couldn't even visit him when he was in the ICU. All those tubes coming out of him. I've never seen Dad like that. I don't know, I just can't handle it."

"My gosh, Steve, you're a vet!" I laughed. But I knew what he meant. It was rough seeing Dad like this. "How did you handle it when Mom called and told you Dad had a stroke?"

"You know, I deal with emotional women all day. I'm trained to deal with crisis situations in a nonemotional way."

"Huh." I didn't know how else to respond. I wasn't too wild about being chucked into a category of "emotional women" as if I had a disability people had to be trained to maneuver around.

"I feel lucky that I didn't have to be there through all this, to tell you the truth," Steve confessed. "I don't think I could handle it."

"I know what you mean," I said. "That's what I thought at first too. But it's good, really. It's intense." Here I was, parroting to my brother the very words my sister had used with me only two weeks earlier. Sharon had become my guide, leading me, willing but green, through the deep woods of the heart.

Steve and I are alike in more ways than I realized—reticent and reluctant in this kind of mess, not venturing too far from the known territory of concrete conversation about concrete things. Sharon, on the other hand, is nimble and fearless, working without a net in her high-wire act of feeling.

How did we come to be so different?

It seems like if you go to the same school, are raised by the same parents, go on the same camping trips, you should end up being more alike than different. Not the case in our family.

One evening we were all lounging around the table and Mom was marveling at our motliness. "I don't know how I could have borne three such different children," she mused, expecting that little nugget to rest unmolested on the table in our midst, a gentle truth.

"I know how, Mom," Sharon said boldly, flinging a few more pretzels into her mouth. "It's the meter reader."

I caught on. "Or was it the milkman—remember that milkman that used to leave milk and butter at our door when we were kids—*after* Dad went to work? I think you kind of look like him!" I said turning Sharon's chin with my finger to get a closer look at her profile.

"Mother!" Sharon said, appalled, as if a family secret had been disclosed in all its garish detail.

Snared once again between two daughters with more energy than manners, Mother dismissed this kind of talk, brushing as it did right up against the topic of sex, by sputtering as authoritatively as it is possible to sputter, "You girls!"

It's true that in many ways we are entirely different, Sharon and I. When we were growing up we fought fiercely and, in the end, went in different directions. She didn't go to college, I did. She doesn't have a career; I do. She lives in the city, I live in the country. She drinks gin and tonic while I dig in the garden (she calls her contribution "supervising"). She has a dog, I have cats. She treats her dog like her child, I think that's ridiculous.

To be specific, Sharon's West Highland terrier is what she calls a "pet-quality dog." I guess that's some kind of pedigree. So I've taken to calling our cats "pound-quality cats." Her dog's name (I am not kidding you here) is Princess Bella Mae Duvall. She dresses this dog in specially made raincoats and tartan jackets and gets its picture taken with Santa Claus. At least she hasn't baptized the thing—yet. Sharon used to call me "Aunt Susan" in relation to the dog, which I really hated. So I treated the dog badly—closing the dishwasher on its snout when it licked the plates after dinner, referring to it as "Lump-o-Lard," and sending it postcards of cats. Now Sharon calls me the dog's "wicked stepsister." I can live with that.

Despite how different we are, sometimes Sharon and I are unnervingly alike—so much so that often Sharon's friends refer to me as "the blond version." We share the trait of fierce competitiveness—a direct inheritance from my father. From the time we were in elementary school we battled to the last breath. We had contests about who could chew the most Bazooka bubble gum at one time. We both crammed thirty-five pieces in our mouths, our heads hanging over the dual bathroom sinks, pink sugary saliva dripping down the drain, our jaws aching from the accomplishment. We went head-to-head on who could eat the most spoonfuls of Crisco without throwing up. Another draw.

I am so miserably competitive, in fact, that I have been banned for life from all card games, board games, and team sports in my family. It's not actually a formal ban, it's just that no one will play with me. Even charades is off-limits. I get too loud and, well, vicious. The whole idea of having fun as a family playing games during the holidays is completely lost on me. I want to win. No matter what.

That doesn't mean I haven't found ways to compete in my family. Unfortunately, in the remaining limited options—variations on what we call "War"—Sharon usually wins. Mostly because she's willing to wait in the weeds a lot longer than I am. I remember in particular the Lamp Wars, which started when my sister moved to Seattle. I was determined to get her the perfect housewarming gift.

Unlike my sister, I hate to shop. But for this occasion I threw practicality to the wind. I ditched the catalogs, cleared my weekend from any distracting duties, and scoured the classified section for garage sales. Money was no object. By Saturday at 8:00 A.M. I was out the door, map in hand. I pawed through tables heaped with old coffeemakers, pilling acrylic sweaters in Tupperware colors, and paperback romance novels by the gross. Florist's vases, stacks of empty egg cartons, rusting cast iron skillets, every edition of *National Geo-*

graphic since 1972, toasters with fraying electric cords, a hot dog cooker ("Never been used!"), yogurt maker ("Used once!"), and an inflatable American flag still in its box. I started to worry. I wasn't finding anything even close to what I was looking for and I'd been at this for nearly an hour. It was hard not to lose heart.

Then, at a multifamily moving sale that had attracted career garage-salers (I could tell because they popped the trunk as they got out of the car, and haggled aggressively over dreck that was priced less than a dollar), I spotted it underneath a table next to the person guarding the cigar box of money. Taking a leaf out of the careerists' book, I curled my lip slightly, showing only disdainful interest in my find so as not to get peeled with the price. But this was it. I would have paid anything.

Within my grasp was a ceramic lamp in near perfect condition. It was about two feet tall, featuring a cartoonish drunk wearing a porkpie hat, rumpled and askew, his eyes rolling into the back of his head and his pink tongue, with a perfect crease straight up the center, hanging, long and shiny, out the side of his mouth. His pea-green sport coat was rumpled, his cuffed pants dragged over the top of his shoes, one giant toe poking through, its nail leaping out like a bayonet, nasty black hairs painted thickly on top. He carried a bottle of liquor (I could only imagine it was cheap, but there was no identifiable label) so loosely that if he hadn't been made of ceramic I'm sure he would have dropped it. He leaned perilously against a black lamppost, surrounded by tufts of green ceramic grass and topped with a 40-watt bulb. The lamp's only flaw was the missing shade. But I considered that part of its charm—a bare bulb sticking straight up into its own dark sky, illuminating the whole comic scene, a moral lesson. I could have wept.

My sister is so tasteful that she hires someone to advise her on decorating her house, to make sure she's au courant—she has her bedspread custom made, her marble table designed by an artist, and her art matches her furniture. So when I came upon the Lamppost Guy, I knew. This was the perfect gift.

"How much?" I asked, pugnacious, looking directly to the right of the seller's nose.

"Two bucks." She answered without apology, trying to intimidate me.

"I'll give you a dollar." I kept my eye right on her.

She paused, appraising my find, calculating how many times it had been passed over, its possible future worth. "Okay," she agreed. But she wasn't happy.

I mailed off my gift and then waited for Sharon's call, her shriek of indignation, the guffaws of laughter before I launched into the telling of my tale. Nothing. Weeks later, the UPS man showed up out of the blue with a big box. Inside, buried in foil confetti that would remain in my carpet for years, was the Lamppost Guy along with a pole lamp hung with three jeweled auburn globes. It must have cost her fifty dollars to send. So I boxed it all up—the Lamppost Guy, the pole lamp, and an additional contribution of a lava lamp without a cord (before they were back in fashion)—and shipped it back. This went on for several more rounds and several more hundred dollars in postage and then things died out. I was relieved. I was worried that for the next round I might have to resort to a refrigerator box and a trucking company. But Sharon never returned the cache, and I assumed I had won. Until Christmas. That year, every single box I opened had a lamp in it.

We've had the Country Decor War, the Icky Food War, and the Dog Purse War. We are currently in the middle of the Girdle War— each of us sewing or gluing more and more lurid decor onto a black bust-to-thigh rubber girdle—tassels, velvet hearts, sequins, zippers, projectiles. This festooned lingerie lies dormant somewhere in either Sharon's house or mine—neither one of us can remember who has the booty. I rummaged through all the places I might have put it and couldn't find it, so I'm frankly a little on edge, fearing an ambush. I find myself eyeing the calendar nervously to prepare for the UPS man's next holiday delivery. Not knowing is part of the torture.

This over-the-top craziness befuddles Mom. Maybe she really does wonder if we're hers. Or maybe she thinks the wackiness skips generations—Grandma had a pretty wide goofy streak. Whoever the culprit, Mom is certain she's not the one to blame.

Once, Mom and I went out to lunch together and headed over to the bookstore to pick up a few things. She'd been complaining about Dad in particular and men in general. How is it, we wondered, that men cannot get the toilet paper roll onto the toilet paper roll holder? What are they doing in there that is so fascinating that they can't go that last step? Then there were the Dad-specific complaints. He always—*always*—makes a phone call to somebody—*anybody*—as soon as you call him for dinner. He won't wear his hearing aid, which forces mother into the bedroom because the television is so loud. Worst of all, he loves those grubby, worn T-shirts that anyone with half a brain and a smidgen of self-respect would be ashamed to be seen in.

By this time we were browsing in the bookstore. I picked up a book relevant to the current topic and slipped it into Mom's hands. "I have an idea, Mom," I said, my voice sympathetic and optimistic. "Why don't you become a lesbian? Then you won't have to worry about how weird men are." She glanced down at the book. *My Coming Out: Becoming a Lesbian after Twenty Years of Marriage*. She dropped it on the floor, probably afraid of catching something communicable and hard to shake. "Just brainstorming!" I said, and put the book back on the shelf.

I recounted the event to Sharon, wicked, conspiratorial laughter peppering my story. Six months later Mom and Sharon were talking on the phone. Mom was giving Sharon the blow-by-blow of some aggravating burr she had under her saddle about Dad. "I completely understand what you're saying, Mother," Sharon commiserated. "You know what I think? I think you should become a lesbian. It would solve a whole lot of problems." Silence. Then Sharon burst into howling laughter and couldn't stop. She had to hang up and call Mom later.

It's not hard to see why Mom can't quite figure us. But whether we were nutty or on her nerves, in those three months when we were thrown together, she must have felt deeply proud. She must have felt that the choice she had made to be the best mother she knew how to be had paid off.

She loved everything there was about being a mother from the very beginning. All of it: our soapy smell after our bath, the way we dug into tuna casserole as if it was a hard-won treat, how our slow shuffle home from school would turn into a hell-for-leather run as soon as we hit the end of the driveway. She loved ripping up a square of old sheet, putting a tablespoon of sugar in it, and securing it with a rubber band to make a bundle for us to suck on when we woke up from a bad dream. She loved whipping up play dough for us out of flour, salt, and water. She loved hiding candy in the corners of windowsills, behind the napkin holder, between books in the bookshelf for us to hunt on Easter morning, carrying our pastel baskets, trailing cellophane straw. She loved being the tooth fairy and Santa Claus. She loved making birthday cakes in the shape of elephants and clowns. She loved it all.

Perhaps most amazing and mundane of all, she loved making us a hot breakfast every morning. It's all I can do to pop half a bagel in the toaster and eat it in the car on the way to work. Mother got up every day, before the sun rose, and by seven she had a full-course breakfast hot on the table. We would arrive in the kitchen to grapefruit halves cut and sectioned so we could eat them easily with a spoon, bacon and scrambled eggs, buttered toast, and orange juice. Lunches packed for all three of us stood at the ready—first in metal lunch pails with a small, bowl-sized thermos of hot soup, a cylindrical thermos that fit in the arched lid of the box full of ice-cold milk, a sandwich, an apple, a sack of corn chips, and homemade cookies for dessert. Then, when we wouldn't be caught dead with a metal lunch box, Mother would pack the same lunch in a paper bag, with two nickels wrapped in a paper towel so we could buy two cartons of milk apiece. She did this every day for seventeen years.

Even now, when being thrown together was so hard, she regretted nothing.

She had planned to have four kids. But after Steve had to have a complete blood transfusion days after his birth, and I was breech, and Sharon came out like a corkscrew, the umbilical cord twisted around her neck, her obstetrician called it quits. He told her that if she had another one, she'd have to find a new doctor. It was just as well. Three was plenty. And two daughters more than enough.

If ever there was a payout for all that work, it was now. Sitting there on the patio reminiscing about growing up, the Montana evening sending a welcome cool breeze over her husband and daughters, Mother had to have known that she had done a good job, that who we were and what we were doing had its beginnings with her.

Dad with the Fleet

17

Oh, Nothing

I needed a nap—needed it with the same single-minded urgency that I usually reserved for chocolate. I had to have it now or I would be unable to continue my life with any sustaining purpose whatsoever. I fell onto the nubby tweed couch that separated the living room from the dining room table, where Dad was intently working on something.

"Nap time!" I announced, settling my head onto the cushion and pulling a light afghan under my chin. I thought I might die of happiness. "What're you doing, Dad?" I mumbled sleepily, unable to see him now that I was sunk deep down into my nesting place.

"Oh, nothing," he answered.

"Me too," I echoed, feeling a pleasant, warm ache as all my weariness drained out into the cushions. My mind went into neutral gear and roamed around through old songs, meaningless memories, skipping over the To-Do list, then circling back to "Oh, nothing." I used that phrase with Mother whenever I was doing a bad thing. I roused myself just enough to speak.

"What's 'Oh, nothing'? It sounds like you're doing *something*."

I heard the sound of an eraser rubbing furiously against paper. I heard the pages of a newspaper turn. I heard Dad ignoring me. I wondered if I was hearing trouble.

"What's 'Oh, nothing,' Dad?" I repeated.

"I'm just writing an ad, that's all."

An ad. That's all. I felt happy. I guess Dad had finally cracked the writing code and now he couldn't be stopped. "What kind of an ad?"

"Just an ad for the planes."

I vaulted off the couch and around the end, smashing my shins into the end table. "Shit!" I hissed, leaning over to rub my leg while I kept powering forward in graceless hops. "What do you mean, an ad for the planes? What planes? What ad?"

"The antiques."

"The BT?"

"And the Fleet."

The yellow *Trade-A-Plane* newspaper was spread open across the dining room table. "My gosh, Dad. There's plenty of time to decide to sell the planes," I crabbed. "Why do you have to do it *right now*?" I was chewing my nails, suddenly wide awake. As he composed his ad, I hopped from foot to foot, eating jelly beans by the handful, pulling the hairs on my arm out by the roots one by one. Anything to keep myself from grabbing all the pencils and paper in the house and making a mad dash for the city dump.

"I've been thinking about this for quite a while, honey. I need to put them up for sale now so I can sell them by the end of summer. I don't want to keep them through another winter. These planes aren't easy to fly."

So that was it, I thought. He doesn't think he'll be able to fly them. He wants to get rid of them so he doesn't have to even *see* them. "You don't know yet, Dad," I pleaded. "You have no idea at this moment how hard it'll be for you to fly them. It's too early. What's the big rush?" The truth was, I didn't know what it was like to fly these planes. I knew they were a handful, took a lot of experience, attention, and piloting skill to get in the air and keep in the air. God knows I had heard plenty of stories of these planes crashing. Maybe Dad really did know that they were too much for him now. Maybe I shouldn't be putting up such a stink.

"No, honey. It's time."

I was in a terrible bind. On the one hand, I believed that Dad needed to make his own decisions about his life and that all our work with Dad was aimed at helping him regain his independence. But selling his planes!

It was a strange reversal of roles. I'd had plenty of conversations with friends about what it was like to break the news to their aging parents that it was no longer safe for them to drive a car, yet here I was urging my father into the air. "Fly! For God's sake, fly the damn thing!" Hearing Dad say the words "It's time" simply gave me the shivers. I had never known Dad to give up. Something else was going on here that I didn't understand. I wouldn't let it go.

"I don't agree with you, Dad. It's not time. In fact, it's exactly the wrong time for you to decide this."

"We'll see."

I knew what that meant. It meant he wasn't listening anymore and he would do things his way.

Fortunately, it wasn't easy to appraise these old antiques. Bud looked around and put a price on the Fleet that was so high not even an idiot would buy it. Bud knew Dad loved the Fleet. Sticking an outrageous price on the plane was the only thing a true friend could do. Dad asked me to e-mail the ads he had written, and I delayed as long as I could—dithering, forgetting, thinking up lots of afternoon errands. But eventually Dad hounded me into doing it. The BT sold immediately. I felt terrible.

Dad's resolve to sell his planes was like a ticking bomb. I was working against the clock. The only way I could beat it was to get him back in the hangar and reconnected to his deep love of antiques.

But Dad wouldn't go near the hangar. Or the Airmaster. This was a plane he had paid too much for. It had rattled him from the beginning and cast a long and dark shadow now. The Airmaster was a massive project, and the problems it presented were crushing. It looked like he would never be able to get back to it, and torn apart as it was, he would never be able to sell it either. The plane tailed him like a secret past he couldn't shake.

Dad tried to dismiss it out of hand, as if it didn't matter to him, didn't occupy a moment of his thought. But his attempt to lay down the law was a lame bit of Irish bull: he told me he couldn't even think about working on the Airmaster for a year; he was too busy.

Too busy. I would have fallen down laughing if I hadn't been so worried.

I nagged him about it, built a watertight case for how good it would be for him, assured him, with virtually no evidence, that he'd be fine in there. "No problem!" I would say so frequently that Mother suggested it be carved into my tombstone.

But it didn't matter what I said, Dad's response was the same: "Nope, I've made up my mind."

The truth was, he had. But what he had made up his mind about wasn't that he would delay working on the Airmaster for a year. It was that he would never work on her again. She was an albatross around his neck, his nemesis. He needed a year to think about how to get rid of her, not how to get back to her.

The case was closed.

Mom's surprise sixty-fifth birthday party, going incognito

18

The Experts Speak

I was pressing forward on three fronts: digging up good material to use with Dad, finding out as much as I could about stroke and stroke recovery, and putting all of this into coherent lesson plans every day. Every workbook I had looked like an unfinished craft project—colored Post-It Notes sticking out from every page, the ones sticking out from the side labeled with the name of the exercise, the ones sticking out from the top indicating the exercises to be used for that day, the ones sticking out from the bottom indicating the exercises that were in the bull pen. The Post-It Notes were color-coded so we could tell at a glance which ones were for building vocabulary, writing, math, or thinking skills. Someone who didn't know might think we were working on a clever centerpiece to enter in the Winter Fair.

So when Sally, the speech therapist, bounded in perky and full of vim at nine o'clock sharp on Monday, kicking off the week with "What would you like to do today?" and looking at Dad sincerely as if she honest-to-goodness expected him to tell her, I was in no mood.

Sally had to go. She was a genuinely nice person and she meant well, but she didn't have the horsepower.

She reminded me of the days when I first began babysitting. I considered it a real job and I wanted to be the best. I always brought activities for the kids. I even ordered magic tricks through the mail and put them together in a hatbox I covered in black-and-white gingham. Hiring me to be the babysitter was like hiring a clown from one of those party places, only a lot cheaper—I got fifty cents an hour. Sally had the entertainment part down fine. For one hour, three times a week, she fossicked around in that big, messy purse of hers and pulled out magic tricks.

One was "playing telephone." She would act like she was the person on the other end of the line and make Dad write down the phone message. She even brought a children's pretend phone, which Dad declined to use. It's not that it was a bad exercise. It's that it was just pulled out of thin air and didn't connect with anything else we were doing. Sally was groping. I realized I was simply much better at groping than she was.

As Sally packed up her purse at the end of the session, she congratulated us all. "You're doing so great!" she sparkled. "I feel like you're doing all the work now and I'm just the support person!" She said it as if this was a sign of progress, as if she expected this would make us all feel happy and relieved.

"I think I'll take Wednesday off," Dad stuttered, squeezing his eyes shut in concentration. "I'd like a little break." Sally couldn't have agreed more. It would be good for Dad to take some time to celebrate and relax. She left as full of pep as when she arrived.

The minute she bounded out the door, Dad looked over at me. "You've got to fire her, hon." He'd made his decision. "I'd do it myself, but I can't quite handle the phone well enough yet."

Sally couldn't have been nicer about it. She genuinely wished us the best of luck and said she fully expected Dad to make a complete recovery. We all knew it was time for her to hand off the baton.

The only trouble was that she was handing the baton back to us. But Dad kept wanting someone to certify that he was making progress. He needed someone with a college degree in speech therapy to tell him how he was doing. It was the only thing that would reassure him.

Even though I had vague feelings of foreboding, we began immediately looking for another therapist.

We hired Bill, the second speech therapist, because a friend of Dad's whose husband had a stroke couldn't say enough about how wonderful he was. When we interviewed him he seemed experienced and confident compared with Sally, who was wet behind the ears. This was reassuring.

But fifteen minutes into the first session I knew Bill was the wrong man for the job. He spent the entire time talking—like he was the one who needed the practice.

I interrupted, a churlish tone to my voice. "I think what Dad needs here is specific exercises to work on particular difficulties he is having with the smoothness of his speech and for getting over hurdles when he gets hung up on words."

"Yes, of course," Bill agreed and prattled on about what a good idea that was, going into various theories about speech. Dad was desperate to get a seal of approval from someone who was college certified, so we stuck with Bill for several more sessions. I hit my limit, though, when, instead of working Dad hard on overcoming his problem with finding the right word, Bill unfurled a clever cover-up strategy, as if it were either unimportant or impossible for Dad to improve. "Carry a handkerchief with you, and when you get into trouble just pull out the handkerchief and wipe your nose—real slowly like." He demonstrated. "That will give you time to slow down and find your words." He tried to get Dad to practice it in front of him.

With Dad's agreement, I called Bill that night and canceled all subsequent sessions. We needed those three hours a week.

The next week two packages came in the mail—one from Wayne State University, one from the Visiting Nurses Association. These were the materials Rick had found on the Web and that I had ordered from the pay phone at Borders Bookstore. Dad was as excited as I was. I pulled out the workbooks, giddy with relief. In here would be the answers to our worries. Competency and surefootedness in a box.

I ripped off the shrink-wrap expectantly. Then I was drawn up short. Cheri, Dad's first speech therapist at the hospital, had told me there was nothing for family members, that everything she had was strictly geared to professionals. Yet here in my hands was the exact same workbook Cheri had used, the workbook we had needed when we started school a month ago. I opened the next workbook. Same thing. Cheri's materials.

Dad didn't know what I was looking at, but he was hopeful that now we would have something developed and endorsed by professionals that would give us confidence that we were doing the right thing. Not that he didn't trust Sharon and me, but we all admitted we didn't have a clue what we were doing, and Dad felt like we were gambling with his life.

Not that Dad was unfamiliar with gambling. His whole life's success had been built on taking gambles and believing in himself without question. When he was in his twenties and had a two-year-old and an infant, he'd decided to go into business for himself. He borrowed two thousand dollars from his mother-in-law, built a garage out behind our house, bought a table saw, and started remodeling kitchens. He didn't hesitate.

Not that the people around him weren't full of doubt. His own mother was vocal in her certainty that he could never make it. Dad pushed forward. He knew what he wanted. He quickly progressed from small remodeling jobs, to building houses on spec, to bidding for houses, to bidding for schools, hospitals, and federal office buildings. Throughout it all he would say, "Every time I bid a job, I'm gambling the company."

I remember bid days. Mother always appeared so placid. I don't know if she was burying anxiety, if she was still in her zone of "everything works out for the best," or if it all flowed over her like water over a rock. Not me. I chewed my nails. I circled around Dad's office on my bike. When I was old enough, I would go with him to bid openings, where all the contractors who want the job submit their price. The lowest bid wins. Dad had a poker face. I did not, although I tried. In those bid openings, seven or eight men—most of them smoking—would sit around a table, the sealed bids piled before someone official. One by one the bids would be opened and read. Dad and I knew what his final bid was, so we would know early if we were high. But if we were low, and Dad often was, the tension remained high until the final reading. We were tense for two reasons—we wanted to be low, but not *too* low. When you were too low, that was called "leaving money on the table." You wanted to be low, but close. If Dad was the low bidder—and especially if he left very little money on the table—it was all I could do not to scream like a lottery winner, beating my hands on the table and pounding my feet on the floor, ending it all with a final flourish of gut-busting laughter. Dad, knowing my predisposition, had given me strict orders that I was not to crack even a smile. Which I didn't. But oh, the joy! I loved bid openings. I loved competition. Mostly I loved winning.

Often we would fly to bid openings. Once I flew with Dad to a bid opening in Sidney, sixty miles south of Canada and eight miles west of the North Dakota border. It was November, a tricky time to fly because the weather could trap you, but Dad had passed his test for instrument flying, so it opened up his options considerably.

Passing the instrument test was no cakewalk. Not only did he have to pass a written exam, but he had to fly wearing a plastic hood with an extended arcing bill that blocked out everything in his field of vision except the instrument panel. No sky. No ground.

When we left Sidney, we were in top spirits. We'd won the bid, driven by the building site for a better look, and celebrated with a steak dinner before heading out to the airport. By the time we took off it was dark, and getting home would take a little over two hours. Looking out my window, it was as if we were flying in a black tunnel, the flashing strobes on the wings of Dad's plane the only lights in the sky.

About an hour into the flight the strobe lights illuminated snow, just a few flakes at first, then a hard, wet blanket. There had been no

hint of this when Dad checked the weather report at the airport before leaving, and it put him in a bind now. He craned his neck to look
out our windows. If ice was building up on the wings there would be
nothing we could do to maintain our altitude—we'd glide right into
the ground. But it was dark, and he was over Garfield County. Plenty
of grass airstrips next to farmers' barns down there, if only we could
see them—a lighted airport was too far away to be a practical solution—but landing in a bare field was not an option in this weather,
because he could plow into cattle, fences, haystacks, or water towers.
He weighed the grim alternatives. There was only one. We had to
climb as high as we could. Instinctively Dad reached over and
yanked my seat belt down so tight I could barely breathe. We flew in
silence. I fixed my eyes on the strobe lights on the wings and watched
the blinking illumination of big wet flakes, blowing sideways.

A little over an hour later, I could see the runway lights up ahead.
Dad brought us in for a landing without saying a word, focusing entirely on getting the plane on the ground. As we taxied up to the
hangar, Dad reached over and loosened my seat belt, his signal that
everything was fine. When the plane came to a stop, Dad took off his
headphones and hung them up, letting his hand rest on the hook in a
moment of thought. Then he shook his head almost imperceptibly.
He didn't like having his kids along when this kind of stuff happened. "You did good, kid," he said to me, patting me on the knee.

"You did too, Dad."

"Yeah, well, we don't have to do that again," he concluded, reaching over to pop open my door. "We won't tell your mom."

"Right."

I asked Mother if having Dad go out on his own bidding jobs,
winning some and losing some, made her nervous. She said she was
too naive to be nervous.

Maybe that was the problem now. We were good at gambling, but
not naive enough to feel comfortable doing it. For his entire life Dad
had depended on himself, and he'd taught us to do likewise. He'd

taken real gambles and landed on his feet. But in this case, Dad was losing the gambler's edge. He wanted professionals in here to certify that this boat could float. In the workbooks spread out around us on the couch, Dad was looking for professional endorsement. I guess I was too. "These are the books Cheri used, Dad." I said, dumbstruck. "We needed these books a month ago. We needed these damn books a month ago!"

We sat down on the couch and pored over them silently. I was afraid I would discover in these workbooks that the last month had been wasted, that we would have to backtrack—or worse, that we had done damage. I think Dad was afraid of the same thing. We looked through every single workbook. There must have been nine of them. I was waiting for Dad's judgment. Did he feel he'd been getting second-rate schooling? Finally he looked up.

"There isn't nothing in here we haven't already done. We're way past this."

"I think you're right, Dad. We're way past this."

"I guess we know what we're doing, then, don't we? There ain't nobody out there gonna do any better for us than we're doing for ourselves." He leafed through the books absentmindedly. "But at least now we know." His voice conveyed both pride and worry. It finally dawned on us that the cavalry would never arrive.

Dad tossed the last workbook aside, then folded my hand in his own. "What would I do without you girls? Think of the mess I would be in." Tears gathered in his eyes. In mine too. "We've done this on our own. And we're way out ahead."

19

Sharon seems to like her present and expresses herself to the wonder of all.

Bugaboo

Everyone around Dad was slaphappy that he wasn't drooling and lurching. As far as they were concerned, anything more than what he had already accomplished was gravy. "No stroke survivor gets back to a hundred percent of what they were," they offered, nudging us toward stopping and settling.

But Dad didn't want to settle. He wanted to fly.

We needed Dr. Hathaway on our side. Dad saw him every week to get a prothrombin time test, measuring how quickly his blood was clotting. People who are on Coumadin, a blood thinner that is an ingredient of rat poison, need to make sure their blood doesn't get too thick or too thin. Dr. Hathaway was also his FAA doctor—the person who would certify to the Federal Aviation Administration that Dad was medically able to fly.

In mid-May, on the last day of Sharon's two-week stint, Dad came home from the doctor's office with a tongue twister written down on a piece of paper. "The big brown bear ate the big black bug and the big black bug bled blue blood." My first day back he read it to me word for word, stumbling through "blig black blug," looking miserable.

"Dr. Hathaway says that as soon as I can say this without making a mistake he'll know I'm ready to fly." That was obviously a joke. Still, it sounded oddly threatening. Dad's goal was to fly again—and nobody really knew if he would ever reach it. It made me furious to have such a deep and elusive hope pinned so glibly on something so trivial—even in fun.

We were trying to get Dad to solve logic puzzles and agree to practice math—something he seemed loathe to do because numbers were so hard for him—and this tongue twister was messing things up.

I was determined that when Dad went back for his next weekly blood test he would be able to recite it word for word.

"When do you see Dr. Hathaway again?"

"I go back next Monday, Tuesday, Wednesday. Wednesday. One day. Week. No, one week from today." Dad still needed to get a running start on things. We would have to work on that. But how? I jotted a note in my spiral notebook. So much to do.

"You'll have it down by then, Dad. No problem."

"I don't think so, honey," Dad snorted. "It'll take longer than that before I ever get this."

Anger churned inside me. I didn't want people setting up contests that Dad felt he had to master no matter how irrelevant they were. Dad needed to be learning how to add, not how to say some dumb rhyme. I had no idea how to help him memorize that damn tongue twister. In seven days.

I laced up my running shoes and headed out down the road. I hadn't jogged half a mile before it came to me. I knew what to do. I sprinted back to the house.

Breathless, I bolted into the kitchen. Dad was sitting at the kitchen table going over the tongue twister, holding the flash card facedown and trying to repeat a few words at a time.

"I'll never get this, Susan." Could it be that a child's simple rhyme would be his downfall, what barred him from flying?

"No problem, Dad. Just a second. I've got it." I took the steps to the basement two at a time and found the toy box where Mother kept the crayons. I grabbed three and a sheet of paper and ran back to the kitchen.

"What are you doing?" he asked.

"Just a second, Dad. I've got it." Quickly I drew a picture of a brown bear holding a great big black bug with huge drops of blue blood dripping out of the bug. I handed it to Dad. "Okay, Dad, put away that note card. Look at this picture and say it." I shoved the picture into his hand, exuberant.

"What?"

"Say it. Say the picture."

He looked down at my crude drawing. "The big brown bear ate the big black bug and the big black bug bled blue blood." He paused for a beat before he realized what he had done, then a big grin spread across his face and he laughed. "Well I'll be damned!"

I took the picture away from him. "Okay. Say it again."

"The big brown bear ate the big black bug and the big black bug bled blue blood." His eyes slid sideways toward me, suspiciously. "How does that work?"

"Visualization, Dad. You can remember anything if you picture it. Visualize. This is going to help us with all kinds of things. If you picture what you want to say, you will probably be able to say it—more than if you concentrate on what the word is. Do you see what I mean?" More keys to the kingdom.

Dad picked up the phone and carefully punched in a phone number. Without any preliminary greeting he blurted, "The big brown bear ate the big black bug and the big black bug bled blue blood."

I could hear my sister screaming on the other end of the line. Dad held the phone out away from his ear and belly laughed. So did I.

I am certain that when Dad hung up the phone, Sharon sank down onto the kitchen floor, put her head on her knees, and bawled.

Sharon and Dad. Amazingly, they were not arrested.

20

Hey There!
Hi There! Ho There!

On one of our biweekly baton passes, Sharon was reviewing with me what Dad had been working on, where he was having trouble, and where he was making swift progress.

She turned to a page of word problems. "Oh, yes!" she exclaimed, remembering. "When Dad finished this page, I did my Happy Dance."

"Happy Dance?"

"You know, I get up from the table and do a dance around the table and clap." She looked at me like I was thickheaded. "Like this." She got up and sang, "Oh, the Happy Dance! Yeah, baby! The Happy Dance! Yip Yip Yip Ki Yay!" doing some combination of the Jerk, a dance we did in the musically unmemorable seventies, and the Hokey Pokey, lurching in one full circumference of the eight-foot table before collapsing in the chair, her head thrown back, big loud guffaws pouring forth. Then, having regained control of herself, she looked at me and asked, all curious journalist, "Don't you do that?"

"I can't say that I do."

"Huh. I do that every time Dad finally gets something he's been working really hard on. I call it the Happy Dance. I think he really enjoys it." She sat up to resume her progress review. "I know *I* do."

I wondered if Dad ever experienced culture shock—jet lag, even—when Sharon and I did our shift switch.

While I ran school like a pedagogue, Sharon ran it like a reconstituted Mickey Mouse Club. After dinner she would often jump up from the table and say, "Hey! Let's play a game!" dragging out games like Twenty Questions, Wordles, Taboo, or I See Something You Don't See. She never actually sang out, "Hey there! Hi there! Ho there!"—at least not when I was home—but if she had, no one would have found it jarring. This was the necessary charm that Sharon brought to the process. She knew how to have fun.

I brought out the games with all the joy and verve of a house matron dispensing castor oil, urging a hearty good-for-you guzzle right down the hatch.

Sharon also dove with cheerful abandon into our family's past. She wasn't the least bit afraid. Where I saw family stories packed in boxes sealed for a reason, Sharon saw lids ready to be tossed aside and contents crying out to be rummaged in. I kept my distance, anticipating an unpleasant stumble over a family skeleton. Sharon skipped ahead like an unworried child, sure she'd find a dusty treasure.

Every night she brewed a pot of decaf after dinner and opened up the family scrapbook. What started as conversation to give Dad practice time for talking became an unfolding of spellbinding family stories. With Sharon's encouragement, I started rummaging around too. We learned how our Great Aunt Pearl and Uncle Leo met in Montana and started cattle ranching after the Great War. How Granddad worked like the devil to make a living. How Great Grandma raised her kids after Great Granddad got killed by lightning on the Fourth of July, the fried chicken and apple pie all packed for a picnic and the dog running back from the field whining. Great Grandma with five kids and a farm and Pearl only two years old.

We talked about Grandma Manley and Grandpa Hartman having

their farm repossessed during the Depression. We talked about what it was like to be in high school during World War II and how Mom spent her hours after school wrapping bandages for the Red Cross. We talked about when Dad was a SeaBee in Guam, and we tried to dig into anything scurrilous about Mom dating other guys when he was away—we didn't get very far with that bit of excavation. They recounted tales of their life in Alaska, how if they couldn't afford a babysitter, they'd go out to dinner with Steve stashed in a laundry basket under the table. We talked about how Dad started his business and what made him want to learn to fly.

Sometimes Dad would unearth a memory he hadn't stumbled across in years, and he'd enjoy patching it together as much as we'd enjoy listening, Mom pitching in with forgotten details. Other times we'd ask him to recount our favorites.

"Tell us the story about the tide," Sharon asked one night.

"Oh, not that one," Mom protested. This was Mother's least favorite story, freshly harrowing with each retelling.

It was mid-September of 1958 and they were living in Alaska. Dad, Kip, and Gene Effner planned to fish and hunt along the shores of the Cook Inlet, about sixty miles from Anchorage. Kip's plane was on floats, so he flew Dad in, unloading him on the shore, where Dad set up camp, waiting for Kip to return with Gene. Dad had hoisted his tent, laid out his sleeping bag, and readied the fire pit. He was sorting through his food pack inside the tent, when water, inexplicably, came rushing through the flap.

"I looked out and saw the tide churning and foaming and knew. It was a bore tide and I was in a world of hurt."

Bore tides were rare and unpredictable, churning so violently that they turned the mud to quicksand in a matter of minutes. Every year people drowned when the mud sucked in their boots—and then their feet—trapping them, unable to move, while the water rose over their heads. Dad grabbed his shotgun and his sleeping bag, abandoning all his other gear, and cast about for the few safe places to run before the sucking mud claimed him.

He tore across the mudflat, scrambling to find firm ground, finally clamboring up on a huge felled cedar log. He perched high up on the root end, shivering with sweat and cold, watching the tide roil and rise. He heard a plane's engine rumble in the distance and knew it would be Kip. When Dad spotted him, he shot his gun, hoping the sound or flare would catch Kip's attention. It didn't. Kip circled and circled but never spotted Dad. By then it was getting dark and Dad knew he was in it for the night.

By sunrise the tide had receded. Dad rolled up his sopping, frosted sleeping bag and tracked back to the shore, confident that another search plane would return that morning. The bore tide had sucked every last bit of his camping gear into oblivion. He'd gotten away just in time. He sat on the hard-packed mudflat for hours, hoping and waiting for rescue. Finally he heard a plane. Kip again. But his plane had floats, and the water had receded so far that he couldn't land. He tilted his wings to Dad, signaling that he'd be back. After Dad spent four more hours in the growing cold, Gene showed up in his plane, which was outfitted with wheels, and landed on the beach.

Dad climbed in, stuffing his sodden sleeping bag and shotgun into the compartment in the back. "Am I ever glad to see you."

"I feel the same way," said Gene. "Close call."

They were both smiling and shaking their heads as they taxied to the far end of the beach, turned the plane around, and got out of there while they had the chance.

Family stories were fun for Sharon not only because they were so transporting, but because they were such a complete departure from what was going on in the rest of her life. She and Jeff had moved from Seattle to Durham, North Carolina, after Jeff took a new job. In less than a year he got caught in a downsizing and, at the age of fifty, was looking for a job. He was panicked and depressed. Sharon was throwing herself into supporting Jeff emotionally, but there was little she could do beyond various versions of "There, there now, honey, can I get you some coffee?" For her, concentrating on Dad was a welcome diversion from worrying.

Although she was a lot smarter than she let on, Sharon excelled at the role of clown in the family. When she was about eleven years old, the whole extended family—all the aunts, great aunts, grandmas, and cousins within a hundred-mile range—were sitting around the holiday table telling stories, filling each other in on the gossip since Easter, when we were last all together.

Sharon fingered the matchbook on the table, her attention drawn to the picture on the cover—a line drawing of a woman aviator with a leather helmet.

"Who was Amelia Earhart?" she asked, curious.

The entire family tree erupted into spontaneous laughter.

Sharon's eyes clouded over and she took on impudence as her well-worn defense. "Never mind," she barked. "I already know. She invented the flag."

"Just squeaking by" was Sharon's familiar gig and one in which she fit comfortably. But now she was doing far more than squeaking by—she was providing the harmony and syncopated rhythm to what would otherwise have been a plunking one-note song.

She flipped to what was in the bull pen for Dad's schooling. "Oh. My. God," she blurted, slamming the notebook shut and placing both hands on it like it might pop open of its own free will. She leaned her head down toward the table, craning it sideways to face me, lowering her voice to a hissing whisper. "It's multiplication tables!" She closed her eyes in dread. "I don't even *know* the multiplication tables."

Then she snapped back up, pushed the notebook aside, finished with her momentary fit. "Oh well," she sang out, unconcerned, "the way Dad and I do it, we help each other. Sometimes he gets it right, sometimes I get it right. We just figure it out together."

Sharon's surprise thirtieth birthday party. That she cried the whole time was not a surprise.

21

The Wild, Wild West

I'm my father's child. Sometimes it's the only way Mother can absolve herself of responsibility for the person I've become—what I would probably call focused, determined, and productive but what others might call driven, opinionated, and incapable of prolonged sitting. Whatever the case, I know that I learned from Dad to discover what you love and throw yourself into it feet first and without a life jacket.

Sharon and I were in Bozeman together for a few days during our shift change. Dad had arranged for me to go on a flight with Dave, who owns an acrobatic plane called an Extra. We drove out to his hangar, and Dave's first lesson was how to roll out of the plane and pull the parachute in case we got into trouble. He made me practice until I felt confident I could do it without getting tangled in the wires. Sharon's eyes widened. Then we climbed into a space so tiny there were only inches between me and the big blue sky, the barrier a nearly invisible Plexiglas canopy. I was in front, Dave piloted from the back. Sharon was doubly impressed when we tore down the runway at 120 miles per hour, took off nearly perpendicular to the tarmac, and then did three loops and a few rolls before heading into airspace farther away from the airport to practice figure eights and barrel rolls and loop-de-loops and God knows what all.

"I bet the first thing she does when she gets out of that plane is puke," Sharon predicted to Dad, on the verge of it herself just from watching.

"I bet within two weeks she'll be calling saying she wants one of these planes," Dad countered.

"You're on," Sharon said, sealing the wager by socking Dad in the arm.

About an hour later, when we finally came in for a landing, Dave popped the canopy and I stood up in the seat of the plane, my parachute still attached. Turning toward Sharon and Dad, I thrust my arms straight up in the air, hollering, "I want one of these!"

"I win!" Dad announced.

"You do?" Sharon marveled, responding to me, not Dad. "How could you?"

In the real wager we had made months ago—that Dad would fly again—we seemed to be gaining the advantage. The further along we got in our rehab program with Dad, the more it seemed we actually might win, that the odds for his recovery were getting shorter.

So it was strange that when we were feeling our most optimistic, Dad worried more rather than less. It gnawed at him that his recovery process might be taking too big a bite out of our lives. He feared that we would tire of our persistent work. "You girls've got to get back to your own lives," he would fret.

Although I had astonishingly little insight about myself in the midst of the process, I did have this one lightbulb: This was my life. Cooking a good meal, changing the sheets, walking down the driveway to pick up the mail, doing laundry, returning a video. This was my life.

Not only that, but I was not even mildly interested in going back to my former life—living in a blur. I was a self-employed organizational development consultant for not-for-profit organizations, and although I enjoyed my work and was good at it, I did not enjoy my idiotic lifestyle, unmoored as it was from reason.

It was unreasonable, for example, to take on as a challenge squeezing as many clients as possible into a three-week coast-to-coast trip, using the same airline so I'd get all those good-luck-trying-to-redeem-them frequent flier miles, minimizing hotel expenses by taking overnight flights whenever possible, and managing close connections by packing everything in a single carry-on. Oh yes, and doing it without a cell phone. (I just hated being so accessible to any Tom, Dick, or Harry who thought they needed to reach me at any time of the day or night.)

I relied on extreme organization to ensure that I never dropped any balls. Slavish devotion to lists kept me on track. At one point early in my career I was not only getting my own business up and running, I had become the volunteer executive director of a professional theater company. It was like I was conducting a physics experiment on myself—how fast can I go before I break apart into a million specs of spangling glitter? When I got home at night I hunkered over the kitchen sink polishing off the remaining pizza Rick had made for dinner, my coat still on and my briefcase still slung over my shoulder, asking Rick—between declarations of "I'm *starving*" and pauses for the globs of cooled mozzarella to slip down my throat—how his day went and what was on the front page of the *New York Times* and if we got any good mail. Then I'd heft myself upstairs to my office to prepare my work for the next day, heft myself back down to take a shower, lay out my clothes for the following morning, and fall into bed. I organized it so I could roll out of bed, get dressed, and be in my car within twenty minutes. I had long ago eliminated eating breakfast from my morning routine.

One particular morning I was making a fund-raising call on a large donor to the theater. I was meeting her at a fancy hotel and needed to dress for the occasion. The night before, I'd laid out a royal purple jersey dress with a tight-fitting long-sleeved bodice, a full swirling skirt, and the highest heels I owned.

It was March and practically spring, so I optimistically left the house early that morning without a coat. Mistake: it was freezing. By the time I got to the hotel I was shivering with cold. I sat across from this elegant older woman making small talk in advance of ordering expensive eggs. I had my arms crossed across my stomach to try to heat myself up when I felt something very funny. It was under my dress, and it wasn't my slip. Continuing to carry on what I can only hope was a coherent conversation, I reached under the tablecloth and hitched up the hem of my dress to reveal my white jersey nightgown. Discreetly, I glanced down. There, embossed at my sternum, was the satin rose adorning my nightgown. I had on no bra. I had on no panties. I had on my pajamas. The last time I remembered doing this I was in kindergarten. Maybe I needed to go to graduate school, I thought. Did they cover problems like this when you got your MBA?

Not long after that, I had a day of meetings in New Hampshire followed by a fund-raising soiree in Vermont, where I needed to be dressed to the nines. I lugged my briefcase, armloads of materials for my day's work, and my evening clothes for the gala out to my car, hanging my fancy dress on the hook in the backseat. I ground through the meetings, drove like an outlaw from New Hampshire to Vermont, wheeled into the hotel parking lot fifteen minutes before the opening toast, and darted into the restroom to do my quick-change act. Only then did I discover that instead of a pair of black ankle-strap heels, I had one black shoe and our cordless phone.

I remember one particularly illuminating moment years ago on a Saturday night. I was watching a documentary on late-night television. A perky woman was enthusiastically demonstrating how she methodically organized all her paper grocery bags. Wow! Admiration and longing welled up in me and I leaned into the television set trying to absorb it all, imagining myself adopting a similar elegant and enviable system. Then—bam!—"*Live from New York, it's Saturday Night!*" I wheezed out a weak, insincere laugh. Of course I didn't care about organizing paper bags. Who would?

The trouble was that none of these incidents were signs to me of a life lived with too much speed. They were merely signs that I needed to be better organized, something to which I aspired. A friend of Rick's commented to him that he had seen me in downtown Hanover. "Every time I see your wife she's always running," he said, amused.

Of course I was running! Dad was the one who got me running in the first place. I remember the moment distinctly. I was nine. My room was painted lilac and had three framed pastel portraits of young girls hung on the wall, pictures we got from sending in boxtops from Ivory Snow detergent. Dad tucked me in that night—covers under the chin, blankets stuffed under the mattress so tight you could bounce a quarter off the top from the tension, a holdover from his Navy days.

Dad kissed me on the forehead, walked to the windows, and parted the flowered curtains. Looking out into the fading night, he said, "You'll never see this day again. It is gone forever." Then he walked out of my room.

I lay there, pressed deep into my mattress by the force of my blankets, wide-eyed with the enormity of the implied responsibility. Never. Forever. I burst into tears.

I've been running ever since.

Once I'd attained such a speed, it was hard to slow down. First, it became what I did. Then it became who I was.

Dad knew how to stop me, though, because he knew how to stop himself.

When I needed a longer detox period than a flight over the valley would provide, I would go up to a cabin we owned on Hyalite Lake. Although it's only thirty minutes from town, it feels like a whole different world, governed by a set of rules so irrefutable that they are immune to my attempts to defy them. Up there you have no choice but to slow down. It happens to you the way drowning would happen if you were trapped underwater. There's no alternative.

I didn't even have to go through decompression when I went up to the cabin. I was slow from the moment the truck door slammed. It was as cool and quiet as the inside of a watermelon. Without electricity, I went to bed when it got dark and woke up when I was done sleeping. Without clocks, I ate when I was hungry. I had no visitors, no radio, and no telephone. I often passed days without saying or hearing a single word.

Some mornings Dad would fly by in his Fleet and drop the plastic-wrapped *Bozeman Daily Chronicle,* getting surprisingly close to the porch, but it was lots more fun to get the morning paper than to read it, and it often went unopened.

Mostly what I did up there was sleep and read and sit and walk and eat. What I never did up there was work or worry or plan—it never occurred to me.

But it never lasted either. The minute I got back in the pickup and headed down the canyon, I turned on the news, constructed my To-Do list in my head, and figured out the speediest way for me to accomplish my errands in time to squeeze in a five-mile run before dinner.

The whole notion of that sensational life I was missing out on was laughable. You couldn't make me go back. This work with Dad, far from being a sacrifice, was a salvation.

It didn't seem that way to other people, who viewed it as a supreme act of selflessness. It wasn't. I never felt dragooned. Frankly, deciding to work with Dad wasn't hard at all. I was propelled by absolute will. You would have had to cut off my head and bury it on another continent to keep me from it. It would have been much harder to stay at home. It helped that Rick was entirely supportive, my clients were flexible, and I had a good travel agent. It was as easy as cruise control.

In fact, working with Dad was oddly invigorating. It gave my life needed focus and meaning, and I was learning so much. Plus, it was darned nice to be back home. It felt lavish to be able to spend so much time with my family. In an odd twist, Dad's stroke was something of an austere second chance.

Forced into the breakdown lane, we had to alter well-worn family routines. Ruts, really. Our family organized itself around getting stuff done—revolving-door activities like mowing the lawn, washing the car, fixing the sump pump, trying to program the sprinklers so they would actually turn on, knitting some more on the interminable afghan, and, in Mom's case, cleaning the immaculate closets in our house.

Projects! This was the organizing principle of everything from chores to romance. We could trace it back to the rainy and muddy sixteen-hour-per-day drive Mom and Dad made up the Alcan Highway in the first months of their marriage—the presumptive beginning of our own get-it-done impulses. We were practical even in our thoughtfulness, surprising one another with sturdy gifts that affirmed our love. A nice new garden hose would make us weepy. Or a year's supply of batteries. Or extra-long Band-Aids for those pesky cuts on your hand. Or, the prize-winner, nose-hair tweezers.

But Dad's stroke pushed us to think less in terms of efficiency and productivity. We all got a little more mushy. How apt, then, that when my forty-third birthday fell on a day when I was in Montana, Rick sent me flowers for the first time—ever. A dozen red roses sticking straight up out of the vase surrounded by lilacs drooping down over the side like overheated hounds hanging out the back window of a car for relief from the heat. Mom and I looked at each other knowingly—despite the freakish floral design, we knew flowers were romantic. What a switch from last year's gift—an electric pencil sharpener. In hearty appreciation of the effort, we sang out in a breathless soprano, "Aren't they beautiful?" and displayed them without alteration on the dining room table.

When Sharon led us into the promised land of storytelling, it was another opportunity to slow down, to do nothing but listen. For me, this was the boonies.

I was transfixed hearing Mother recount her life on the farm. Not that I hadn't heard these stories in bits and snatches over the years, but to hear them in one long narrative, a chapter after each evening meal, was captivating. Sometimes it was hard to believe that the mother telling me these stories was the same little girl who starred in these stories. I had to suspend my disbelief to imagine my stylish mother peeing in a piss pot and bathing in someone else's suds.

Mom never thought of herself as poor, but she'd had a rough beginning, and it went downhill from there. Her first year of school was in a one-room schoolhouse with fifteen kids ranging in age from six to eighteen. Mom had no idea how to read. When she failed miserably, reading the words from right to left, the exasperated teacher heaped on her a torrent of ridicule that drove Mom, a six-year-old child, to desperate action. Every night she asked her mother to read to her, and Mom memorized every word. Daily she got up in front of the class, held her book open in both hands, and recited her assigned pages word-for-word without breaking so much as a little pink sweat. That's how she made it through first grade.

Hartman, her father, was desperately trying to hang on to the farm, the Depression relentlessly snapping at his heels. He sold his cattle to help pay the bank loans and kept his sheep, hiring himself out to a nearby ranch to bring in extra needed cash. But it wasn't enough. By the summer of 1934, the Depression finally decimated their finances and the bank repossessed the farm.

Grandma, an aspiring but thwarted socialite, couldn't bear the humiliation, and that fall she made a break for it. With Mom only seven years old and her brother, Dave, just a newborn, they boarded a train back to Grandma's home in New Richmond, Indiana, leaving Hartman behind. Mom felt like she had entered an unimaginable world of plenty. Great Grandma Miller had an expansive three-story house with five bedrooms, a library full of books, and a bathroom with a flush toilet, a porcelain basin, and running water. Great Grandpa Miller, a pig farmer, had chosen his wife for her brawn. She had a large, long face with a hank of gray hair parted in the middle and slicked back into a bun and big flat ears the shape of prickly pears—but she could bale hay, milk cows, and slaughter pigs, which is what that farm needed and more. Great Grandpa Miller died when the oldest of their seven children was only fifteen, and after that Great Grandma Miller ran the farm on her own, raising pigs and chickens, growing corn, minding an apple orchard, and making lye soap. Eventually she laid by enough money to send all seven of her children to college—even the girls.

Mom and Grandma stayed there through that whole school year. Hartman visited once to tell Grandma that he had bought another dairy farm—this one in Bozeman—and Grandma dreamed about what it was like. She lavished upon the social crowd in New Richmond romantic stories of the breathtaking beauty of the landscape and chronicled the bucolic nature of farm life out west. Soon she came to believe her own tales. She described an expansive dairy farm with neither shit nor flies, a big white house with basins and toilets and porcelain fixtures, and a barn surrounded by sturdy fences. When she boarded the train headed west as a landed woman, she waved to her envious sisters, teary-eyed on the platform, doomed to the stale town life of New Richmond.

Hartman picked them up at the train station. When he drove up the drive to their new dairy farm, a tiny yellow shack with no running water, a one-hole outhouse, and a lidded white enamel piss pot in the single bedroom, Grandma squalled, consumed in disappointment, and laid it all at the guilty and irresponsible feet of Hartman, who had failed, once again, to please her.

Mom lived in that house until she was in high school. In addition to the sole bedroom, there was a parlor and a kitchen. The only running water in the house came from a hand pump next to the wooden sink in the kitchen, which pulled water from a reservoir out back. She and her brother slept on a rudimentary pull-out couch in the living room.

Every Saturday night they heated water to fill a round galvanized metal tub three feet across that they hauled into the middle of the kitchen for the family's weekly bath. Hartman bathed first, squatting into the tub, then bending his skinny legs over the side to let his feet balance against the floor. Grandma bathed next, followed by Mom and then Dave. The pecking order was by family status, but nobody lingered. A five-minute bath was always sufficient to get clean enough for another week of work.

It wasn't until 1943, when Mother was in the eighth grade, that they scrounged together enough money to install an indoor toilet.

When Mom was in high school they moved into the "white house" on a newly acquired piece of land adjoining the farm. Even though it was considerably more spacious, Grandma wasn't satisfied. Her dreams of high-society living were buckling under the crushing weight of cooking for thrashers, keeping the cattle out of the alfalfa, and finding mouse droppings in the silverware drawer every morning. Grandma whined and howled, but none of her protests stopped the monthly obligation to the bank. Hartman leaned into his work like he would lean into a winter blizzard, Grandma's tearful conniptions merely the whining of the wind.

Until the winter of 1945. That February, Hartman quit. One morning he got up, sat in front of the wood-fired stove in the living room, a blanket over his lap, and stared into the fire, wordless. In the afternoon, he lumbered over to the couch to sleep. In the evening, Grandma brought his supper to him in his chair. The pattern continued. He neither talked nor worked till spring.

Bill Smith, the hired man, ran the farm that winter, milking the twenty-five cows by hand every morning and evening, a job Hartman used to do. Grandma and Mom helped him bottle the milk in the mornings, and then Bill delivered it in town. For three months Hartman shut down, and for those three months Grandma quit complaining.

Finally, he came around, started talking again, slept in his own bed, and ate meals with the family. But it was a close call, and no one ever knew if it was farming or Grandma that pushed him over the edge.

I was riveted to Mother's stories as she told them. No wonder she bought cheap plastic wrap. Had I grown up like she did, I would probably genuflect to the flush toilet every morning and stop getting so huffy when it got plugged up. These stories helped me understand who Mom was and whetted my appetite for more. There was life in stories, and passion, and pathos. They made my blood run.

I called Rick. "Tell me about swinging on hoses off the Shenley Park bridge."

"What?"

Rick had been accustomed to me efficiently rifling off the details of Dad's recovery and reading from my list of things I needed him to find out, inquiring about the cats, referencing anything singular in the news. "Tell me about how you used to swing down off the bridge."

"What do you want to know?" Rick had no idea what I was after here.

"Who'd you do it with?"

"Schmeggy Terlecky. Him and a bunch of other guys. We'd steal garden hoses. Then we'd screw them together and hang them in a big loop from the bridge girders. We'd swing out as far as we could. It must've been three hundred feet down. Did I ever tell you about my Superman routine?" He let out a long and marvelous laugh. So did I.

Rick told me about his Superman routine. I told him stories about Mom. He told me stories about his mom. That night we must have talked for an hour—storytelling instead of updates and new requests for information.

It was only then that I realized how lonely I had become. Phone calls are no substitute for sitting together drinking coffee, reading the paper, musing. It was spending time I needed to do more of, which meant a dramatic reordering of my life.

"I miss you," Rick said when we were through.

"I miss you too," I echoed.

We both felt happier than we had in months.

The lure of storytelling finished off any lurking fondness I had for my hard-learned habits of working too hard and too long. I was done with counting things: my income, how little sleep I could get by on, how many miles I could drive on cruise control without touching the brake, how many bulbs I could plant before the first frost. No more counting. I was thirsty for the music and messiness of family stories. Getting to know my family like this felt like riding bareback across the prairie at a full gallop, the wind blowing the tears out of my eyes. For me this was intimate work, and as far as my heart was concerned it was the wild, wild west.

The Girdle War begins. (Where is the girdle now, anyway?)

22

Incomprehensible

It wasn't long before my mornings with Dad took on a predictable rhythm. After a warm-up exercise, Dad would read aloud an article from the paper. Midmorning he would read aloud from *Flight of the Gin Fizz*, a book written by Henry Kisor, a deaf pilot recounting a cross-country flight he'd made in an antique airplane. Right before lunch he would read aloud from *An Ornery Bunch*.

Dad liked reading *Flight of the Gin Fizz* because it gave him ideas. He still didn't feel confident in his ability to speak. He was particularly worried about the rapid-fire code he would have to both comprehend and speak if he was ever going to fly again, using the radio to talk to the control tower. But the pilot of the *Gin Fizz* couldn't use the radio, and he'd flown across the country using airports that weren't controlled by towers. By reading the book out loud, Dad had practically become friends with Henry. It was like starting his day by talking shop with another pilot who obviously understood what it meant to overcome a handicap in order to fly. Dad gobbled up this book, stockpiling the story as if hoarding hope.

Early on Dad's reading was so slow that it interfered with his comprehension. By the time he got to the end of the sentence—and had labored over several words to get there—it had become a string of words that didn't make any sense. He understood the meaning of each word, but didn't grasp the larger story the words were meant to convey. Increasing his reading speed would help with that.

At first when he got hung up on a word he would stab at it intently and get it wrong every which way. I would interrupt him and bark, "Sound of the first letter," like a military command. This was his clue to sound it out.

As we progressed Dad became quite skilled at sounding out; now he needed to practice substituting words. Often it wasn't that he didn't know what the word was, he just couldn't get it out of his mouth. I would interrupt him and say, "Substitute," or, "Give me another word, that particular word isn't important," or, "Tell me what he means, Dad, you know what comes next." Word substitution was good practice for when he got hung up in everyday speech. Our work in the evenings on sons-a-bitches came in handy here.

I made a copy of each day's book reading and followed along while he read, tracking both his reading speed and his errors. I made a flash card for every error, which we would review at the end of the reading. When he was finished he would count the lines he'd read and, using his calculator to figure out his words per minute, dutifully record his "score" in the book, comparing it with the previous day's. On our first foray, he read at 25 words per minute. We were aiming for 110, average for an adult.

One morning we started as usual reading something from the paper out loud. This was hard, grinding-it-out work. The local paper, sometimes poorly written and therefore difficult to read, was filled with dull local news about zoning commission meetings, shoplifting scandals, and engagement announcements. Dad picked an article titled "Phone Company Investigates Charges."

"Damn phone company rates. It's as good as any." He began reading, haltingly.

The headline required a phonics lesson on why *ph* sounded like *f* and a grammar lesson on how *charges* could be both a verb and a noun. I started making flash cards with *ph* words, *f* words, and sentences containing the word *charges* as both a noun and a verb.

Once Dad labored through the headline, he started in on the body of the article.

"Local off. Off. Offish. Offish. Officials . . ." I waited while he worked. "Announced today . . . that they . . . are . . . in-in-invest-invest-i-gat-ing, investigating, investigating, okay, a company calling . . . them . . . selves Gal Pals. This company has alleg-alligat. Huh?"

"Allegedly. That's a hard word. See how you can sound it out." Then I had to explain the difference between a hard *g* and a soft *g*. I made more flash cards and thought about that nifty water-into-wine trick in the Bible. I swirled my coffee and wondered what it would take to turn it into a stiff little vodka and tonic. Even a beer would do.

"Allegedly set up a serv . . . ser-service . . . to . . . provide phone . . . sex to clients."

Pause.

Dad tilted his head to one side, a puzzled frown animating his face. "That don't make no sense." I wondered, feverishly, if it was lunchtime yet and glanced at my watch—eight-thirty.

"That's okay!" I chirped. "Let's try the next paragraph!" I must have looked like I just had plastic surgery, my face frozen into an optimistic smile. Maybe the subject of this article would change dramatically in the next paragraph. Maybe they'd launch into something new, like how to order call waiting.

Dad continued. "In addition, authorities believe the company also had an operation for . . ." Dad got quite hung up on the next word.

My reliable strategy to roar "Sound it out!" or to demand that he substitute a word seemed wholly inadequate. My urge was to holler, "Oh, let's just forget the whole damn thing!"

Dad, however, was well trained and chose the sound-it-out strat-egy. I could read that damned article upside down, and I knew what was coming. I tried desperately to have an out-of-body experience.

"Cy-ber-sex . . . cy-ber-sex . . . cybersex." Dad kept repeating it, assuming that its meaning would click in like it did with *candle* and *doghouse*. "Cybersex."

By this time Mother was in on the act. Whenever she heard Dad struggling, she would hover around the edges to make sure Sharon and I didn't torture him too much. But this time morbid curiosity re-placed her urge to protect.

"What on earth are you two talking about?"

"Cybersex." Dad said it perfectly. "We're not talking, we're trying to figure out what it means." Dad looked directly at me for a reason-able explanation.

Regrettably, I did not die.

I decided a clinical, straightforward approach would be best. "Phone sex is when people pay someone to talk dirty to them on the phone, and cybersex is . . ." I had absolutely no idea what cybersex was. It sounded weird to me, too. I improvised. "Cybersex is the same thing only on the computer." There. That was done. Could we please now go back to work?

"On the computer!" Mom gasped, failing to imagine it. "How can they do it on the computer? You mean with *cameras*?" She pictured the social fabric of our society worn threadbare.

Deftly, I decided to forgo asking her to explain what she meant by "do it." In this matter I was as clueless as my parents, but I was pretty sure cameras weren't involved. Besides, my point wasn't accuracy, but getting out of the conversation lickety-split.

"No. They get into chat rooms and type in dirty things to each other. It's all the rage with twenty-somethings. You know how they are with computers."

"Huh," Mother puffed, deeming my answer unsatisfactory.

Dad shrugged. "What them kids won't come up with." He snapped the paper to indicate he wanted to get back to work.

Starting from the top, Dad reread the entire article out loud, then methodically calculated his words per minute—93. Like clockwork, he held out his hand to review the flash cards for the words he'd missed. I handed them over like I always did.

There was no flash card for *cybersex*.

Dad is King, in case you were wondering.

23

Am I Wrong?

We set up a reward system for sticking with our plans. By now we were taking weekends off, and Dad was on his own in the afternoons. A daily reward for Dad, though, was ending each night by sitting down with me to watch *The O'Reilly Factor*, an obnoxious Fox News program that was on every night at nine. This was not a reward for me. I would rather eat dirt than listen to Bill O'Reilly repeatedly ask, as if he really wants to know, "Am I wrong?" and when the person on the receiving end responds appropriately with something very close to "Yes, as a matter of fact you are dead wrong," he interrupts them with another, louder version of his point of view, which he offers as if it has been presprinkled with holy water flown in directly from Rome.

Dad loves him.

Weirdly, Bill O'Reilly and Sharon's husband, Jeff, are childhood friends, having grown up in the same neighborhood, and go on vacation together every year—what Sharon and I call the Male Bondage

Weekend, since being with O'Reilly for any length of time seems like it could be nothing less. So when Jeff told O'Reilly that Dad watched his show every night and that he was working to fly again after a stroke, O'Reilly sent Dad an *O'Reilly Factor* baseball cap, which Dad would wear when we watched the show. Now and then he would offer it to me, but I declined.

Under ordinary circumstances, our difference in attitude toward this political icon could be a problem. Previously, when his shouting match came on, I would just walk out of the room and go read. But in these extraordinary circumstances I learned to just let it all wash over me. Getting wound up about O'Reilly would only shorten my life span.

So we would watch every night and talk to the television set. Dad would shout, "That's right!" or some close approximation, and I would shout, "You have got to be kidding me!" Then we would both laugh, Dad patting me on the knee and me slugging him on the shoulder.

The most fun, though, was just sitting there with Dad for an hour, eating popcorn and acting stupid, instead of working all the time. In fact, sitting with Mom and Dad became one of my favorite things to do—after lessons, after games, in midafternoon when we had a few minutes. The more time we spent together, the more stories we told, and the more we cried.

I described what I was experiencing to a friend of mine who is a nurse, and she cut me off.

"Oh, yes. That's typical of stroke patients. They cry more easily. It's because of the damage in the brain."

I didn't think this increased ability to express ourselves emotionally was because of something broken. It seemed to me like something got fixed. I was loath to explain as a medical malady something that had been spiritually transforming. If this was all due to damage in the brain, I wanted to ask, then why did I cry more? No damage happened in my brain that I knew of.

This was a big deal for us. Dad had embraced help—gripped a lifeline—for the first time in his life. Pitiful, inadequate, and scared, we pulled and heaved and hauled with all the strength we could muster. We were afraid, and we were thankful, and that was new.

Even Bud noticed. "Now he's so much more open than he ever was," he said. "Down at the airport he was trying to tell us about some gal who had a bed and breakfast over there in Sidney. Damned if he couldn't say 'bed and breakfast' for the life of him. Finally he said 'sleep and eat' and everyone broke up. He laughed too. He doesn't give a shit. He knows this coulda been a lot worse."

It wasn't even that it could have been a lot worse, but that it could hardly have been any sweeter. There was far more than stroke recovery going on. We were discovering a Dad that wasn't scary.

Ever since we were little kids, Dad had seemed scary the way God seemed scary—in fact, it was hard to tell them apart, and, given he was actually *there*, Dad was more real and therefore scarier. He meted out punishment, was the court of no appeal, harbored no doubts, and, although we'd never experienced it, wielded the power of executioner if the situation warranted it.

That he had his version of the Ten Commandments was another likeness. Unlike God's, Dad's commandments changed over time, but they still carried all the heavy penalties—and in the end, that was the scary part. The penalties.

This had early beginnings. I was about seven years old. Sharon was five and Steve was nine. Every night during dinner—and I mean every night—one of us would spill the milk.

Finally, Dad had had enough. "The next kid that spills the milk gets the whole carton poured over their head." I'm sure he thought that would be the end of it. About forty-five seconds passed, and then, thunk, I spilled my glass of milk. I remember looking at him, my eyes pleading for pity. I have to believe he hesitated. I didn't think he would really pour the milk on my head—partly because he didn't want to and partly because we couldn't afford to waste all that milk. Still, he followed through. He took me into the bathroom, stood me in the tub, and poured the half-gallon of milk over my head while I bawled my eyes out and Mother called from her powerless place at the dinner table, "Wayne! Wayne! Oh, Wayne!" I don't think I have ever spilled a glass of milk in my forty years since then.

The stakes for infractions and consequences got higher as we got older. Curfew was a particularly thorny one. When we were in high school we were to be in by midnight. This was nonnegotiable. But when I was making out with my boyfriend in the back of my parents' car, it was easy to lose track of time. At least it was easy for *me* to lose track of time. Dad had no difficulty. I was lost in another world in the back of that steamy car when I heard a thump on the window. It was Bob Johnson, the chief of police, tipped off by Dad. He ordered me out of my car and into the police car and drove me home. I was, of course, furious. (Not to mention completely humiliated. How was a girl supposed to have a boyfriend under these conditions?) Not only was I faced with having to stomp and huff past my father into my bedroom downstairs, but the next morning I had to ride with him in his truck to go pick up the car—in absolute silence. I didn't get a chance to plead my case or even to cry and get a little absolution, like a pat on the knee or a tissue. Dad just walked into my room, said, "C'mon," and ordered me into his truck.

Driving up to the scene of the crime and actually getting inside the car, where the steam of the night before had condensed and dried, leaving telltale dots on the windshield like fossils, was an inflaming humiliation. Then being followed home in the truck, as if I might otherwise bolt for the border, gave me a hybrid of lockjaw—I didn't speak for at least two hours, maybe not even the whole rest of the day. I communicated by slamming doors and cupboards and phone receivers hard.

Dad's was a clear and reliable system of cause and effect—even more consistent than God's, since there was no praying in the mix to get you out of a pinch.

But now we were in entirely new circumstances, where the laws of black and white were irrelevant, the thought of sinning made us too tired to move, and nobody drank milk anymore. Plenty scared us—right out of our wits, in fact—but it was never Dad.

Dad wasn't scary anymore. Maybe he never had been.

Mom and Dad with the Tiger Moth, 1988

24

Gun Control

Dad couldn't sleep at night. Left without the distractions of school and errands, he lay on his back and worried. About everything. He called it "drilling." Even though he was improving dramatically, he had it fixed in his mind that he would always be disabled, spilling jam on his shirt, garbling his words, unable to calculate in his head. He would never fly again. In the quiet of the night, he matched up all his incapacities with all of what needed to be done and came up short every time.

"How'd you sleep last night, Dad?" This was always the first question of the morning as Sharon or I stood at the kitchen stove making a protein-packed smoked salmon omelet for his morning breakfast.

"Not very good" was his most common answer. "Drilled all night."

He worried about his construction business, which he'd sold to Joe when he retired. The construction industry was so competitive and litigious, so different from when he went into it. What if Joe didn't make it? He worried about the Airmaster. What would he do now? Who would buy a plane that was torn apart and strewn all over the hangar? He kicked himself for ever starting in on the project in the first place. He worried about Sharon and me, that we would tire of teaching him and deliver the news that we had to get on with our lives. His worry list was endless.

All this drilling left him exhausted in the morning and made it that much more difficult to concentrate during school. The problem eventually eclipsed all others as our chief concern. One night I called just to check in and asked Mom the standard question. "How'd Dad sleep last night?"

"He did pretty good. I think I've finally been able to do something right around here for a change. I put on classical music from the radio station real soft. It calmed him down. I feel like tits on bacon around here. I'm glad I could finally come up with something useful."

That stopped me cold. Mother never said "tits." Ever. Much less "tits on bacon." She was so ill-practiced that it came out of her mouth as if she had learned it phonetically—it sounded memorized. I was so shocked that, in that tiny frozen moment, I finally realized that we had pushed Mom to the brink. She resented being benched. Sharon and I had come in and taken over the whole situation—we developed the lesson plans, we spent hours and hours with Dad every day, we cooked breakfast, lunch, and dinner—and we got self-righteous about protein, fish, and fruit. We shot holes in everything Mom did, said, or bought.

In the seeming eternity between "tits on bacon" and whatever else she said, my mind rolled with an instant replay of when I'd been there the week before.

"This is the worst treadmill I've ever seen," I barked one afternoon, inspecting the exercise machine she hoped Dad might use as part of his rehab.

"It's a fine treadmill."

"If it's so fine, why doesn't anyone ever use it? It's impossible to walk on, Mother. Have you ever tried it? Im-possible."

"We walk up at the cardio unit at the hospital, and that is *just fine*," Mother said with finality. "Susan, don't get started."

"I'm not 'getting started,' Mother. It's just that this is a completely stupid machine. It's impossible to walk on. I don't know why you don't just get rid of it."

"A larger treadmill wouldn't fit in that room anyway."

That was my opening. I marched to the phone book, looked up Exercise Equipment in the yellow pages, and dialed. I got the footprint of what I considered a decent machine and sat at the kitchen table making a to-scale layout of their bedroom showing how the treadmill would fit.

"Daisy! Stop that! Right now!" Mother yelled at the dog, and Daisy, Mom's sweet little West Highland terrier, went hightailing it from the kitchen to the back bedroom. I doubt Daisy had ever been yelled at by Mother in all her seven years.

I closed my eyes, trying to shut out the memory. We were wearing Mother down to a nubbin. She wanted things back to normal. She was sick and tired of the whole chaotic mess, a mess that I spent every waking moment planning and carrying out in meticulous detail. I hated myself. I wanted to lay my head in my mother's lap and cry. I wanted to say I was sorry a thousand times over until she could believe me. But I couldn't. I was too afraid. I dared not say "I'm sorry" even once for fear I would give foothold to any ideas she might have that we alter our course.

The only thing that gave Mother comfort was her steadfast belief that there was a larger purpose to all of this. Her mantra was "Everything happens for a reason," and she believed it with the same certainty that she believed the sun would rise tomorrow. The trouble was, I didn't.

It was vitally important to me at the time that everyone believe the same thing. That is to say, that everyone believe what I believed. We were a family that had concentric circles of belief. Mom was at the core. She believed in God, Jesus, and the Holy Ghost— deeply, literally, and without doubt. Next came Dad. He believed pretty darned hard, but he didn't really get too specific about it. He just believed in the American God. Steve and Sharon were probably in the middle. Neither one of them got too worked up about anything having to do with religion. They prayed in a pinch. They could sing loud and spirited hymns in church without getting the heebie-jeebies.

Then there was me. I was like Pluto—way out there on the outer reaches of the known solar system and possibly not even a planet. I adamantly refused to pray even under the most dire conditions. I didn't bow my head during public prayers, and I had a nagging theoretical concern that if I ever had to take an oath in a courtroom, I would have to refuse when they came to the part about telling the whole truth and nothing but the truth *so help you God*. I would have to go to jail. Not believing in God meant a lot to me.

So, of course I couldn't think of any single idea that could give less comfort than "Everything happens for a reason." When Mother invoked this incantation, I unraveled, snapping and whipping like a flag in a high wind.

"Dad's stroke did not happen for a reason," I erupted. "It was *bad luck*, Mom. It's *unfair*. It's *life*. Some people get hit by cars. Some people have strokes. It shouldn't have happened. It's not okay." I hammered away. "Jesus, Mom. What's the reason? That seems to me like discovering someone crapped on your porch, then rushing around trying to find out who did it so you can thank them for what you learned from it."

Mom knew enough not to argue with me. She couldn't win. My coldly rational arguments, delivered with such derision, were just one more thing to silence her.

Dad was the one who felt the most at the mercy of chaos and the least able to even pretend to get a handle on it. This probably bothered him as much as losing his ability to communicate. He could no longer control events, which, for him, was like not being the head of the family anymore. He was just one more mouth to feed. This was why he "drilled" all night long.

One afternoon, he and I were on an afternoon walk down the airstrip. "I guess it's a good idea we got that security system installed after all," he said. This comment came straight out of East Jesus.

"Why do you say that, Dad?" Dad had always scoffed at Mother's insistence on a security system. We lived in a small town. It wasn't that many years ago that, during the summer, we slept with the doors wide open to keep the house cool. Now we had alarms wired into a security company in Texas that had a whole system of calls and callbacks. Now and then, someone would get the commands mixed up and the alarms would go off in the middle of the night while a centrally installed loudspeaker would bray "Burglary! Burglary! Burglary!" causing us all to hurtle out of bed, our hearts racing. It's a wonder we all hadn't died of heart failure.

Mother was the only one who really knew what buttons to push and what 800 number to call when that happened. Luckily she was always around. Mom and Dad never set the alarm when I was there because when I got up early to go running I would invariably have to wake up Mother to make sure that if I opened the door all hell wouldn't break loose. The entire procedure confounded me, so I was curious why all of a sudden Dad was warming to it.

"Because I'm really in no shape to protect my family anymore." We always knew that Dad's first priority was providing for and protecting his family. When we were kids he made us do annual fire drills so we would know how to escape from the bedrooms. We knew where the fire extinguishers were and how to operate them. We knew that Dad had a pistol in the drawer of his nightstand and a rifle beside the back door. We also knew that if any of us so much as touched that drawer or cast our eyes sideways upon that rifle . . . well, it was better not to speculate on what would happen. Dad was The Family Protector. No funny business.

"What do you mean, Dad?"

"If anybody was to break into the house, what good would I be?"

I didn't know what to say. Factually, Dad would probably not be as quick on his feet as he used to be if we were to be attacked by marauders. It didn't matter that the likelihood of that occurring was about the same as that of waking up to find zebras snacking on the lilac bushes instead of deer. Dad wasn't calculating the odds of rape and pillage, he was mourning the loss of his ability to protect his family.

"I don't know, Dad. But I'd take you over that security system any day." I was sidestepping the issue, in violation of my rules. "I don't think we're in any imminent danger, Dad, do you?"

"No. I guess we're not." He grabbed my hand and we walked the rest of the way hand in hand, silent.

The next afternoon, when Dad was up at the hospital doing his cardiac rehab program, I found Mother sitting on the edge of her bed, wringing her hands and crying, her eyes ringed red and frantic.

"Susan! You've got to help me!" she begged. "You've got to help me get rid of your father's guns."

"What are you talking about?"

"You know the rifle that's been by the back door for years? I found it today in his closet." Mother put her head in her hands and cried. "I can't take this anymore!"

"What are you talking about, Mother? You think Dad wants to kill himself?"

She couldn't speak over her anguish. She covered her mouth and gave the slightest nod.

"Mother," I told her sternly, "Dad isn't planning to kill himself. He feels good about himself. He feels like he's making progress. We talked about it just this morning."

"Then why did he put his rifle in his closet?" she hissed.

"Mom. Listen to me." I relayed to her my earlier conversation with Dad and reasoned that he put the gun in his closet as a way of feeling more in control if something went wrong.

She would have none of it. She just knew that if she didn't act that very day, we'd be cleaning bits of his brain off the closet walls tomorrow. "I have to get rid of his gun. You have to help me get rid of it. Now. Before he comes home."

"What do you mean?"

"I want you to take it to Bud's house. Give it to him. Just get rid of it!" She looked at me, pleading. "We have to do it now, before he gets back from rehab."

"I won't do it, Mother."

She stopped crying and looked straight through me. Her eyes lost their spark of neediness and hardened into drab utilitarian lenses, flat and set as riprap on a riverbank.

"You know what that would do, Mom? Sneaking around behind Dad's back and getting rid of something that for his whole life has been the symbol of freedom?" I hated spouting the NRA line, but Dad directly equated freedom with the right to own a gun—unregistered. "That would really depress him. He feels like he has no control, Mom. If you do this, all you'll be doing is saying that you don't trust him and that he needs to be kept away from sharp objects. I won't do it, Mom. If Dad wants to kill himself, taking his rifle away won't prevent it. Far from it, it might push him to it. I won't do it."

"You won't help me?"

"No. I won't. Why don't you talk to Dad, Mom? Tell him how you feel. Tell him what you're afraid of. Talk to him. Tell him you don't like guns in the bedroom. Suggest that he store them in the basement."

She laughed, a mocking snort of ridicule. "Ha! You and your high-and-mighty ideas. You have no idea. If you won't help me, I'll do it myself."

"You do what you need to do, Mom. But think about the consequences. They might be worse than the risk of leaving things the way they are."

I watched as she lugged his rifle out to her little purple Chevy and stuffed it into the trunk like it was a dead body, a look of revulsion on her face. Then she lugged out his shotgun, too. I didn't have any idea where that had been kept. She slammed down the trunk and got in the car without a word to me. She drove carefully down the driveway, a felon making her guilty getaway.

I got on the phone to Bud and explained the situation.

"Sure. I'll take them for her." Bud, in his desperate desire to be helpful, would agree to anything any member of my family asked of him.

"No, Bud. *Don't* take them for her. Do you know what this would do to your relationship with Dad? You're his best friend. This would be a supreme betrayal. Don't you see? He would see you as trying to control him. He already doesn't have any control. Now his best friend is in on the act?" I was as persuasive and urgent as I knew how to be. I feared Mother would be pulling into his driveway any minute, and I knew Bud hated conflict. Not only did I have to persuade him to refuse Mother's request, but I had to give him step-by-step instructions for how to handle her.

"I see what you're saying, kid. Damn. What if your mother calls? Or drops by?"

"Tell her the truth, Bud. Tell her you understand she's upset, but that you can't do something behind Dad's back. Suggest she store them in the basement."

"Good idea. I'll do that. Thanks for the heads-up."

Thirty minutes later Mother returned. "I guess you talked to Bud, huh?"

"No, Mom. I didn't." She knew I was lying and I felt ashamed.

We were brought up in the age where spanking was on the hit parade and I got spanked a lot—for sassing, flagrant disobedience, or slatternly behavior. But lying was an offense far worse than any of those. Lying was a personal and family betrayal and was met with the most feared discipline: my parents' wordless disappointment.

When I lied this time, Mom said nothing. She went back into the garage and popped the trunk, lugged the guns into the laundry room, and leaned them heavily against the washing machine. Then she got out a rickety stepladder and tried to balance on it while hefting the guns onto the uppermost shelf of the sewing closet, teetering with the effort.

While I watched.

I felt cruel watching her frantic struggle, her fears for her family consuming her. Finally, I broke down.

"Let me help you, Mom."

Much taller and stronger than Mother, I lifted the guns up to the top shelf and tucked them in the back where they couldn't be seen.

Mom and Dad dancing in the hangar, which is better than them dancing in public. (Notice the bread basket on her head?)

25

Invisible

Sharon and I didn't appreciate the extent to which Mom had become the casualty in this whole process. We romped over her like she was invisible. It wasn't that, feeling overwhelmed and preoccupied with Dad, we stepped on her toes occasionally. We ruthlessly cut her out of the action. We didn't realize how cruel we were being. We were straining to do the best we knew how. It was irrelevant that it wasn't good enough. It was all we had. But being sidelined in the process was the single thing about this experience that hurt her the most.

Sharon and I took over the grocery shopping in the afternoons because we were preparing the meals at night. If Mom unloaded the dishwasher, we shushed her because the clinking of china was distracting Dad. If she suggested oatmeal for breakfast as a little change of pace I gave her the Protein Glare. When she walked down the hallway during school with a load of laundry, Sharon pounced. Didn't Mother know this bustling around was throwing Dad off?

Instead of sitting us down and saying, "Now hold on here just one minute," Mom pulled out her old standby strategy: don't make a fuss. I don't blame her. She had tried to make a fuss at the hospital and all she'd gotten from me was ridicule and sarcasm. She had probably done a simple cost-benefit analysis and realized it was better to keep her head down and plow, holding fast to the Biblical promise "This too shall pass," than try to stop me from my single-minded purpose.

Mom had had a lifetime to perfect the don't-make-a-fuss strategy. It enabled her to endure the nearly constant criticism she got, starting with her mother. When Mom decided she wanted to study nursing in college, Grandma scoffed that Mother wasn't smart enough and sent her to secretarial school. When my grandmother was housebound and Mother did her grocery shopping at her bidding, she was met with criticism that the cottage cheese was the wrong brand, the expiration date on the milk was too soon, and the bread was sliced too thick. Then Grandma withheld forty-three cents when she was reimbursing Mother for the grocery bill because Mother hadn't been frugal enough to drive across town to buy the ground meat that was on sale at Safeway.

Not making a fuss also made Life with Father a lot easier. When Dad was working out in the yard and wanted Mother for some reason, he wouldn't come in and look for her. He wouldn't shout her name. He would whistle. It didn't cross her mind to bash him over the head with a lead crystal vase. Instead, she would put down what she was doing, hurry to wherever he was, and do whatever he needed done.

So Sharon and I were surprised and thrilled when, after we had all graduated from high school, Mother decided to take a job managing a gift shop in town. It sold high-end dishware, beautiful glass, candles, and unusual gifts. It was the shop where every bride in town registered, and it was a perfect job for Mother. She helped these optimistic young women pick out silverware and glasses, napkins and place mats, candle holders, casserole dishes, soup ladles, and steak knives. She attended to them like a lady-in-waiting, and they loved her. She made sure each gift was wrapped to perfection, no wrinkles in the corners, no twists in the shiny flat ribbon.

Having that job meant that every morning she got to dress up and go to town. She got to wait on countless people who were glad to see her and lavished her with thanks for her help.

She always packed herself a lunch, so I made her a lunch container, a bulbous wicker basket with a lid, handle, and blue quilted fabric lining that fastened to the rim with Velcro so she could launder it. I bought matching cloth napkins and a blue coffee mug. It suited Mom, who did everything with style and good taste.

But working from nine to five meant that Dad ate lunch by himself and dinner was often later than usual. If he got a hankering to fly down to Elko, Nevada, on the weekend to see friends they had down there, Mom often couldn't go because she worked on Saturdays. She had only two weeks of vacation as part of her employment, and it needed to be planned.

That didn't work for Dad. He hadn't struggled all these years, finally creating some independence, to have Mother's minimum-wage job determine when they could leave and when they had to stay home. They didn't need the money, and they certainly didn't need the constraint.

So Mom quit.

I was outraged. How could she do this? I lectured. This wasn't about the money, this was about enjoying your work. It was about what Mom wanted, not what Dad wanted. Since when did Dad have all the votes anyway? I railed about the injustice, about Mom going soft, about men. Mother tried to explain that it was she who was making this choice, that no choice was independent of its effect on others, and she had to take that into account. She tried to explain that it wasn't worth it to her to have this job if it meant hurting her family. Her job didn't mean that much to her.

I would hear none of it. Mother had on her hands a girlchild as foreign and confusing to her as someone raised by Bella Abzug—or wolves, for that matter. I didn't shave my legs, had no intention of getting married, and if for some reason I did, I certainly would not change my name, and furthermore I fully intended to have a career.

Mom raised a family in the chasm between two different worlds: she was a fifties housewife whose daughters fully and shrilly embraced seventies feminism. Whichever way she faced she was looking square in the eyes of criticism that ranged somewhere between "What do you *mean,* Mom, he won't *let* you?" and "What time is dinner?"

It's amazing that my mother rose from bed cheerfully each morning. I should freely grant her any coping mechanism that enabled her to continue to love us as ferociously as she did. Lucky for us she chose prayer over a daily fifth of gin.

What Mom knew better than anyone was that, given time, everything comes around. Kids grow up. Edges soften. Voices lower. People learn. "Everything comes out in the wash," she would say. In the meantime she counted on God. Whatever solace she could not get from her family—and there was precious little in those three months when Sharon and I invaded her home—she got from God. During Dad's recovery from his stroke, God is who Mom spent most of her time with, and it was there, with God, that she cried.

What I didn't acknowledge, because I didn't know it—or if I did I wouldn't have given it any credence at the time—was that Mother's daily prayers supported our sweaty labor. We had succeeded in cutting her out of the action in every other way, from participating in Dad's schooling to cooking meals, but we couldn't cut her out of her communion with forces bigger than ourselves who were helping us along. Our lack of appreciation for the role of her faith did not stop her prayers, however, nor her belief in their importance and power.

We had decided as a family that Mom would not be part of the process of school. Her job would be to be Wayne's wife, to carry on as much as possible with the life the two of them had forged before the stroke. It was upside down enough that Dad had the reading capacity of a kindergartner and was taking orders from his daughters. Being a husband to his wife would at least give him a small corner of the world in which he had a familiar role, where things were a little more normal.

The biggest flaw in our strategy was that Dad was too tired to be a husband or have a wife. Every waking minute we had him either in school, doing errands in town, or playing word games after dinner. By the time he got to bed at night he had no energy left for pillow talk as they drifted off to sleep. If he didn't collapse in exhaustion, he thrashed and worried that he wouldn't get enough sleep to do it all over again the next morning.

Even when they did have moments alone, Dad was preoccupied with whether he was making progress, whether he would fly again, or what to do about the Airmaster, the worry above all others that would sink him. Any other more mundane concerns that often pepper the conversation of a household—what night would be best to have Martha and Glenn over for dinner, what to do about the weeds growing in the rock beds, how to discourage the deer from eating the lilac bushes—had no audience.

Mom's role as wife in these three months had narrow boundaries: encourage him.

One afternoon, Dad was sitting on the couch working on the morning's flash cards. Inch by inch his head fell down to his chest, then, when his chin dropped low enough, his head jerked up, as though a bitter schoolmarm with a switch had forced him back to attention.

"Here, honey," Mom said, reaching for the afghan. "Why don't you just lie down and take a nap."

"I don't need no nap," Dad protested, picking up the note cards that had spilled across his lap.

"You've studied enough for today. Things will come to you better if you just let them rest for a while." Mom sat down next to him.

"How will I ever finish that Airmaster?" Dad stammered out, confessing the worry that preoccupied him. "I've put a lot of money into that thing. Nobody will buy it in pieces like it is—all over the hangar." It took him forever to get his thoughts out. Even though Mom knew what he was thinking and what he wanted to say, she waited patiently while he said it for himself.

"Give it time, honey. You don't know you won't be able to handle it. It's too early to decide that."

"It's too big a project, Marcia. I won't be able to finish it."

"Take it one step at a time, honey. You'll be able to tackle it eventually. You don't have to decide anything right now."

But Dad was the deciding type. He didn't like things dangling. "You don't know that, Marcia. That project is too big for me."

"I do know, Wayne. If there's one thing I know it's that. You'll get back to the Airmaster. But you have to give it time." She held his hand in her lap. "It's too early to go off half-cocked. That plane sitting there a few more months won't hurt anybody. You can decide later." She got up and grabbed Dad's ankles, lifting them onto the couch. He willingly lay back, his head on the pillow she had placed there. She pulled the afghan over him, bringing it up under his chin like she had done thousands of times over the course of their life together.

"What would I do without you, love," Dad said as she slipped the flash cards out of his hand.

"The same thing I'd do without you, honey." He was asleep before he felt her kiss on his forehead.

Mom understood Dad better than anybody and knew instinctively how to be his partner—she'd even become a pilot herself, which scared the pisswillies right out of her. Still, it seemed to her at the time like the right thing to do. She was twenty-eight years old, with a six-year-old boy, a four-year-old girl, and another daughter in arms. She had decided to surprise Dad by adding "pilot" to her credentials. She knew it would please him. Plus, having her license would be a good safety net if anything ever went wrong while they were flying and she needed to take the controls. It would make her feel more secure. "I want to learn to fly," she'd told him at lunch one afternoon, and he didn't even wait to listen to the weather report on the radio before he hightailed it to the airport and arranged for lessons for Mom with Roger Strong, a friend of his and a good teacher.

Twice a week she went to ground school where she learned about aerodynamics, airplane engines, and the physics and mechanics of flying. She learned about the forces that cause lift, the speed and angle at which planes stall, and how to maneuver in the air. She didn't tell any of her friends that she was learning to fly, and she swore Dad to secrecy. She didn't want to seem like she was showing off, and she didn't want it advertised if she failed.

After ground school came the actual flying. Roger took things slowly, moving Mom through gentle turns, changing altitude gradually, flying over broad valleys. He knew how Mother learned and didn't rush her, gently coaxing her into the pilot's seat. Then one morning they taxied out and when they got to the end of the runway and Mom turned the plane around to take off, Roger opened the door and jumped out, announcing to Mom that she was on her own, that she knew enough to solo.

So there she was.

She hadn't quite expected to be in this situation. She'd known she would have to solo, of course. But until now it had always been in the future, nothing to worry about yet. Now, with no warning, she had to do it. To hell with Roger, she thought, she would.

Gripping the control wheel, she watched Roger trot off into the grass, grinning and snortling, his arms folded across his chest, giving her the thumbs-up. Then she glanced over at the hangar, and had she not been buckled in, engines running, feeling responsible for the safekeeping of this machine, she would have hopped out of the plane herself. Dad was standing there with Sharon in his arms, me next to him in my purple shorts and purple and pink striped T-shirt, holding his hand and sucking my thumb, and Steve in his cowboy outfit, complete with a fringed shirt and a holster. Her three sweet children, waving and smiling, stood watching. We had no idea what we were looking at except that it was Mommy in an airplane.

So Dad and Roger had this surprise solo flight planned all along. She looked at her children, she looked down at her instrument panel, she looked at the runway stretching out ahead of her. She didn't want to back down now. She knew how to fly. She gave it power and took off.

Unlike Dad, Mother didn't feel free, exhilarated, or powerful flying alone. It scared the hell out of her. They were talking to her on the radio and she wasn't answering back. Nobody had taught her how to use the radio. She got away from the airport, where the commercial planes were taking off and landing, and flew around the valley. She got used to it up there, but she didn't like it. There was too far to fall. She brought it in for a landing, smooth as butter, then took off again, landing it a second time just as perfectly.

Flying solo got Mom her student license and she was proud of that. But to get her operator's license she had to fly solo to two other airports in Montana and back again. That meant she would have to follow aeronautical maps and geographic landmarks, to find the right airport and land on the right runway. She didn't want to do it. Her three little babies needed their mama a whole lot more than she needed to be a pilot. She had done enough. She could fly the plane if she had to, if there was an emergency, and that was all she needed. She liked life on solid ground, and her decision was irrevocable. She never piloted a plane again.

One evening when Sharon and I were both home at once, we'd managed to infuriate Mom even more than usual. To make matters worse, she knew Sharon and I would probably try to bribe her out of her fury with some baked offering and she fully intended to stymie our little plan.

Mom routinely goes to bed at nine—sometimes earlier, never later. Sharon and I had planned to make her a pie she could take to her Over the Hill Gang dinner the following night. We were cocksure that would buy us her forgiveness. The trouble was, Mother would not go to bed. She didn't say anything, she just sat in her chair and read. Ten, ten-thirty, eleven—this was ridiculous. Sharon and I kept cutting glances at each other. What was wrong with Mother?

Finally I had to throw in the towel. My plane was leaving at six the following morning. I needed to get some rest. I was asleep within five minutes.

It was almost midnight when Sharon snuck into my room and gave me the all-clear. Mom had gone to bed. I dragged myself out of bed, and we tiptoed down the hall.

We decided to make Mom a Lemon Pucker Pie. I busily cut the butter into the flour to make the crust, preheated the oven, soundlessly slipped all the dishes into the dishwasher, while Sharon stood sentinel. The crust was out of the oven and cooling and it was time to whip up the custard.

Then a terrible thing happened. In a moment of inattention—it was, after all, two in the morning—I let the sugar syrup boil over onto Mother's unscathed glass cooktop stove, which she wouldn't even allow the housekeeper to run a wet cloth over for fear it would get scratched.

This was a big problem. This was a bigger problem than Mom being mad at us.

Thinking fast on our feet, we quickly tried to wipe it up but managed only to smear the burning syrup into a wider swath across the heated surface. We both grabbed for the special stovetop cleanser and a nylon scrubber and scoured, smoke rising as the nylon scrubber melted onto the surface in tacky globs.

Desperate and near panic, we decided to burn off the char. We turned the stove up high and watched helplessly as the mess soldered itself onto the surface. From what we could tell, the sugar syrup, the cleaner, and the nylon scrubber were now an inseparable part of Mom's once-pristine cooktop.

Taking turns rubbing frantically and picking at it with our fingernails, we calculated how much it would cost to buy a new stovetop— five hundred dollars? How disruptive would it be to replace? How soon could we get someone in to do it? Could Sharon arrange for that tomorrow and somehow distract Mother so she'd never know? We were delusional.

Sharon put the full weight of her backside into her scrubbing, complaining, "Mother should know better than to buy this stupid kind of a stove. People with kids shouldn't have stoves like this."

I agreed heartily. This was Mother's fault. She had shown lack of judgment when purchasing by not taking into account childproofing.

Approaching 3:00 A.M. we had to give up. I had to leave for the airport in two hours. In between scrubbing we had managed to get the pie baked and it was beautiful—yellow and glistening—but its beauty hardly offset the damage to the stove. It would take a lot of baking to make up for this.

Casting about wildly for salvation, I read the directions on the stovetop cleanser. In our family, we always read the directions last. Except for mother. She reads the directions first, which is why she is the only one in the household who can program the VCR. The instructions read, "For really tough jobs, use a razor blade to scrape debris from the surface." There, next to the cleanser, was a razor blade in a special holder. Of course Mother would have all this organized and in the right place. In a matter of three minutes, we had the stove completely cleaned.

The next morning, Mother noticed something amiss with the stove. Sharon pulled the newspaper up over her face, intently reading the high school sports section.

"Did you clean the stove?" Mother asked, her head level with the stove's surface, her hands expertly palpating the glass top, feeling for nicks.

"Huh-uh," Sharon lied, sounding bored silly.

Mother knew. She just didn't know how to prove it.

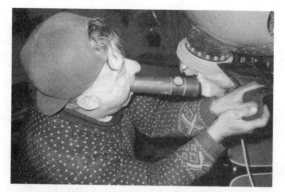

A perfect use for Dad's mouth—holding a flashlight

26

Battle of the Bulls

I knew that the hardest job yet awaited us: math. This was becoming the toilet-bowl subject—something everyone wanted to avoid. I didn't know how to teach it, Sharon didn't know how to do it, and to Dad it was nothing short of leprous. He didn't run screaming from the room when I mentioned math, but it was always a risk. I was the only one holding firm here—he didn't have a choice.

Whenever I pushed, Dad pushed back. Numbers were far more difficult than words in every way. He would read the numbers backward, like he was dyslexic. He couldn't do simple math problems in his head, like four plus eight equals twelve. Most difficult of all, he didn't get math concepts, like what division was, and I was at a loss for how to teach him.

I started by introducing flash cards with simple addition problems on them. When Dad looked at the cards, all he saw was a bunch of scribbled lines. This must have been both shocking and worrying to him. Knowing numbers and doing math were a portal to his former life. He couldn't get there without going through it.

I lowered the bar. I wrote numbers on the cards and had him read them out loud. I started with single digits—8, 4, 7, 2. At first he would get about half of them wrong the first time through. "Six, no seven, no eight. Eight." In his mind, he knew the number was 8, but when he went to "reach" for it with his language, he would grab a number next to it.

More irritating to him was that he wouldn't know that was happening until the wrong number was out of his mouth—and at first it completely surprised him. He didn't even know he'd said the wrong number until I pointed it out.

But still he couldn't add, subtract, multiply, or divide whole numbers, let alone fractions.

Finally, he agreed to do addition flash cards. Simple math. Once he got the hang of that we started simple subtraction. Dad put the brakes on. This was like backward adding and it flummoxed him. I retreated and moved to multiplication, since it was more like adding. I went right back to my memories of third grade and made a multiplication grid on the computer, 1 through 9 across the top, 1 through 9 down the left-hand side, and blanks in the middle. I printed out fifty copies. At first he would fill all the boxes in by row and I could tell he had a system going—he wasn't really multiplying, he was moving across the rows by twos, then moving across the next row by threes, and so forth.

"Okay, Dad. I think you're cheating."

He feigned a look of innocence in the face of injustice. I was unmoved. I grabbed a blank table and highlighted random boxes in yellow marker for him to fill in. I did this over and over and over. It was stultifyingly boring.

Then, every day, we did the multiplication tables at least twice, me calling out random combinations and Dad doing the math in his head. I kept score. We did it until he was able to do the whole table without errors twice a day for a week.

We managed to muscle our way through adding, subtracting, and multiplying, but when it came to division, Dad knuckled under.

First I explained division and how we use division every day in our lives. I built a rock-solid case for the nearly infinite ways that division makes life on earth possible—cutting firewood to length, halving a recipe for brownies, calculating gas mileage.

"Let's say I have a recipe and it's for six people, but I only want to make it for us. What would I do?"

"You'd only make half the recipe," Dad said, in a tone that indicated I should pick up the pace a bit.

"Okay, so that's division. I would *divide* the recipe in half." Having laid such a strong foundation grounded in the real world, I thought we might just sail right through.

"So, what is twenty divided by four, for example?"

Dad looked stumped.

"Twenty divided by four—you know, four goes into twenty how many times?" I lost him in the rubble.

Groping for a prop of some sort, I spotted a bowl of marbles and scooped up a handful. "Here's twenty marbles. See? Twenty. Put these marbles into four equal groups." I smiled. Dad did not smile back. I rephrased it. "What I mean is, this is one pile of marbles right? There are twenty marbles in this pile. But I want to have four piles instead of one pile. Put these marbles into four piles."

"Why do you want to have four piles?" Dad asked.

"Good question!" I chirped through a frozen, panicky smile. "Okay. Imagine that you are working on the plane. You have a board that is twenty inches long and you need to cut four segments out of it. How long would each segment be?" He pulled out his calculator and punched in 20 divided by 4.

"Five inches. But what's that got to do with marbles?"

"Forget about the marbles," I said, swishing them back into their bowl. "But you should try it without a calculator."

"Why do I need to figure it out if I can use the calculator?"

I knew the argument. I had used it many times myself. I even believed it. The only cogent answer that came to me was "Just because." Then I supplemented it with something straight out of my seventh grade math class. "You can use the calculator. But sometimes it might be faster to do it in your head, and if you can learn it, why not?"

I knew the answer to that one, too—because it was drop-dead dull, that's why. I dropped math for that day and decided I needed a whole plan for math, not these off-the-cuff little games I was inventing. That night I worked out a whole series of activities that I thought provided enough diversion that they would make learning math tolerable.

For subtraction I would go through mental math drills like "What is the change from five dollars after spending two dollars and fifty-one cents?" I found a book at the bookstore called *Mental Math* so I didn't have to make these up. For division I would pull out moth-eaten story problems like "Jane is buying dinner rolls for twenty-six people. There are a dozen rolls to a package and she figures two rolls per person. How many packages should she buy?" These dumb word problems made me cringe. I couldn't believe I was torturing Dad with the same brutal instrument used on me when I was in school. But Dad slowly, painfully plowed his way through it all.

All of this was aimed at hoisting Dad over the biggest hurdle yet—getting him back into the hangar and working on the Airmaster. He resisted it at every turn. Every day he'd walk the airstrip for exercise. That meant he had to walk right past the hangar. He never even looked in the windows.

Dad's reluctance had put Bud out of commission. Dad and Bud's friendship was as old-fashioned as the planes they rebuilt. Their lives were so intertwined that what happened to one happened to the other. With Dad waylaid, Bud was furloughed. He would go out to the hangar and look at the Airmaster and wonder what it would take to finish it by himself. He flat-out lost enthusiasm to do that. It wasn't just rebuilding antiques that was fun, it was rebuilding them with Dad. For Bud, the prospect of finishing the project solo was a grim one.

Bud would go out and clean up, put things away, sweep. He probably cleaned the hangar about nine times. He dinged around on his own airplane a little bit. Finally, he turned the lights off and locked it up and dug in for the Big Wait. Bud was waiting for his friend to make a decision. The hangar was their playground and their language. Without it, what would be left, finally, to talk about?

Bud knew it was up to him to get Dad into the hangar. So, immutable and relentless as the eastern Montana skyline, he leaned harder on Dad. Every night he called, worming his way into Dad's mind. "When should we start?" Bud would ask.

"Not for a while," Dad would answer. "I'll let you know."

The next night, Bud would ask again. Night after night after night.

In the meantime, another battle was taking place in Dad's mind. To get the Airmaster done they had to have a plan, and he couldn't put a plan together in his mind. He couldn't keep his thoughts straight, couldn't get his numbers together. He was overwhelmed. He had no idea where to begin or what to do next, and it terrified him. That's why he couldn't go to the hangar. Lacking self-confidence was unfamiliar territory for Dad.

It was Alan, a fellow pilot, who inadvertently broke the logjam. Alan was rebuilding a 1947 Aeronca Champ and getting ready to paint the wings bright yellow. He wanted to borrow Dad's paint gun. Dad was happy to oblige. Pilots shared tools and equipment all the time. The trouble was that to get the paint gun, Dad had to go into the hangar. There was no way out.

Dad went on his usual afternoon walk down the airstrip. But this time when he got to the hangar, he walked up to it, put his hands up to the windows to frame his face, and looked in. Then he walked around to the front, reached up to the top of the doorjamb, and felt around until his hand landed on the key. He held it in his hand and turned to look at the sun reflecting off the snow that never melted off the Spanish Peaks. Flying weather. He breathed in a big gulp of air. His thumb traced the smooth sides of the key and settled on the beveled edge. He slid it into the lock and turned, pulled it out, replaced it on top of the jamb like he always did, and opened the door.

The hangar was just the way he had left it. The boom box, covered with a thick coat of dust, sat silent on the workbench. Giant tin cans labeled "fabric rivets, washers, grommets," "access rings and ring covers," and "fin tapes" were stacked underneath the workbench. A broken wing, inscribed with Bud's blocky writing in black felt-tip marker, hung on the wall: "Tiger Moth. Landed on the Interstate, 1974. Not Fun." The sheetrock that butted up against the doorjamb held a long list of penciled notes—"February 23, 1993, Bob Green, 16 below," "March 10, 1997, Tim, Cub on skis, still 14" snow," "May 10, 1993—Sasha and Yogi got killed"—chronicling years of memorable events, both those we celebrated and those we grieved.

Dad turned and faced the hulking Airmaster, dismembered and abandoned. The crippled wing—impossibly long—sprawled across a yoke of sawhorses, taking up nearly the entire width of the hangar. Its wooden nosepieces, exposed and broken on one side, stared back accusingly. The unwieldy skeleton of the four-passenger fuselage, stripped of its outer skin and without seats or instrument panel, laid squatter's claim to a good portion of the far corner. The engine had been removed, flattening the nose of the fuselage as if it had incurred a comic injury. Bolts of white felt, used to cover the wings, leaned against the back wall, rolled up and waiting. Pots of glue, paint, and epoxy sat next to cans full of cleaned brushes. The smell of glue and paint and oil still lingered in the air after all these months.

Dad didn't move for a long time.

Then he remembered his task and began digging around for the paint gun. He found it, but nothing about it looked familiar to him. He didn't know which end was up. He knew the pieces were all there, but he had no idea how to fit them together. It stunned him. He was in the deep end and it was only a damn paint gun. He would never be able to rebuild the Airmaster. He would never be able, again, to fly the Fleet.

Sheer bullheadedness kept him there. He stared at the paint gun, trying to discern how it worked. He played with the levers. Was this the nozzle? Was this the lever you pushed to operate the spray? He turned his back to the Airmaster. He fiddled with the paint gun long enough so he got it figured out, got it assembled, and understood it enough that he could explain to Alan how it worked. What should have taken him ten minutes took nearly two hours.

He walked home and called Alan to tell him that he could come by anytime.

The next day he went to the hangar again. By himself. And again the following day.

The third day he walked into the house and sat down in the comfortable chairs where I was poring over the puritan low-fat recipe books. After weeks of salad and broiled fish, I had a hankering to sink my teeth into a sizzling piece of barbecued pork fat and a side of fries. Perhaps I was losing my edge, no longer as afraid of food as I knew I should be, but it was hard not to notice that these enthusiastic cookbooks were full of hokum, suggesting, for example, lemon ice for dessert. Ice? Ice was for when you were hospitalized and couldn't eat anything upsetting. Fried ice cream—now that was dessert. I was certain that if I wanted to sneak out for an under-the-radar dessert run this afternoon, I could shanghai Dad. I was steeled to lead this mutiny when Dad interrupted my plans.

"I went to the hangar today," he said, not realizing that I'd been watching his every move for the last three days. "There's a lot of work to be done out there." He paused, taking in a huge breath like he was afraid of suffocating. "I could almost bawl. There's no way I can get back to doing this. I feel like selling the whole shooting match."

"Bad idea, Dad."

"I know it is. But it's how I feel."

I didn't know what to say. I knew that if I pushed he would push back. I laid low and kept reading my cookbook.

He knew he had two choices: fix the Airmaster or get rid of it. Being in there, with all the smells of paint and oil, the metal cans, the nosepieces for the wing, the boom box waiting to blare out the Mills Brothers, pulled at him.

When Bud called again that night, he wheedled him a little harder. "Whadaya say we take a gander at that Airmaster, Edsall. You up to it?"

"No, I don't think so quite yet."

Like a fly fisherman feeling the slightest tug on the line, Bud knew it was time to make his move. "Edsall, you stubborn bastard, my ass is getting flat as last night's beer sitting here waiting for you. All I been able to do is clean the damn thing and I done that about nine times. Let's just try her."

"I don't know."

Bud had his fish on the line.

On the fourth day Dad came back from his walk and sat down next to me in the living room. He jumped right in as if simply continuing the conversation we'd started the day before. "I've decided to make a pass at it," he said. "But I need Bud."

That Saturday, Bud met Dad at the hangar, on time for a change, acting as if it was a day like any other. Except he couldn't talk.

"Big sky day!" Dad said, pushing the door of his truck closed and rubbing at a spot on the window.

"You bet!" Bud responded, picking up a rock from the parking area and lobbing it at a magpie.

Dad put his hand on that familiar spot on top of the doorjamb, retrieving the key and turning it over and over in his hand.

"Been a while since we been here."

"Too long," Bud replied.

Dad unlocked the door and they both walked in. It was cold and dark and silent. Bud flipped the lights, which fluttered on as if they needed prodding.

"You done a good job cleaning up," Dad said.

"I finally got that broom figured out. Took some doin'."

Dad laughed. "I bet it did."

They walked around, Bud intent on Dad, Dad intent on the Airmaster. "Look familiar?" Bud asked.

"Some."

Dad didn't touch a thing. He just stood, hands crammed in his
pockets, and stared at the wing splayed out unadorned. He heaved a
sigh so hard it cleared his throat. Bud knew Dad was overwhelmed.

"We'll need to reskin the wing here, don'tcha think?" Bud was
chewing hard on his gum.

"Yeah," Dad said, but sounded uncertain.

"This is where we were at," Bud said, running his hand over the
broken nosepiece.

Dad just shook his head. "I'll never live long enough to get this
thing done."

"Shit, Edsall. You say that about every project," Bud answered.

Bud tried to keep it light, reminding Dad that they'd start with the
easy things. But Dad didn't have a clue where to begin. He didn't even
know how to read a tape measure. Dad couldn't bluff his way through
with bullshit this time. He knew he didn't yet have what it took, and
he knew that Bud knew, too. They stayed in there nearly an hour.

But being in the hangar with Bud primed Dad's pump. The next
few afternoons, Dad sketched the nose rib and tried to work out solutions, inscribing a big X through ideas that hit a quick dead end, till
the dining room table was littered with abandoned alternatives.
Their evening phone conversations zeroed in on how to tackle the
seemingly intractable problems. There wasn't an obvious solution,
and Bud was as stumped as Dad. In the past, they'd been on more
equal footing. Now, when Bud thought a particular idea wouldn't
work, Dad didn't press, like he would have in the past. He had no
confidence in his own powers of reasoning.

It wasn't long before Dad would go out to the hangar every afternoon. Bud would join him in the evening and straighten out whatever had been confusing for Dad. Bud was in charge now, and this
was entirely new—almost harder for Bud than for Dad. Bud knew
how to be the straight man, ribbing Dad and losing most tussles.

They'd grown accustomed to their roles, having rebuilt so many planes. But now, Bud had to do a lot over that Dad got wrong. There was no finessing it. Dad took his place as student with grace, unspeakably glad to have a friend willing to take on the formidable role of his teacher.

They'd been in the middle of rebuilding the Airmaster's right wing when Dad had his stroke. The difficulty then was figuring out how to custom-build the nosepieces without a pattern because each nosepiece was different. The only measurement they had was from the exposed nosepiece on the left wing, the one closest to the fuselage and the biggest. When they got that measurement they could mathematically figure out how to scale down each subsequent nosepiece so the leading edge ran true.

In theory anyway.

Dad worked on the problem alone in the afternoons. First he transferred the nosepiece measurements from the right wing to the plywood so he could cut a new nosepiece for the left wing. He got the first one done. Then, from that, he worked on the second. Then the third. He got about a dozen of them done—nearly three-quarters of the job—and then began attaching them to the main spar.

That evening, when Bud showed up, he saw immediately that the nosepieces were wrong. Once Dad had them attached, Bud could sight down the wing and see they weren't aligned. When he showed Dad, Dad could see it too.

They took the nosepieces off to find out what had gone wrong. Bud showed Dad that the problem was in the measurement of the first nosepiece. Dad must have made an error in reading the tape, transferred the error to the plywood, and when he built all the subsequent nosepieces off that first measurement, the errors just multiplied.

"I think we'll have to start over, Edsall."

"Well, it won't be the first time."

"Hell, I'm just glad we're tearing things out because of you for a change. Usually I'm the one doing some dumb-ass thing."

"Dumb-ass is right. I say to hell with this measuring bullshit. Give me a dry line and a level and I can build anything. Here. Hand me that string."

So they started over. They strung a series of string-lines at one-inch intervals from the main spar to the leading edge of the wing.

"That'll give us something to build to," Dad said when they had the lines in place.

"Don't go getting smarter than me, now, you clever bastard," Bud joked. "I'd kinda like to come up with a few good ideas myself on this thing."

"You been doin' plenty."

"I suppose we ain't built an airplane yet we didn't have to do some things over two or three times."

They adjusted some of the strings, and stood back to admire their breakthrough.

"I appreciate you sticking it out with me, Bud. I know it ain't easy, fighting this battle with me. A few times I've just wanted to quit."

"Don't you worry," Bud finally managed, busying himself with a twisted string. He was getting his buddy back. "I know you'd do the same for me, you ever had to."

27 *Annual fly-in breakfast at the house*

Flyby

Dad was a surprisingly model student, given he'd had no previous experience. In high school he was a shining example of mediocrity. He did the best in things that were hands-on—shop, football, and summer. He had a lifetime of black-diamond experience in being infuriatingly mulish, however, and that served him quite nicely now.

Nothing would deter him from grinding away at his work, and he set out a hard-boiled rule to secure it: During school, visitors and phone calls were strictly off-limits.

Only one thing would crumble his resolve—planes buzzing the house.

Dad's pilot friends were like him: they lived to fly. When word went out about Dad's stroke, it sent a chill throughout the flying community in Montana. "Son of a bitch" was all Arlin could summon when Bud told him the news. Grounded. Arlin ran a Fixed Base Operation, chartering planes, fixing people's planes, servicing pilots who flew in from out of town. He had a little kitchen area in the back of his gigantic hangar with a percolating coffeepot that I'm sure wouldn't sell for a quarter at a garage sale. Every morning he would make a whopping urn of coffee that boiled and burned all day, a magnet for local pilots, who would congregate there for doughnuts and gossip. "It could happen to me" must have been on their minds.

They wanted to be able to do something, but there really wasn't much they could do. Except wait. And hope. Quite a few pilots let Bud know that as soon as Dad was ready to fly, they'd be glad to take him up in their plane, or fly copilot in his.

Sometimes they would call the house, sounding hesitant. "This is, uh, Joe, I'm a friend of Wayne's. Just calling to see how he's doing." Their tone was funereal. If I knew who it was and Dad wasn't too tired, I would say, "He's doing great, would you like to talk to him?" It was good practice—for everyone.

The little kids were the most at ease. Children who had been on plane rides with Dad wrote him letters. One boy, Dustin, drew a picture of an Air Force jet—silver ink on black paper—and wrote, "Dear, Mr. Edsal, I hope you recover soon so you can take me flying. Sincerely, Dustin. GET WELL!" He folded the paper in half, drew a stamp in one corner, and had his father hand-deliver it to Dad.

Pilot friends from across the state, across the west, and Canada sent letters. Every note was upbeat. They believed Dad would fly again and told him so, told him they were thinking about him. Friends who weren't pilots wrote moving letters about their own recovery from stroke. These letters, astoundingly personal and self-disclosing, must have been hard to write. Dad knew he had a whole crowd rooting for him, and we felt an obligation to live up to their hopes as well as our own.

Still, except for Bud, Dad's friends stayed away. They worried that being around pilots would only make Dad feel depressed because he wasn't in the air. Or else, knowing what a private person Dad is, they didn't want to intrude on his recovery. Or they stayed away out of their own discomfort. When I came back to Montana in May, I put in a call to Bud.

"Where the hell is everybody, Bud?"

"They're right here with their engines running, you little shit. We're waiting for you to give the word."

The next morning Dad and I were sitting at the dining room table, the Tobacco Root Mountains brilliant outside the picture windows, drilling on analogies.

"*Dry* is to *desert* as *wet* is to what?"

Dad had both his hands balled up in fists, one on top of the other, his forehead resting on top, like a sculpture of a head. "You know, I wasn't very good at these in school."

"Well, I guess you'll be smarter after your stroke than you were before. *Dry* is to *desert* as *wet* is to . . ."

"As *wet* is to, as *wet* is to . . . *Dry* is to *desert* as *wet* is to . . . ocean?"

"Right! Let's do another one. *Window* is to *pane* as *book* is to . . ."

Suddenly Dad's head popped up off its prop.

"Hear that?" His face lit up.

"What? I think it's the dog. Okay. *Window* is to *pane* as *book* is to what?"

"It's planes. Listen. There's a biplane in the distance." He got up from the table and ran outside onto the porch, then into the yard. He shaded his eyes from the sun as he peered intently off to the southwest. Sure enough, three biplanes were headed his way. By this time he was halfway to the grass airstrip behind the house and they were coming in straight on. He put a fist in the air and pumped his arm up and down in greeting as each plane buzzed him low and then made a steep climb to circle back around, their engines growling in greeting.

I watched him through the picture window. He didn't belong on the ground. I knew he was wondering how he could ever progress enough to fly again. He had to be able not only to read but to read his Flight Guide—that thick six-ring binder, stowed snugly next to his pilot's seat, that had the runway specifications, radio frequencies, lighting systems, and common traffic patterns for every airport in the United States. He needed to be able to talk to the tower on the radio and understand the cryptic code flight controllers used to indicate which runway to take off from, the direction and speed of the wind, and instructions regarding altitude.

Then I noticed that the three pilots had landed on the grass runway. I could tell by their planes that it was Ben Mikaelsen, Steve
Kleimer, and Bud. They were taxiing right up to the back porch, and
Dad was grinning from ear to ear. He stuck his head in the door and
without any stumbling shouted, "Susan! Put on the coffeepot,
wouldya? Do we have any cookies?"

This was the first time I had met Ben, a children's author in his
late forties. He flies a "classic" plane, a 1949 Navion painted white.
His wife, Melanie, is also a pilot. She flies a 1952 Birddog—the same
plane that Bud flies—painted camouflage green and brown. About
fifteen years ago they had rescued an abandoned baby black bear
who had been lost in the woods and christened her Buffy. The two of
them had built a whole operation out behind their house up Bridger
Canyon to accommodate the bear, including a place where Buffy
could hibernate. Buffy would ride around in the back of Ben's truck
when he went to town.

When Dad asked me if I could get together a plate of cookies, I
couldn't have thought of a better reason for ditching class.

"No problem, Dad! Give me ten minutes!"

For the next half an hour I ferried out coffee and cookies. Dad
motioned for me to stay on the porch and join in, but I wanted to
give him a chance to be with the guys. These were guys' guys and
Dad was the guys' guys' guy.

Bud came into the house hopping on one foot and then another,
wanting to help in some way.

"Don't treat him like a retard, Bud."

"Well how in the hell am I supposed to treat him? I always treat
him like a retard."

"Just don't finish his sentences for him, you jerk." I shoved a plate
of cookies at him.

I stood back from the door, but watched the whole scene. Dad
was laughing and staying in the conversation, even though he sometimes struggled. Steve hung in there with Dad, relaxed, not rushing
to fill in for Dad's blank spaces. Steve had been working for years on
rebuilding his 1940 Stearman. Dad always described it as a work of

art. Now Steve sat out underneath the summer sun and asked Dad's advice about covering the wing, and they puzzled on the problem together.

Ben downed cookies and gave an update on Buffy and on Melanie's progress in getting licensed as a physician's assistant. Bud filled in around the edges with his reliable self-deprecating humor, greasing the conversational skids. They talked about airplanes, Dad's plans for keeping the airstrip mowed, how his "schooling" was going, and whether he wanted to take a ride.

He was whistling after the guys left. The spontaneous gabbing slaked his thirst for his old life. Recharged, he was ready to go back to the salt mines and tackle analogies like he was killing snakes.

Watching him out there with his buddies made me worry more. There was Dad's ongoing struggle with math. If he didn't learn math—and not just basic math, but how to add and subtract fractions—he wouldn't be able to finish rebuilding his Airmaster. It was that simple and that hard. Reconstructing and recovering the wing had been slow going before the stroke. Having Dad fozzle around in the hangar in the afternoons, and having Bud rescue him—and the Airmaster—in the evenings, was fine in the short term, but to get airborne, the Airmaster needed Dad's brain.

I made a mental note to push him harder on math, both drills and story problems. I had promised him he would fly again in a year. We had no time to lose.

I remembered what Bud had told me when he visited Dad in the hospital. He said they'd had a good thing going, but that it was over. He couldn't fathom how Dad would keep from going crazy from the terror and the confinement. "Trapped all day with only women around," he bellyached. "Jesus." But as the work we were doing started paying off, Bud confided, "Maybe there's gonna be a miracle here."

Dad perked up when the phone rang each evening.

"Hey, Edsall, you slackin' off?"

"Hell, no, Hall. You come over here and try it. You ain't never worked this hard in your life."

"Yeah, well. I'm working pretty hard. Had to go over to Miles City today. Damn company won't let me take the plane—goddamn lawyers and their liability suits—so I had to drive the whole damn way. Jesus. It's so far out in the boonies they have to pump daylight to the hoot owls over there."

Dad laughed. "That's what I hear."

"Damn lucky the road's as straight as it is and not a patrol car within a day's drive. I bet I was pushing eighty-five, ninety, the whole way."

"Yeah. Last time I went that direction I bet I hit a hundred."

"Jesus, Edsall, the first liar doesn't have a chance."

In every phone call, Bud would push Dad to go on a ride with him in his Birddog, a little two-seater plane built in 1951 and used in the Korean War and in Vietnam as an artillery spotter. These planes were used as "forward air control," which meant they went out as scouts, marking targets with white phosphorus rockets, so when larger planes flying higher came in after them, they could see their targets. They call planes like these "Warbirds."

I would often eavesdrop during these evening calls from Bud—assessing Dad's progress, how he was doing with his language, if he got worse when he was tired. One evening when Bud brought up the idea of an airplane ride I heard Dad say, "Not yet. I have apprehensions." Apprehensions? I was still doing flash cards for *doghouse* and *motel,* and here Dad was having "apprehensions."

We had to walk Dad down this road one mile at a time. I wasn't sure why he didn't want to ride, what his apprehensions were. I wondered if going up as a passenger without any certainty that he would one day be a pilot again held the specter of more disappointment than he could handle. But Dad would not be rushed. Dad is a private man. His losses because of the stroke were public beyond measure.

He kept to himself all that he could, and whatever was stopping him from flying he didn't share.

For a fleeting moment I thought that the notion of flying with Bud might be what was stopping Dad. We always teased Bud about his loony flying habits.

"I sure wouldn't fly with you," Sharon stabbed. "In fact, I don't know how you ever came to be a pilot in the first place, since you can't even read a map."

Whenever Bud flew anywhere, he would navigate using his Rand McNally road atlas. He always said that flying IFR, which in the pilot world means "instrument flying rules," really meant "I follow roads." When he had to land his Tiger Moth on the interstate, it only reinforced in his mind the wisdom of his peculiar navigational habits. What if there hadn't been a paved road nearby?

During Sharon's next two-week stint, Bud called during class. "Get your dad out on the front porch in ten minutes. We've got something for him to see."

"What is it?"

"Just get your skinny little ass out there and stop asking so many questions."

Sharon hung up the phone.

"What was that about?" Dad asked.

"Bud wants us on the front porch in ten minutes," she reported.

They filled their coffee cups, grabbed the bowl of jelly beans, and sat out on the front porch to wait. Soon they could see a whole caravan of trucks approaching, their lights flashing and horns honking. In the middle of the parade, strapped to a big flatbed truck, was the fuselage for the Airmaster. Dad had been planning to transport it to his hangar the weekend he had his stroke.

He stood up and pumped his fist in salute. All the guys pumped their fist back at him from the windows of their trucks, whooping and shouting.

Bud persisted. Every night he would call. Every night he would work
in the idea that it was time for Dad to take a ride, scraping away at
Dad's resistance, relentless. Bud was worried that Dad had lost the
spark to fly. He thought maybe Dad was afraid to rekindle his love of
flying because the idea that he would never be pilot-in-command
again was gaining on him.

If Dad didn't fly again, it would change Bud's life too. The evenings in the hangar, the winter weekends, the summer Sundays flying off for breakfast three hundred miles away. Bud kept poking
away every time they talked. Let's go flying. Let's go flying. Hey, let's
go flying.

Dad wasn't ready.

Dad started going down to the airport on the weekends, though,
where he could be with his friends and get out of the house. Saturday, May 20—three days before my birthday and only two months
since his stroke—Bud and Dad were down at the airport dinging
around.

"Why don't we take a ride," Dad said, glancing over at the Birddog. Dad had decided. This was the day.

They pulled up the door on Bud's hangar, which was spit-shined
just like Dad's—complete with a refrigerator full of beer, neatly organized racks holding cans of oil, and memorabilia on the walls—the
hangar of someone trained as a Marine. One person behind each
wing, they pushed Bud's airplane off the crushed gravel floor and
onto the concrete apron as if it were any Saturday from the past
twenty summers.

Bud sat in front and Dad in back. The Birddog is a tiny Marine-
green plane, only twenty-five feet long, and with a wingspan of
thirty-six feet. The two of them in it were probably as much weight
as it could carry. It was what Dad called "Fleet weather"—above
sixty degrees and sunny—a clarion call as clear as "Gentlemen,
start your engines." From the looks of things, everyone had done
just that—every hangar door was up, and every hangar was empty.

The sky was swarming with planes. Bud took off and left the world behind—school, Dad's struggles, Bud's worries, the house full of women. They were high above it all and out of reach.

"You can't believe how much I'm enjoying this and how much this means to me," Dad told Bud as they flew over the headwaters of the Missouri River, looking for bald eagle nests.

"I always hoped I'd be the one to take you up first!" Bud said back. "Are you ready to take it?"

Dad hesitated a second. Then he grabbed the controls and flew the plane from the back. Everything came back to him. Bud undid his seat belt and slid over to the right so Dad could see the instruments—the air speed indicator and the turn and bank indicator. They flew out over the Madison and Dad performed maneuvers, banking left and right, doing S-turns. They were both electrified.

Bud switched the radio to 122.75, the bullshit frequency.

"Hey, boys! I got Edsall here in the back flying the Birddog. He hasn't lost a damn thing! Even has a little finesse for a change!"

Right away, 122.75 crackled with the poetry of pilots who had held their breath too long.

"I knew it wouldn't be any other way!" Kleimer responded.

"The old boy hasn't lost it!"

"You haven't missed a beat, you old son of a bitch!"

"You're back in the air, Wayne! You're back in the goddamned air!"

From the back of the plane, on the intercom that was just between Bud and him, Dad said, "You can't believe what this means to me, Bud. You'll never know." He paused, using the stick to bank the plane over a herd of elk. "I hope you never will know."

The first time the Tiger Moth didn't make it off the ground.

28

Once Burned

Now that Dad knew he could fly a plane, he was itchy to get in the air again. Only this time he wanted to fly his own plane.

Of course, he couldn't go up alone. The stroke meant he'd automatically lost his license. He had to wait six months before he could even reapply, and for that he had to ace a flight physical. All his numbers had to be stellar: blood pressure, stress test, cholesterol, weight, prothrombin time—everything. The bar for getting back his license was higher than it had ever been.

Less than a week after his flight with Bud, Dad was at the kitchen table with Sharon and Mom listening to Paul Harvey, a habit of a lifetime. Every summer day since we were old enough to feed ourselves, Paul Harvey had fed us our medicinal dose of Republican common sense, complete with a daily story illustrating the sad fact that there wasn't a single government employee that could park a bicycle straight. As if concluding a prayer, we would always join in at the end with his closing flourish, "Good day!" Even now, when we were fully

capable of refusing his spoonful of sugar, we still mimicked the closing salutation. Then it was on to the farm report, which detailed the
progress of the wheat crop and the current price for pigs.

Then came the weatherman, predicting a cloudless weekend—
sunny and warm. Sharon and Mom were finishing their last spoonful
of soup when Dad flipped through his Rolodex, punched in a phone
number, and asked John Stickney if he would take him flying in his
Cessna the next day. John would ride in the passenger's seat while
Dad flew. John, a flight instructor, was "checked out" in the kind of
plane Dad owned, a Cessna 185.

It was settled. Dad acted like it was no big deal, as ordinary as can-
celing the subscription for the paper. So Mom and Sharon acted like
it was no big deal, too, Mom loading the dishes into the dishwasher
and Sharon scraping her spoon along the bottom of her soup bowl.

Dad got up early the next morning and headed off to the airport
without any hoopla. Sharon didn't linger in bed—even though it was
her day off. She knew Dad would buzz the house, and she didn't
want to miss it. It was only May—we had been working at school for
less than two months. It was hard to believe he had improved so fast.

All morning, Sharon and Mom strained to hear the sound of the
plane's engine. They pretended to read the paper, fussed over the
dishes, refolded the afghan, and puttered around. They didn't want
to betray to each other the breathless scale of their hope, the nagging fear of their doubt, the wishing and bargaining with God they
were both doing. They opened the windows as if in need of air, but
really in need of sound.

No sound came.

Mother swore at the dog. Sharon complained that all that the
crappy local paper had in it was ads and high school sports. She
slammed the refrigerator door after looking for the third time and
finding nothing to eat.

"You'd think Mother Hubbard lived here for the amount of food
we have. What do you think, Mother, we're poor?"

Then they heard the sound of the garage door opening. They
shared their only glances of the morning. Sharon hurried off into the

living room so she wouldn't have to face Dad and the enormity of his certain disappointment. She was scared to find out what had happened, what it meant.

She heard Dad join Mother in the kitchen. A brief conversation. Then Dad walked down the hall to his bedroom and shut the door.

Sharon stood at the entrance to the kitchen, facing Mother's back as she peeled oranges into the kitchen sink. "What happened, Mom?" Sharon whispered.

"Stickney didn't show up."

"What?"

"Dad waited for two hours, and he never showed up."

"He finked out on him?"

"Don't worry about it. It's just the way John is. I'm not surprised."

"What do you mean?"

"He doesn't know how to keep a promise, Sharon. It's not the first time he hasn't shown up for things. It's just too bad it happened today, with your Dad, that's all."

Moments later, Dad walked into the kitchen. "Why don't you call John, Dad?" Sharon groped, trying to sound casual. "Maybe he ran out of gas or got a flat tire. Or something." Even as she was saying it, it felt weak.

"I'm not calling him." Dad was unwavering. "I won't be an airport bum. A hanger-on riding shotgun." Dad had unreserved contempt for airport bums—freeloaders who hung out hours on end at airports looking for free rides, free food, free beer. Dad would not become an airport bum. Even if it meant he never went to an airport again.

I knew Dad was planning to fly on that Saturday, and I was back home in Vermont keeping as busy as I could with anything that didn't require thinking. I scrubbed the waffle iron, ran vinegar water through the coffeemaker, refolded and straightened the lifetime supply of paper bags I had crammed into a drawer.

When the phone rang I lunged for it.

Sharon spoke in a monotone. Our conversation probably lasted little more than a minute. We had considered countless scenarios of what might happen that day, but we hadn't anticipated this. I was stunned. I didn't even feel angry. I felt revulsion, like I had just watched someone swerve to hit a dog.

How could someone be so mean? What was he thinking? I crammed on a baseball cap and headed up into the woods by our house, hands in my pockets, looking at my shoes, shutting out every sound except the clatter in my brain.

I had been stood up before. Everyone had. It's inconvenient and aggravating. This wasn't that. This was flagrant disregard—like being mocked—and I couldn't stomach it.

I kicked a rock hard out ahead of me, caught up to it and kicked it again, following it up the hill.

But you do stomach it, I thought. What else is there? It was Dad who had taught me to stomach things when I was getting divorced nearly twenty years ago. I had moved back home until I could find an apartment. I was in college. I was poor. I was determined I would not rely on my parents to make ends meet. I was also devastated emotionally—dangerously thin, sleepless, and withdrawn. I think Dad would have suffered any pain willingly if it would have relieved me of my own. I believe what pained him the most was that he had to watch me on my solitary journey. He had to stomach it—and he knew I had to stomach it too. But he did what he could, small things that mattered. I was leaving for a movie one winter evening. As I pulled on my mittens I found a fifty-dollar bill inside with a note attached, "Love, Dad." I wished now that there was something small I could do for him, but I couldn't think of anything.

His heart was enormous and could break enormously when it came to his family. Now my heart was breaking for him. I knew how important flying was for him. But so did his flying buddies. That's what was so confounding to me about John not showing up. Hadn't he been part of that gaggle of pilots that had been having fun for years and years?

Every year John and the other pilots organized and pulled off the

Three Forks Fly-In. Billed as an air show for the public, it was no secret that it was really a three-day weekend for pilots to park their
planes and then sit in lawn chairs and drink and tell stories about the
pickles they'd gotten into flying, the close calls, the details of someone else's crash. Now and then through the course of the three days
they would get in their open-cockpit planes and throw ten-pound
sacks of flour out, trying to hit a bull's-eye on a target painted on the
ground. Or give people rides in their antiques. But mostly it was
about the camaraderie.

Dad's job, after he parked his plane, was to drive the beer truck.
He loved it. Beers were two for a dollar. Or two for five dollars. Or
two for ten dollars. Really, they were two for whatever bill you
handed Dad. All bills were worth the same amount when it came to
the beer truck. Dad didn't make change. When planning the event,
the pilots were always clear that the beer truck was one of their mon-
eymakers. No wonder.

Dad was driving the beer truck once when an antique airplane
pulled onto the runway. As a lark, Dad pulled the beer truck up right
behind the plane. The pilot added power. Dad added power. That
beer truck was going as fast as it could go behind that plane, when an
announcement came over the public address system, "I don't think
Edsall will be able to get that thing in the air, folks."

He probably could have, I thought. Dad can fly anything.

I dropped down onto McGiver Road and kicked the rock the remaining mile and a half home, crisscrossing the road and jumping
down into the weeds when my aim was off. I adopted the strange
childhood superstition, like stepping on a sidewalk crack and breaking your mother's back, that if I didn't kick the rock, something bad
would happen. But if I *did* kick the exact same rock all the way
home . . . *If I did* . . .

It was a small thing I could do.

The guy who dies with the most toys wins.

29

At a Loss for Words

Right before Memorial Day—a little over two months since his stroke—I went with Dad to buy three birch trees for the yard. When it came time to do the paperwork and arrange for their delivery, the sales clerk fired off the standard questions without glancing up.

"Address?"

He paused. I waited. "Fifty-three-oh-six Mac—Macmur—ington Road." Then he gave her specific directions for how to get there while she copied them down on the delivery sheet. He rattled off his phone number without a hitch.

We climbed into the truck. I looked over at Dad. He looked over at me. "Pretty good, Dad."

"Not bad!" he agreed.

We drove home, down through the blue mountains of the Bridger Range, the sun blazing through the windows, lulling me into peaceful silence. Everything's going to be okay.

I knew things were getting back to normal when, several days later, Dad decided he needed to buy a new truck. Dad had a thing about trucks. And he always seemed to have a new one.

"I'm going over to Livingston. I think the dealers there are a little hungrier than the dealers here." He was going solo on this one. I wasn't worried.

When he came home several hours later, he looked whipped. Something had gone wrong.

"How'd you do, Dad?"

"Bad. Damn!" He sat at the kitchen table with his elbows on his knees and his head in his hands. He was clearly shook up.

"What happened?" I sat down, alarmed.

"We had a deal all worked out, and he was working up the papers." Dad didn't raise his head as he related the story. "He shoved them across at me to fill in my name and address and I couldn't do it, Susan, I just couldn't do it. Damn! I just couldn't do it."

"What do you mean, you 'couldn't do it'?"

"I couldn't fill out the papers."

"So what *did* you do?"

"I told him I couldn't read and write. And I got up and left."

"You told him you couldn't read and write?" I blurted, aghast. Imagining the humiliation left me reeling. "Why on earth did you say that, Dad?"

"I didn't know what else to say. What could I do? He shoved those papers at me and I went blank. Plumb blank. Damn!"

"But Dad—"

"What's so frustrating is that I have something one day and then I completely lose it the next. When am I ever going to get it, Susan? When, when, when?" I could see him pulling back in, drawn toward the comforting seclusion and safety of classroom work. I could imagine him reluctant to go out again, to put himself in anything close to that situation again. It is exactly how I would feel.

"But Dad"—I was still back at the couldn't read and write part of the story—"why didn't you tell him you recently had a stroke and had trouble writing? Why did you tell him you couldn't read and write? It's not even true."

"I didn't know what else to say. I couldn't find the words."

30

Let's celebrate Mother knitting! Why not?

Go Down in Flames Trying

Dad knew how far he had to go, and he really didn't know if he had the stamina to make it—or worse, the brains. Fear of failure was his constant companion.

Mine, too. The well-developed Voice of Judgment in my head would often mock me, jeering "Who do you think you are?" as I went about preparing exercises or researching stroke recovery. I could tell that some people thought we were nuts to think Dad would ever fly again. How did I know, maybe we were. Sometimes I felt numb with the backbreaking weight of responsibility I felt for his recovery coupled with the fear that I was completely incompetent.

What was there to do but plod on?

And plod on in the face of a pervasively negative profession. I talked with a nurse who was following twenty-six people who had had strokes. "Twenty-five are not motivated to recover," she declared.

Those were her words: "not motivated to recover."

"That's ridiculous!" I blurted. "I don't believe it."

"How else can you explain it?"

I told her about our experience with Dad, how successful it was and how much work.

"Well, you are the exception. I only have one patient who has that level of motivation. The others just plain don't care. People in general are unmotivated. It's why so many people are fat and why so many people smoke."

"Being fat or smoking and not being able to speak are two different things," I argued. "Smoking and eating give people pleasure. Not being able to communicate your thoughts is misery. Think about it. Inner speech is almost incessant. Talking connects us with other people. If not being able to talk was so much fun, more people would be doing it voluntarily." I didn't go on to say that in many cases I wished they would.

"All I can say is that practically all my patients are unmotivated."

I can believe that some of these people have had strokes that damaged parts of their brains that impact motivation. I can believe that nobody has helped them put together a concrete plan for what to do on a daily basis. I can believe that they don't have a caregiver who feels able to carry out the plan. I can believe that they have been given such a vague—perhaps even discouraging—prognosis that it feels hopeless. I can believe that platitudes, generalities, good wishes, and spotty therapy has *de*motivated them. I can believe that the caregiver mistakes his or her role and doesn't know how to demand participation from and push the patient. I can believe that the caregiver has misconceptions about what it means to help and therefore "takes over" the patient's work, leaving the patient dependent.

I cannot believe that the majority of stroke survivors (in this nurse's case, 96 percent of them) are unmotivated. I cannot believe that people with strokes are kicking back in some lazy lethargy, thinking, "Gosh, I just don't feel like being able to communicate with anyone for the rest of my life."

This excuse struck me as a thinly veiled way to blame the patient for what the profession hasn't figured out yet. Or perhaps, since the majority of the stroke population is elderly, we ourselves don't care enough. Would the urgency around research on stroke recovery be higher if the majority of people getting hit were, say, in their thirties? Perhaps it's not the patient but the medical community that is unmotivated.

I kept coming across families who were not unmotivated but were in need of direction. One day Mom and I ran into Louise, an old friend of hers.

"Marcia!" she exclaimed. "I saw Wayne the other day and he is doing so well! It's hard to believe how much he has recovered."

"Well, he has really worked at it," Mom beamed. "Every day. He's very committed to his therapy."

"You know, my Bob had a stroke about eight years ago." Louise stared off into space, pressing herself to remember. "Yes, eight years. He was seventy-four then. And he never really recovered. Nobody ever suggested therapy." It was as if this was the first time in eight years the thought had crossed her mind. "I wonder if that might have helped him."

Instinctively Mother reached over to put her hand on my knee, patting it, a signal for me to stay calm and, above all, not to pop off with a stream of criticism.

Part of the problem is that families struggling with stroke recovery don't have a track record. Usually they're dealing with all of it for the first time. Naturally they rely on professionals to give them guidance. When that guidance is to "make do," too many people take it, not knowing there is another path.

My brother, Steve, admitted that he too had felt that way. "Until I saw how you worked with Dad, I thought that was the way it was, that there wasn't any other way. I trusted the medical professionals to know what therapy would work. I thought that was the way it was— an hour a week on the treadmill and alphabet cards." Steve was a veterinarian. He expected his clients to trust him, so it was only natural that he would trust doctors.

We had to believe there was another path. That other path was to figure out what we wanted and go down in flames trying, if that's what it took. We figured that if it was worth wanting, it was worth

failing at. It was as simple and profound as that. In the middle of it
all I was reminded of one of the lessons Mom taught me when I was
about nine years old and learning to knit. I was worried that I
wouldn't know how to make armholes when I got to that point in my
project. "Don't read ahead in the directions, honey," she instructed.
"You'll figure out how to do it when you get there."

That's what we did with Dad. We figured it out when we got there.
The program Sharon and I cobbled together was not particularly inspired. We weren't this rare specimen of motivation and ingenuity.
Our program came directly off the shelves of Borders Bookstore in
the reference section for teachers. Had their book buyer had different
inclinations, our program would have looked different.

I was talking about all of this with my friend Phoebe, whose
grandmother had a stroke several years ago and never recovered. In
telling me the story, Phoebe said, "Grandma Minna loved men. She
loved to dance. But when she had her stroke, they moved her from
California to Philadelphia where she didn't know a soul, made her
wear pants—which for her was a great indignity; she had never worn
pants in her life, not even once—and put her in a small room where
she had to walk on the treadmill. She hated it, and it didn't take her
long before she up and died. She probably figured it was her only
way out. I'm sure if she saw that her therapy would mean she would
get to dance again, it would have been quite different. The chance to
get to dance again"—Phoebe laughed, recalling her grandma—"she
would've gotten into pants for that."

Who couldn't love this guy? Especially since he doesn't know we just short-sheeted his bed.

Victory Lap

By June 1, a little over two months after his stroke, Dad stammered very little, read aloud at 110 words per minute, and easily substituted words when he got hung up. He still got all balled up with numbers in general and math in particular, but we hammered away at it every day—I no longer had to chase him down to get him to do the drills. He walked without any trouble on his right side and had been driving his truck since about the first of May.

Like one of his planes, we had him pretty much put back together again—just in time for a scheduled checkup. Sharon and Jeff flew in early so we could all go as a kind of celebration. We piled into the big car and took the victory lap to the hospital, Dad in the driver's seat with Mom next to him, the way it's supposed to be, Sharon, Jeff, and me in the back. We chattered the entire way to the hospital.

"I can't wait to see Cheri! She'll be so proud, Dad. The last time she saw you, you couldn't even say a whole sentence! I can't wait to see her face." My stomach did a little flip just thinking about it.

We walked into the hospital together, Dad leading the way. We made a beeline for Cheri's office. Even though she hadn't shared her workbooks, she had been helpful with Dad. When Dad saw her, his eyes filled with tears. He reached out to hug her and to tell her that he was great, that everything was turning out fine, and to thank her for getting the whole recovery process rolling. He talked flawlessly. We stood behind him, blinking back tears and beaming at each other and then at Cheri. We're the family!

We'd all expected her to exclaim, "My God! I can't *believe* how well you're talking, Wayne! When I saw you last, you couldn't even say a whole sentence. Wow!"

Instead, Cheri cracked a little professional smile and said evenly, "I'm glad you're doing better."

She nodded to us all and then moved on—to her next therapy session, I suppose.

Dad looked momentarily lost—embarrassed even—his eyes following Cheri down the hall. He turned to us as if for an explanation. We looked back blank and stunned. He shrugged his shoulders and took charge. "Well? Where to next?"

We made our way to a large examination room to await Dr. Lilly. Dad and I sat on the table, Mom, Jeff, and Sharon in the various chairs and stools scattered about. We were brimming with too much pent-up energy to carry on a normal conversation. Jeff and Sharon and I got wacky, blowing up the latex gloves and watching them fly around the room when we let out the air. We laughed hysterically. Mother was appalled.

When the door popped open and Dr. Lilly entered, we instantly morphed into adults.

Dad's checkup started off sideways and never did straighten out. I had printed out a sheet with the names, addresses, phone numbers, and Web addresses of the places where family members could order materials to help provide therapy or get more information on brain injury and recovery. I expected Dr. Lilly to say something like "Well, thank you so much. This will be so helpful for families. We can copy this and give it to them before they leave the hospital. That was very thoughtful of you."

Nothing was happening according to my script. Dr. Lilly silently accepted the sheet and gave it a little toss so it landed on a nearby counter, a mere flick of the wrist from the edge of the trash can. He handed Dad the latest edition of *Time* magazine and asked him to read the first two paragraphs of an article. In unison Sharon and I crossed our legs, a good luck talisman.

Dad read without a hitch. I had to pin myself to the table to keep from leaping into the air and leading the whole family in a hearty cheer. "Give me a *D*! Give me an *A*! Give me a *D*! What's that spell?"

"That was acceptable," Dr. Lilly said without feeling. "But you did substitute a word."

I'd had enough. "That's a skill he's learned. It's what he's supposed to do instead of getting hung up on a word."

Dr. Lilly ignored me and kept his focus on Dad. "I'd like to put you on Ritalin." I felt suddenly disoriented. Where was I? Wasn't Ritalin the wonder drug that kept students activity-free? Didn't it do schools a service by putting lead in the britches of those little monsters? Maybe Dr. Lilly had noticed the stray, stretched exam gloves littering the floor and meant *we* needed Ritalin.

"Can you explain more about that?" Dad asked.

Dr. Lilly told us that there was some research evidence that stroke survivors were able to retrieve words more easily once they were on Ritalin. I had never come across any of this in any of my reading on stroke, so I was curious. If there was something that could help Dad, bring it on. Even though Dr. Lilly hadn't been appreciative of my effort to produce a helpful handout for families, I wouldn't let that lapse in gratitude spoil the chances for Dad.

"I haven't heard of that. It sounds interesting. Do you have an article we could read on it?" I asked.

"An article?"

"You know, a summary of the research that you mentioned."

"No. I don't recollect exactly where the study was done, just that it was successful in enough patients that I think it's worth a try. The results are immediate. You would know within a week whether it was helping."

"Do you know anything about who did the study? My husband is a medical librarian. I could have him do a literature search." As hard as this might be to believe, I wasn't being sarcastic or pushy. I was genuinely curious to dig into this idea.

"No. I don't. It can't hurt him, and I think it would be worth a try." I had this funny feeling that Dr. Lilly wanted to blast me with his disappear gun. Maybe it was the funny way that he wouldn't look me in the eye. It was as if he wanted to give us a refresher on the rules, the first one being "Doctors are right, so you don't need to ask pesky questions."

The Ritalin idea died.

Dr. Lilly turned his attention to Dad and did some physical tests to measure responsiveness to feeling on his right side, poking his ankles and knees with a sharp object to determine the extent of Dad's poststroke neglect. He was surprised and satisfied with the results—all Dad's feeling had returned.

Then came a barrage of questions.

"Are you eating well?"

"Yes," Dad answered.

"Sleep normal?"

"Yes."

"Your sex life, has that resumed?"

I froze. What in the hell kind of a question was that to ask in front of the whole family?

Ten minutes later we climbed back into the car without having heard a single "Congratulations" or "Good job" or "How wonderful," but knowing, straight from the horse's mouth, that Mom and Dad were back at it in bed. There was sullen silence.

"Well, I've got a bellyful of that malarkey," Dad weighed in. The rest of us slumped down into our seats and closed our eyes, trying to think of something else.

For the next two hours, nobody uttered another word.

Until we got to the outskirts of Livingston, thirty miles from home. "They're just jealous," Sharon said, as if the bats had finally cleared out of her belfry and she'd had a sudden blinding insight.

"Well they sure as hell ought to be," I agreed, my eyes still closed. "Those pricks."

"Girls! Goodness!"

"Next time we should wheel you in there in your pajamas with your tongue hanging out of your mouth and baby food smeared on your shirt. Maybe that would make them happy." Sharon acted like she was hatching a plan.

"Next time, schmext time," Dad warned. "If they ever want me back there again they'll have to catch me first."

"They are so *fucking parochial* that they can't bear it when some-body else does something better than *they do*," I railed. "Those pigs."

"Weasels."

"Carp."

"Kids. Come on, now," Mother protested. "Heavens." Despite her better judgment, she was laughing.

With every epithet our spirits lifted. In no time, we were in top form—having launched into an impromptu contest of spouting out lower and lower forms of animal life—and ready for a celebration. Dad gladly pulled off the interstate and we thundered full tilt into the Livingston Bar and Grill, Sharon, Jeff, and I catapulting through the heavy oak door and pleading for their private room. Given our peals of laughter and seemingly random socking and shoving of one another, they were more than glad to oblige.

"Beers all around!" Jeff ordered without consulting anyone.

"Beers?" I protested. "What about margaritas?"

"And a pitcher of margaritas," Jeff amended his order.

Dad decided on a first course of appetizers before we each or-dered our meal.

We didn't even wait for the basket of bread to arrive. We just leaned in and let it rip, a final torrent of invective that mended our transgressed souls.

Dad and Kleimer

Sky-High

There is nothing more glorious than Montana in June. The sky is huge and blue. The sun is brilliant. The air smells of pine and green and water. Everyone heads for high ground so they can see forever—hikers, picnickers, Sunday drivers.

Pilots head for the skies.

It's also in June that the Saturday evening parties at the airport hangars rev up again. This particular evening the party was at Bob Greene's hangar. Bob is a tall, reticent farmer. Absolutely nothing pretentious about him—or about his hangar. An oil barrel had been cut in half and turned on its side for a makeshift barbecue. Pounds of sausages as thick as your wrist were piled next to it, waiting for the fire. Dozens of buns, sacks of charcoal, and bags of potato chips stood at the ready. Pickup trucks had their tailgates down, groaning under the weight of cooler upon cooler of beer and soda. By six-thirty there must have been about thirty-five people there.

Widebody had parked himself in an old aluminum reclining lawn chair he'd pulled out of the weeds and dragged onto the tarmac in front of the hangar, an ice cold beer in one mitt, jawing about his latest aeronautic feats. Greg and Bill and Leslie were teetering in frayed deck chairs, balancing paper plates and plastic forks and bottles of beer. Cindy arrived in her typical splendor, wearing coverall shorts starched so stiff she probably wouldn't be able to sit down and her trademark costume-jewelry earrings so ornate and magnificent they took on the appearance of a tiara slightly askew.

If you stood back a dozen yards or so and let your vision go fuzzy, it was an attractive enough bunch. But the group lost a little shine when compared to the upper-class crowd having a party across the runway. Golf carts transported guests from the parking area to the spotless hangar, decorated with balloons and crepe paper in teal and lavender. The hoity-toity crowd nibbled on catered food and drained good liquor out of glasses, holding forth to each other from the comfort of matching chairs.

Widebody needled them loudly from the safety of his lawn chair. "Come over here! We'll show you how to have a good time!" He took a big bite out of his sausage sandwich and pork, peppers, and onions cascaded down his shirt. Everyone laughed.

Mom, Dad, Sharon, and Jeff arrived as the food was coming off the barbecue. Sharon was nervous. She felt like putting on dark glasses and tailing Dad, to give a stern stare to anyone who tried to finish his sentences for him or rescue him if he got in a bind.

She leaned over and whispered in Jeff's ear, "I should have brought my water pistol."

These were Dad's friends, but sometimes friends had the worst instincts when it came to helping. Besides, it was the first time since his stroke that he'd been in a crowd, and Dad sometimes up and lost it for no reason.

A raucous party wasn't the ideal environment for anyone to have a decent conversation, come to think of it. People were shouting to one another to get them a beer, give them help with the charcoal, or meet their brother in from Philadelphia. The noise rose into the rafters and then cascaded back down like fireworks. People would barge into a conversation, leave in the middle, or grab someone by the arm and drag them away midsentence. It was the first party of the summer and it had the feel of an entire prison on an early-release program.

Dad didn't hesitate. He made a beeline to Steve Kleimer, at the opposite corner of the hangar. He got stopped five or six times before he got there, pilots glad to see him, cooks plying him with a sausage sandwich, potato salad, and beans, others hawking beer.

Steve had a heaping plate of food too, and they leaned against a workbench at the back of the hangar.

"I need a favor," Dad told Steve.

"You name it," Steve said, leaning over his plate as he bit into his overstuffed sandwich, shaking his head at the mess he was making. "A man's likely to starve here tonight," he added.

Dad's food sat untouched on his plate, but he took a long swallow of beer.

"You're checked out in the Cessna, aren't you?"

"Yep."

"I want to go flying."

Steve swallowed a good three-inch section of sausage without chewing it. The lump must have skidded whole down his throat.

Dad took a bite of his sandwich and chewed.

"Sure, Wayne, anytime." Steve stabbed at his potato salad.

"Tomorrow."

"Sounds good," Steve said, taking a long swig of beer. "I'll need to get fuel. How's eight-thirty sound?"

"I don't mean your plane, Steve. I want to fly mine. Early. Before anybody gets there. How about seven? She's been fueled."

Steve stared at his plate, pushing at his beans, a grin spreading across the full width of his face. He looked up. "You're on, Wayne," he said, giving Dad a nod. "I'll be there. You bet I'll be there."

"Appreciate it," Dad said, and bit into his barbecue sandwich, wiping his mouth with a napkin. "Mmm. Good, isn't it? Been a long time."

———

Mom was sitting at a table with several of the wives, Jeff had crashed the fancy party across the runway, unable to resist someone else's free food, and Sharon was on self-assigned lookout duty but, having lost Dad in the crowd, had pretty much given up. The situation didn't require much policing after all. Gene, a fast-talking, fast-flying pilot, bounded up to her and gave her a sharp poke in the ribs, spilling beer onto her shoes.

"Hey, Gene!" she greeted him. "You're not finishing Dad's sentences—"

He cut her off. "For him? No. I'm good. Really, I am! Hey!" He was hopping around like his pants were afire, but this was Gene. We often thought someone should get a blowgun and blast him full of Valium. He sidled up to her and spoke in a conspiratorial whisper. "Your dad couldn't have made anyone's day brighter," he opined.

"Yeah? Whatdaya mean?"

"Your dad asked Steve Kleimer to fly with him tomorrow." The word was already out. "When your dad asks someone to fly with him, that is a great day." Gene rocked back on his heels, satisfied. Gene clinked his beer bottle onto Sharon's Diet Coke can and offered a toast. "Here's to your dad!" Sharon's heart squeezed into an anxious wad. It was only five days ago that John had ditched Dad.

"To Dad!" she cheered, and drained her drink.

The hangar turned into a blur of people and noise. Usually Dad would have cut out by now, before the drinking began in earnest, but he was operating on high octane even as the rest of the family was drooping. Mom slumped lower into her chair. Sharon reached for another Diet Coke for a caffeine infusion, then reconsidered. One more and she was sure to have to use the Port-a-Potty, affectionately termed the Honey Bucket. Last time she did that Bud locked her in, and it had made her jumpy ever since. Even Jeff was wilting—and usually a beer and something to sit across from, living or dead, could keep him going for hours.

Dad simply wouldn't go home.

He was, for the first time since March, his old self.

"Hey, Wayne! Did you hear the one about the two broads in a bar?"

"If it's a joke about Hillary I'm all ears."

"Didja see those hang gliders this morning, Edsall? Don't that look like fun? Whadaya think? Wanna do it?"

"Nah. I'll take a pass. That seems about as dangerous to me as guessing a woman's weight."

They stayed long enough to help with the cleanup and then piled into the car, Dad the only one still fully operating.

"I haven't had that much fun in years," he said.

The next morning, Dad was up at dawn, scarfing down breakfast and heading for the hangar to pilot his own plane.

The rest of the family took up a high-strung vigil, abandoning all routines. No sleeping in, no cinnamon rolls and newspaper at the Western Cafe, no church—and certainly no talking. They each took up their posts in a chair or couch and stayed there, propping up a section of the morning paper in front of their faces, too jittery to read. Everyone was straining to hear the sound of a plane. The water heater in the basement roared on, generating a collective and involuntary near-bounce out of each chair. But nobody laughed or spoke. Everyone just snapped their papers straight and kept on not reading. The room was filled with nerve-racking, pigheaded silence.

Then came the unmistakable sound of an engine. No one moved. Glances went around the room. Sharon was the first to blink. "It's Dad!" she screamed, which sent everyone springing for the door, tripping over the dog, the coffee table, skidding on the Sunday comics scattered on the floor. Sharon grabbed a broom.

There he was, coming from the south, his yellow and white Cessna 185 a glorious, speeding torch in the sky. He banked steep over the East Gallatin River, the wings like outstretched arms, and for a moment they lost him, the plane swallowed up in the gleaming blue of morning. Then he emerged again, parting the sky, and climbed, seeming to graze the floorboards of heaven, as if declaring that he was no longer bound by the grip of earth. Then he dove homeward, exploding toward them as if driven by the force of God. Roaring full throttle, the din of the engines a chorus of joy, the plane grew in size and meaning. Dad was home.

Sharon climbed up on a bench and hoisted her broom in the air, as if she didn't think Dad could find the place without a signpost.

Dad dipped down low, buzzing the house so close they could see him in the pilot's seat, his maroon polo shirt, headphones, and smile. Steve Kleimer waved from the passenger's seat, grinning and laughing and giving them the thumbs-up. They whooped and hollered and waved and shouted, "Go Dad!" until it all gave way to unbridled screaming and clapping. They were laughing and crying and finding it all hopelessly inadequate in expressing how explosively joyful they felt.

Then Dad circled around for a second pass, buzzing them all straight on, pulling up and over the house, a growl swirling in the yard, while the plane continued northwest, up the valley, Dad tilting the wings back and forth in his traditional airplane wave. Sharon, Jeff, and Mom watched silently, riveted to their hope borne skyward, until the plane receded into the boundless horizon, a tiny speck.

Hours later, Dad walked through the kitchen door whistling and grinning. He grabbed Mom and Sharon as they met him at the door, hugging them hard. They pummeled him with questions.

Dad started to talk. Fluently. Without groping for words. Without prompting. About how great it was to be in that plane. How he didn't have a problem with the radio, or understanding the tower. How everything came back to him. How everything clicked. Everything. It was like he hadn't been away. He knew everything was going to be fine.

Nobody else said a word. Dad just talked and talked and talked.

*This woman knows
how to dress!*

33

The 103rd Day

It was the end of June. Dad had been in school for almost three months. At the outset he had set July as the end-point of school—not because we knew anything about the magic of July or of three months but because we just needed some light at the end of the tunnel.

Now July was upon us. It was summer, the weather was perfect, and Dad could fly. It gave him a serious case of senioritis. He would show up later for school, seem less interested, and take people up on invitations to meet for coffee at the airport during school hours. I was preparing for his wholesale sprint from the classroom. He wanted to get out in the real world—and stay there.

When Sharon arrived the next day, I told her I thought school was over and that we needed to plan a party. Her less-than-helpful response was to run into the bathroom and throw up. Then she crawled under the afghan in our big easy chair and moaned.

"I'm sick."

"You can't be sick," I ordered. "We have a party to organize. How long are you planning to be sick?"

"I don't know," she whined. "I feel like I might throw up again."

"Okay. Well, I'm heading to town, I'll be back in an hour. Will you be done being sick by then?" She simply couldn't be sick. We had dinner to arrange and party favors and gifts and cards to buy. She could be sick later if she really needed to.

"I'll try."

"Try very hard. I'll be back by eleven o'clock."

By one o'clock Sharon and I were scouring the length of Main Street looking for gifts for Mom, Dad, and Bud that would be memorable and appropriate. All we found were stuffed animals and paperweights made out of turquoise and agate.

We knew what we wanted. We wanted rocks that had words carved into them. All summer we'd seen those carved rocks everywhere—PATIENCE, PEACE, LAUGHTER, HARMONY. But now, nobody had them.

Think! We'd been making Dad think for the last three months, and now we could barely do it ourselves. The party was tomorrow and we were without a single gift. Then it hit us. We hotfooted it down to the cemetery. If the stonecutter could carve gravestones, surely he could carve rocks.

The stonecutter led us out back to look at his rock collection. There were plenty to choose from. The trouble was they were all about two feet square and weighed 150 pounds apiece. He agreed to have smaller rocks carved by four the next afternoon if we brought them to him by eight the next morning.

"No problem," I assured him. We bolted out the door.

"So, what's so 'no problem' about that?" Sharon grilled me. "Where will we find three round rocks?"

"The river. There's got to be rocks in the river."

Sharon looked skeptical.

"Do you have a better idea?"

"Okay! So let's go to the river! You're driving—it's not my foot on the brake."

On the way, we passed a mall under construction. Big islands in the parking lot kept the cars corralled in the right lanes. These islands were filled with big gray rocks. I veered in and drove up next to one.

"Rocks," I said. "Good rocks."

"We're going to be arrested," Sharon predicted.

I popped the lid to the trunk. "Not if we work fast."

I was bursting with our astonishing good luck as we hefted a pile worth considering into the trunk of Mom's car.

Our plan was to wash them up that night, pick out the ones we wanted, and I would drive them to the stonecutter the next morning.

On the way back from the gravestone shop the next morning, I stopped at the bridge and dumped the remaining rocks in the river. I wondered if someone would think I was dumping a body. I had my ear tuned for sirens all day.

Sharon and I arrived at the restaurant early to decorate the table with dozens and dozens of origami birds I'd folded to represent flight. We showered the table with foil confetti that said "Congrats!" and tied helium balloons to the back of each chair. More balloons, tied to bags of sand, stood like jocund butlers. Graduation tassles dangled out of the wineglasses, and across each plate we placed a picture of Dad in his airplane, rolled up to look like a diploma and tied with a ribbon. The waiter chilled a worthy bottle of champagne.

We dressed up like people do in Montana—everyone wore something besides jeans. Mom and Bud's wife, Barb, looked their usual put-together selves. But the rest of us upgraded. For the first time since March, Dad wore his bolo tie—a black braid of leather straps hitched at the neck with a piece of elk horn, a biplane carved in the bone. I wore lipstick. Sharon wore a dress. Jeff had on his khakis and signature bow tie. Bud had on a button-down-the-front shirt.

"That you?" Bud squinted hard at me, holding his glasses out from his face and frowning. "Geez. I hardly recognize you all cleaned up like that."

"You oughta talk," Sharon butted in. "Barb help you part your hair? Musta hurt after all these years."

We ordered our meal and then, much against the sniffy waiter's well-bred sensibilities, decided to pop the champagne. Dad lifted his glass in a toast. "To the end of a long, hard road," he said, shaking his head at the memory.

Dad's voice choked so bad that Bud took up where he left off. "And to all the work of you girls, much as I hate to say anything nice about you, and to you, Wayne, you bullheaded son of a bitch, your goddamn stubbornness finally paid off."

Dad took it up again. "And to that damned Airmaster. Sheez. I put way too much money into that thing, but you know, I think it saved my life." Then he paused and looked at Mom. "And to Marcia, I think it's been as hard on you as it's been on me. Ain't no way around it—it's been a long, hard road."

"Okay, let's down this high-class stuff before we all start bawling," Bud urged. "Then let's bring on the feedbag!" We clinked glasses and drained them.

We sopped up the last bit of juice off our plates with a final swipe of bread and laid our silverware across the plate signaling we had thrown in the towel. That's when Sharon and I brought out our presents—shiny bags stuffed with colored tissue paper. We had it all planned. I would begin with a sweeping tribute to the importance of friends and family, followed by my lucky discovery that not only does the mind seek meaning, but so does the heart, and in this work I had found a treasure store of meaning and love sufficient for a king's ransom. Then Sharon would finish off with a specific appreciation for Mom, Dad, Bud, and Barb.

Sharon looked at me to begin. I couldn't do it. It wasn't that I forgot what to say, it's that I knew if I opened my mouth I would cry.

Everyone waited while Sharon and I stood there. "You go," I whispered, fumbling with my bags.

"No, you first," Sharon deferred.

"I can't."

"Neither can I."

Thankfully, we had written cards. Looking at the tags, we word-lessly thrust the glittering packages into their laps.

Bud's rock said "Friends." Mom's rock said "Faith," and Dad's rock said "Family" on one side and "Courage" on the other.

"No," Dad said, turning his rock so the "Family" side was up. "I think all I needed was this."

Dad's surprise sixty-ninth birthday party—and it really was a surprise!

34

Snail Mail

Every pilot knows what conditions require their pilot's license to be surrendered: heart attack, bypass surgery, stroke. It so rattles them that they joke about it, adding blindness, drunkenness, and debauchery to the list. Not only do they have to wait six months before reapplying for the license, they usually have to wait an additional six months for the application to wind its way through the maze of offices, a process so precarious that pilots threaten to tie a string to their application, just so they'll know where to find it if they have to.

Dad made certain that on September 25—six months to the day after his stroke—Dr. Hathaway, his physician, had completed all the medical paperwork. Even with that keen punctuality, Dad would be without his license for a year. Without that license, he could never fly solo.

From the moment the application disappeared into the engulfing maw of the mailbox at the post office, Dad's whole future rested in the hands of . . . who? The decision, he worried, would be based less on his application than on the luck of the draw. "That damn reviewer could have indigestion and that would be the end of it," Dad said gloomily. "That application could be in the wrong place at the wrong time."

If only he could meet with the reviewer, talk to him, take him on a flight over the majestic expanse of the Gallatin Valley to see where the bald eagles nest or where herds of elk graze by the hundreds. "It's out of our hands," Dad intoned, a sour prayer.

It must have looked like our lives had returned to normal. Dad was out in the shop working with Bud on rebuilding the Airmaster. He went down to the airport every Saturday morning for coffee and doughnuts. Every Sunday that the weather was good, he flew with other pilots to some small town in Montana where they ate breakfast at a local diner. Dad piloted, Bud copiloted.

That license would close the book on Dad's stroke, fully restoring his independence. No news could only be a harbinger of bad news. Biding our time was leaving stretch marks on our nerves, making us jangly. We should have heard by now.

After six months of dashing to the mailbox, full of expectation, only to return disappointed, nobody really believed that Dad would get his license back, except for Mom. I hoped he would, but it was entirely out of our control, and that was the horror. Bureaucrats were in charge of this process, and that did not bode well—our distrust of the government was bred in the bone. Other pilots didn't say anything, but they knew. It was just a matter of time before we all knew.

I tried to imagine what it would be like for Dad, how he would take the disappointment. How I would take it. A joke in the flying community is that every pilot is one physical away from an ultralight. You can fly an ultralight plane without passing a medical exam. But Dad in an ultralight? It would be a public indignity, like trading in your Dodge four-by-four with a plow for a shiny new trike.

We didn't talk about it. To raise the issue was to jinx it. We let it lie, a rankling, fulminating silence.

I was home visiting the first week of March. It had been nearly a year since Dad's stroke. I was standing in front of the open refrigerator, hanging on the door and staring in, hoping some warm rice pudding with raisins would appear. Dad was sitting at the table opening mail. He always did it the same way—slicing all the envelopes with an ivory-handled letter opener, holding each one up to the light to discern the contents, and only then taking the letter out.

He held a sliced envelope out to me. "Here, Susan. I can't read this," he said, his weary, near-resigned tone indicating that he'd received yet another notice for a public hearing on the proposed development on the land surrounding our house. My mind still fixated on dessert, I tore myself away from the empty refrigerator and took the envelope. I hated the development too. Oddly, Dad's hand was shaking and he stood back a step or two to lean against the kitchen counter. Baffled, I turned the envelope over to look at the return address. Federal Aviation Administration.

How glad I was to be there—whatever the news. How very grateful I was to have come so far, to feel free to celebrate or to grieve without fear. Was it only a year ago that I clutched when Sharon had said, "Susan, it's intense," when describing the work with Dad? How hard I had worked to shield myself from that intensity. But this had changed me. Holding that letter in my hand, knowing I would be the one to deliver the news, I felt a deep yearning for my father, a desire so much a part of me that I could taste the salt. How powerfully I wanted, by the force of my will, to make this letter say the right thing.

I pulled out the letter. Three pages. Hastily I scanned, desperately searching for the words CONGRATULATIONS in all caps somewhere. Then I got to the sentence that mattered.

An octave high, I forced my voice past tears and read aloud, "Based on the complete review of the available medical evidence I have determined that you may be granted authorization of special issue of the enclosed 3rd class airman medical certificate, under section 67.401 of the FARs."

I looked up at Dad, tears streaming down my face. "You're an official pilot, Dad. You got it."

Dad took a step forward and grabbed for the counter to keep his balance. He let out the breath he had been holding for nearly a year. He nodded as if in acknowledgment. Mom appeared out of nowhere. She wrapped her arms around Dad's waist and looked up into his disbelieving eyes. "I knew," she said, shaking him as best she could. "I always knew."

35

On his own, in the Fleet

Home

Dad had one more thing to do: fly the Fleet.

It wasn't an easy plane, not like the Cessna. Flying the Fleet wasn't the hard part. It was getting her in the air and getting her back down on the ground that was so difficult.

She was a dream once she was in the air. Dad flew this plane not from the instrument panel but from the sound. He knew her murmurs and her growls, what they meant and how to respond. When he flew, he listened to that plane like he listened to a lover.

Only a year ago he'd battled Sharon, Bud, and me about selling it. But the real battle was with the Fleet herself. She would not be sold.

The Fleet stood sentinel in his hangar at the airport, a gleaming orange silence. She loomed in his mind like a phantom, appearing sometimes as unfinished business, at other times as a death wish. Really, she was his final teacher, his most exacting taskmaster. One false move in the Fleet, one momentary lapse, and it was over.

Only a couple of years back he'd shelled the engine in the Fleet, blown it out completely—poor Bob Taylor in the backseat, scheduled for heart surgery in just a few days. One of the cylinders blew off, the spark plug wires still attached, and engine parts thrashed around inside the engine before spewing out the front of the plane. Dad, flying from the back, leaned forward, hit Bob on the shoulder, and hollered, "Buckle up 'cause we're gonna crash!" Dad smiled, remembering how Bob disappeared down into the cockpit, bracing for a smashup.

Somehow Dad set her down without a scratch in a farmer's field, sending the cows scattering. He'd known what to do then. He'd always lived on Roy Lindsay's early advice: You just have to handle it. Could he handle it now? Every scrape he'd been in was because of a problem with the plane. If he got into a scrape now with the Fleet, he knew the problem would be with him.

Dad started slowly. First he went over every square inch of the engine, reacquainting himself with it. He examined the prop hub bolts to make sure they were tight. If you lose a propeller, it doesn't matter how good you are, your plane becomes an instant glider.

He made sure the spark plugs were tight and the leads were in place. He opened the small door that gave him access to the space between the engine and the firewall. There, he checked the fuel lines, the oil lines, the primer lines. A crack in the fuel lines and the engine could go up in flames.

He knew that no matter how prepared he was, things could still go wrong. He changed the oil, recalling the time in Alaska when he was flying his Piper Clipper up to Desko Lake to pick up his dad. He was ten minutes out from the airport when the engine blew and he lost all his power. The plane's cabin was spooky with the quiet, the wind whistling past his windshield the only sound. He had enough speed to keep it in the air, but it was just sheer luck it didn't happen any further out. Ten more minutes and he'd have been out over the Susitna River country in the dead of winter with few choices about where to land and nobody who knew where he was. He always packed emergency gear, but it wouldn't help much when the temperature dropped to forty below. He'd turned the plane around and made it back to the airport, urging it on as he lost speed, oil spraying out of the engine and blackening the windshield in an unforgiving slick he could hardly see through. Somehow he'd managed to land it.

He closed the door to the Fleet's engine compartment. She was ready to go.

He filled a three-gallon bucket with soapy water and took an entire day to wash the plane with a sponge and a toothbrush, scraping every gnat off with the tip of his thumbnail. It reminded him of why, when they flew, they said they were going to "go smash bugs." Then he used a screwdriver to pop off the lid of his high-grade airplane wax, its distinct perfume jolting him back to the memory of the first time he waxed the Fleet, nearly twenty-one years ago to the day, after he'd flown back from New Mexico.

Starting with the bright orange tail feathers, he rubbed on the wax in a circular motion and watched it turn a dull gray. Then, planting his feet and leaning in hard, he rubbed it to a high sheen, section by section.

He whistled, losing himself in the rhythm of the work, in the memories, in the satisfaction of making her gleam. When he got to the door panels he saw stenciled: "Wayne Edsall, Pilot" and underneath that "Bud Hall, Chief Mechanic." It stopped him cold. Wayne Edsall, Pilot. He rubbed over it with the wax.

He believed he was ready to fly the Fleet. But still, he was tormented with self-doubt. He was a bold pilot, but always safe. Now he just didn't know if flying her was safe. If *he* was safe. It wasn't that he was afraid of dying. He was afraid of finding himself a has-been. Of discovering, and having others discover, that Edsall didn't have what it takes anymore, that his real place was in the passenger seat, riding shotgun. This was a monster of a plane. You lose it and it's lost for good. What if he failed?

Dad went over the flight in his mind. The plane was tricky to take off and land. There was one problem and it was a big one: you had to keep the plane going straight. No matter what. The minute the back wheel got away from you, you were in a ground loop and just along for the ride.

It would be easier to take off if he were on the grass airstrip at home, but he wasn't. Grass is more forgiving—if the tail goes sideways, the grass lets it slide. But on tarmac, the runway just grabs the wheel and tosses the plane, and there's nothing the pilot can do.

At least the brakes weren't as squirrely as the brakes on the Tiger Moth, but they were lots tougher than the Cessna's hydraulic brakes. The Fleet's brakes were mechanical and required more muscle and more runway to bring the plane to a stop. If he touched down too late, he'd run out of runway and smash into the chain-link fence.

There was a lot to think about. Paying attention to every detail mattered with the Fleet. Losing your concentration meant losing your plane. It could also mean losing your life. Dad had not yet been tested in the way the Fleet would test him.

This year he had passed nearly all the trials of his stroke by learning to compensate. If he stumbled over a word, he just substituted another one. If he couldn't even think of a word, he visualized it. If reading silently gave him a headache, he read out loud. The Cessna allowed him to compensate. With it, there was wiggle room. Not so in the Fleet.

He wouldn't get to compensate. He had to nail it. The first time. There would be no second chance.

The Cessna required him to be skillful. The Fleet required him to be a master.

Six weeks had passed since he'd gotten word of his license. It was late April and the weather was turning. Fleet weather. His blood was running with the desire to be up in the air, his face against the wind in the open cockpit. Dad couldn't put it off any longer. He knew he had to try it. Flying the Cessna was exhilarating, but flying the Fleet was like being with God. If he could make it, then he would be satisfied. If he bunched it up, well, at least he would go down swinging.

Dad didn't tell his plans to anyone except Bud. Not even Mom. He ate his breakfast, cleaned off his desk, and kissed Mom good-bye.

He promised he'd be back by noon. Then he grabbed his leather flight jacket off its peg on his way out the door. He didn't want Mom to worry, and he didn't want anyone else around. Faced with the chance he would fail, he'd rather fail by himself than with a crowd of people.

He and Bud stood for a while in the quiet of that big metal hangar. Then he put on his leather helmet and goggles and zipped his flight jacket up to his neck. It would be cold up there. He rubbed his hand across the sleek, slick fabric of the polished wing. They stood motionless as the oversized electric hangar door folded up into the ceiling. Then they each put one hand on the lower wing and one hand on the strut and pushed the Fleet out of the hangar and onto the apron. Dad felt the pressure in his chest where the heart surgeon had cut through his ribs. He heard the thumping of his heart.

"Didn't think this day would come so soon, Edsall."

"Couldn't come soon enough for me."

"Yeah, I'll bet."

The plane was in position. "Now tell me your flight plan, Edsall. And stick with it this time. Not like every goddamn other time before when you tell me something and do the opposite. I'd just like to know where you're going and when you think you'll be back." Bud eyeballed the flaps and rudder while Dad checked the gas and oil. "I'd just like to know, is all."

Dad told Bud his plans, knowing full well that Bud wanted to know where to look for him if he went down.

Dad climbed up on the wing and swung his leg over the side of the fuselage to climb in. Gripping each side of the fuselage with his hands, he wedged himself into the pilot's seat. This was where he belonged—the joystick between his legs, the throttle lever to his left, nothing between him and the sky.

Bud helped him fasten his shoulder harnesses down tight, a sharp click letting him know they had locked into his lap belt. Dad plugged in his headphones. "Remember, this son of a bitch glides like a brick," Bud reminded him, then smacked him on the shoulder. "Go get 'em, Edsall," he said, and climbed down to take his position in front of the propeller.

"Clear!" Dad yelled, a signal to Bud that he was about to crank the engine.

"Clear!" Bud answered back.

Dad turned the key.

Both hands on the prop, Bud pulled down hard. It sputtered and popped and stopped. Dad smiled, thinking of how long it took for Bud to hand-prop the Tiger Moth the first time they flew it. He probably pulled down on that propeller thirty times before it finally caught. Bud had worked up a sweat before he even climbed into the pilot's seat. Now Bud pulled down several more times, until the Fleet finally sputtered and coughed and caught. The sound of the engine galvanized him, a welcome, thundering ovation from all the antiques he had ever rebuilt and flown, and now his sole audience.

Looking out toward the Bridgers in the direction of Mom and the house and the hangar, he took a deep breath. He was doing the right thing. Wasn't he?

He pulled out and saluted Bud, shouting, "I'm going Fleeting!" Bud saluted back, then blew his nose and wiped his eyes. "Goddamn hay fever," he muttered.

Dad called the tower to get the go-ahead to take off.

He taxied toward the runway, pushed two levers on his left, the throttle control and the mixture control, performed his engine check, and when the fuel was at full rich, he powered onto the runway. The tarmac stretched out ahead of him, its black length as straight as if he'd laid it himself with a dry line and a level. *Keep it straight. No matter what.* His right hand on the joystick, he pulled the throttle lever with his left. He had to concentrate. Keeping the nose of the airplane straight down the line, he picked up speed. He tuned his ears to the music of the plane. He riveted his eyes straight ahead. *Keep it straight.* He heard the tail of the plane lift up, felt it, then almost immediately he felt a giant palm of air lofting his front wheels.

He was in the air.

The wind whipped up hallelujahs around him and he hollered like hell, tears streaming down his face and blowing away in the wind. He was six years old again, looking up into the sky, dreaming. He was eleven years old on his first flight. He was standing outside a barbed wire fence looking on as planes took off and landed. He was in Alaska landing on lakes, on snowplowed roads, on frozen rivers.

He was Wayne Edsall, pilot of the only Fleet Series 9 left flying in the world.

He felt more like himself in the air, in the Fleet, than anywhere else on earth or above it. Euphoria flooded through him, filling up the empty spaces he had grown accustomed to, empty spaces he didn't even realize were there until that very moment.

Dad flew out to the Three Forks Airport, a tiny airport about forty-five miles from Bozeman. Without a tower, small planes come and go as they please. Nobody was there, so he could shoot landings all by himself, first on the grass airstrip, then on the tarmac. He did hand-eye-foot coordination maneuvers to practice operating the rudder, maneuvering the plane in the air, and controlling the landing. He practiced until he felt absolutely sure, absolutely confident. He practiced until he ground his self-doubt into a fine powder and felt it blow away in the wind.

Heading east toward the Bridger Mountain Range, Dad cast back to the hallway in the rehab center at the hospital, where he'd sat, hopeless, in a chair, gripping my small hands while I made him my promise.

"Give me a year. You will fly in one year, Dad. I promise. You will fly me for my birthday."

In this year he had traveled an inconceivable distance in his heart and in his mind. He had never spent so much time in a landscape so breathtakingly barren, so unrecognizable, so full of terror, with no landmarks, no maps, and no end in sight.

He banked the plane over the Bridgers, leaning out over the edge of the fuselage. This landscape he knew. He knew where the eagles nested, where the elk grazed, where the moose hunkered down in the snow. He knew where Lewis and Clark traveled, where they split up, where they got confused. He knew the migration of the birds and where the buffalo gave birth. He knew the location of every Bunkhouse Bar in Montana.

With this year behind him he also knew another landscape. The landscape of his heart. He knew where despair lodged, and where frustration smoldered, smoky. He knew where the bitter damp fog of humiliation churned like a bore tide, and where the chapping winds of exhaustion blew. He knew where the hot iron of fear had, without mercy, burned its brand.

He also knew, finally, his own headwaters—he'd bushwhacked through sprawling thickets to find in himself a well of unguarded love, spilling out clear and cool and generous. He knew the landmarks and how he'd gotten here. He would neither forget nor leave.

He flew back toward the house he'd built for himself and Mom. Mom heard that familiar engine sound and ran out on the deck, shading her eyes with her hands to see. Oh, good Lord, Wayne, the Fleet! Here came Dad in that big orange biplane, buzzing her low and hard, just like he always did, framed by the cloudless blue sky, the Tobacco Root Mountains standing in salute on the horizon. She put both her hands in the air and waved like a schoolgirl. She tilted her curly red head to the open sky, kissed her hands, and flung them up to my father. Then she put them over her eyes and cried. She hadn't lost him. Once again, she hadn't lost him.

Dad gripped the joystick and moved it, slowly, back and forth—to the left, the right, and back to the left again. Flying the plane as smoothly as a trout swims in a brook, he waved back to Mother with his wings. He was waving hello, not good-bye. He'd been away a long time and he was back. She waved until she lost him from her sight.

The Fleet at home

Epilogue

Almost a year later, I was in the Cincinnati airport with about thirty minutes between flights, so I decided to check my messages. The only one was from Dad. "Hi, Sue," he said, pausing long and sighing. "Call me as soon as you get this message. It's important. I have some bad news."

Dad had missed the training in phone message protocol: leave full and complete messages, including the names of the deceased and the phone number of the hospital or funeral home.

I was frantic. I called Dad and he wasn't home. I called Sharon. Gone. I called the local hospital and asked to be connected to my mother's room. There was no one by that name. I called every hospital within two hundred miles. Same answer. I called Bud. Nobody home.

Then it hit me. Everyone but me was at the funeral home. But which one? And who had died?

I called Dad again and got his answering machine. "Dad, it's not okay to leave a message like that. You need to call my machine back as soon as you get this and give me all the details. I'm about to get on an airplane. All the details, Dad."

Three miserable hours later, I got back to Vermont and played back Dad's message on my answering machine: Bud had had a widow-maker. That's how the doctors described his massive heart attack. This time it was Bud who was shithouse lucky. Before he went to the hospital, he'd spent several hours at home pacing the floor trying to "walk off" what he had self-diagnosed as indigestion. He'd been flown to a big-city hospital and was undergoing bypass surgery right now.

Dad was there when Bud got out of surgery.

"How ya doin', Hall? You look pretty green around the gills." Bud was in his blue-striped hospital johnnie, a pillow hugged against his sawed and stitched rib cage, his mouth dry and caking.

"They gave me a shot of that juice and I was feeling pretty good. Thought I might even be able to give them a hand with the surgery. Then everything got black as the inside of a cow," Bud told Dad. "They tell me they did five bypasses."

"I've only ever heard of a quadruple. I wonder what they call five?"

"I believe the term is 'quite-a-few.'"

Bud tried to be perky, but he was exhausted and depressed from the surgery. Barb was there with their three kids—Jane, Jill, and Slade. Barb said out loud what everyone was thinking: "The stroke is next." They were just waiting for it to happen because they had seen it happen to too many of their friends. In some deep, swampy place in their minds, they knew a stroke would follow, they just didn't know when. Or what life would be like after.

Bud had always told Barb that if he ever had a stroke she should just take him out in the backyard and shoot him. He wasn't sure he still thought that. He wasn't sure what he thought.

For three slow, worried days Bud's family hovered in shifts around the clock at his bedside, ready to pounce at the slightest sign of the stroke that had felled Dad after his bypass. Finally, on Friday, the doctors declared Bud out of danger. Sick, sore, and relieved, he went home with a red heart-shaped pillow to hug to his chest when he sneezed or laughed, several handouts with illustrated suggestions for a better diet, and a trial-size canister of lavender-scented baby powder that was included in his room charge.

What he didn't have was his pilot's license.

Bud hated more than anything to be without his wings. He said it made him feel homesick, and the last thing he wanted to do was start acting like a goddamn sorry-ass girl. His tasteless new diet of scrambled egg whites, broiled chicken breasts, and enough salad to start a rabbit ranch weren't nearly as hard for him to swallow as the lengthening days of summer stretching out before him while he was nailed to the ground. Dad would pick Bud up in the afternoons and drive him to the rehab unit at the hospital where they would work out together. They'd talk about the Airmaster, the Three Forks air show, and all the fur that was flying about the new grass runway at the airport. All they could do was talk, because Bud was too tired to do anything else.

After six weeks, Bud was full up with talk. He couldn't be tied down any longer. He could pilot his own plane without a license as long as he had another pilot with him. Two years almost to the day that Bud took Dad on his first fearsome flight after Dad's stroke, they went up again. Like then, Bud was in the pilot's seat and Dad flew shotgun. But this time it was Dad who stood in the breech while his friend spread his wings.

"This sure as hell beats fat-free food!" Bud sang out over his headset as his wheels lifted off the ground, his seat belt pulled snug over a pillow that protected the flaming red incision that ran from his clavicle to the middle of his belly. "It's amazing how life goes, isn't it, Edsall? Sometimes the ass you kick becomes the ass you kiss." Bud had bullied, cajoled, and lured Dad to work on the Airmaster, taking the lead when Dad didn't have what it took to solve problems by himself. And now it was all reversed. Dad had set up a stool and a small painting project for Bud in the hangar so Bud could work for thirty minutes on the Airmaster before he had to go home to take a nap. Amazing how often the Airmaster had been coming to the rescue lately. It made him glad it had been such a miserable cuss to work on. The headset crackled to life again. "Thanks, Edsall—for everything. You know I mean that, don'tcha?"

"I can never pay you back, Hall. This ain't nothing." They banked near the Bridgers to head down the valley. "Been a pretty cockeyed couple of years."

Whatever else there might have been to say was better said by the pageant spread out before them—the wild mountains, the oxbowed rivers, the vast valleys of winter wheat barely poking up above the snow, and most of all, the wide swath of crackling blue sky and the freedom they both felt, not just by being in the air, but by being in the air together.

The next summer, August of 2002, Dad and I flew the Fleet over to a grass airstrip near Boulder, Montana. We taxied to the side and peeled ourselves out of the seats, hopping down onto the brittle grass, parched from a rainless summer.

"I'm thinking of taking another trip to the Arctic next summer," Dad said. "Bud'll have his license back by then. He's back in the saddle now—just has to get a sign-off on his numbers."

"That sounds great, Dad."

"I don't have that many summers left," he said, so out of the blue that I had the same ambushed feeling I had when I was riding my bicycle through the woods and got thrown end-over-end when I hit a near-invisible strand of wire.

I laced my fingers through his and walked back to the plane. Maybe I didn't have many summers left either. Who does?

We both looked off across the broad yellow late-summer valley, little clouds of dust the only sign that farmers were driving combines, at work putting up the harvest. Then we climbed back into the Fleet, strapped on our helmets and goggles, and lifted off into another blue Montana sky.